Pursuing Public Policies Through the Patent System

Pursuing Public Policies Through the Patent System

Dos and Don'ts of Drafting the Patent Statute of a Developing Country

Nuno Pires de Carvalho

Wolters Kluwer

Published by:
Kluwer Law International B.V.
PO Box 316
2400 AH Alphen aan den Rijn
The Netherlands
E-mail: lrs-sales@wolterskluwer.com
Website: www.wolterskluwer.com/en/solutions/kluwerlawinternational

Sold and distributed by:
Wolters Kluwer Legal & Regulatory U.S.
920 Links Avenue
Landisville, PA 17538
United States of America
E-mail: customer.service@wolterskluwer.com

ISBN 978-94-035-3539-5

e-Book: ISBN 978-94-035-3549-4
web-PDF: ISBN 978-94-035-3559-3

For Ana, forever
For André, Hugo, and Carolina
For Theo, Felipe, Pedro, Sofia, and Mateo

I dedicate this book especially to Doctor Marco Matías Alemán, currently WIPO Assistant Director General. For several years, we worked together at WIPO's service, seeking to help developing countries write good patent laws. During that period, we entertained many discussions on the best avenues that could be proposed to countries. Marco, a large part of this book's content, I owe it to your intelligence, your sensitivity, and your deep understanding of patent law.

Table of Contents

Preamble		1
Introduction		9
	Are There Patent Statutes That Are Proper for Developing Countries?	9
	What Objectives Should a Developing Country's Patent Statute Pursue?	13
1	The First Public Policy: To Protect Inventors' Rights as Human Rights	13
2	The Most Frequently Mentioned Public Policy Undergirding Patent Statutes: To Promote Economic and Technological Development, in General, and Invention, in Particular	15
3	A Rarely Admitted but Frequently Present Goal of National Patent Statutes: To Attend to Trade Commitments	20
4	Another Objective: To Promote the Country's Competitiveness and Capacity of Luring Foreign Direct Investment (FDI)	23
5	Stating a Wide Range of Objectives	24
6	Conclusion	25
Chapter 1		
On the Right to Apply for (and Obtain) the Patent		27
1	The Problem(s)	27
2	Examples of Answers Given by National Statutes	28
3	*Dos and Don'ts*	36
Chapter 2		
On the Examination of Patent Applications		41
1	Substantive Versus Merely Formal Examination Prior to the Grant of the Patent: The Dilemma of Small Patent Offices	41
2	Getting Help in the Examination of Patent Applications	52
3	Fast-Track Procedures	54
4	*Dos and Don'ts*	57

CHAPTER 3
On Patentability 59
1 Inventions That Offend Morals or That Are Contrary to Public Policies 59
2 Diagnostic, Therapeutic and Surgical Methods for the Treatment of Humans or Animals 63
3 Plants and Animals (Other Than Microorganisms) and Essentially Biological Processes for the Production of Plants and Animals (Other Than Non-biological and Microbiological Processes) 65
3.1 Some Examples of National Provisions Dealing with Plant and Animal-Related Inventions 68
3.2 *Dos and Don'ts* 71
4 Discoveries, Scientific Theories and Mathematical Methods 71
5 Second Uses 72
5.1 Examples 73
5.2 Discussion 77
5.3 *Dos* 79
6 Schemes, Rules and Methods of Performing Mental Acts, Playing Games or Doing Business, and Programs for Computers 79
6.1 Computer Software 80
6.2 *Dos and Don'ts* 82
7 Business Methods 83
8 *Dos and Don'ts* of Making Patents Available for Abstract, Yet Useful Inventions 85
9 Utility Models and Innovation (or Petty) Patents; The Case of Handicrafts 85
9.1 *Dos and Don'ts* 87
9.2 Patents for Handicrafts 88

CHAPTER 4
On Formal and Substantive Requirements of Patentability 91
1 Formal Requirements 91
1.1 Unity of Invention 91
1.2 Enabling Disclosure 92
1.2.a Defining the Person Skilled in the Art for the Purposes of the Enabling Disclosure Condition 95
1.2.b *Dos and Don'ts* 96
1.3 Best Mode 98
1.4 Information Concerning Foreign Applications and Patents 100
1.5 The Requirement to Disclose the Origin of Genetic Resources and/or Traditional Knowledge Used in the Making of the Claimed Invention 105
1.5.a *Dos and Don'ts* 111
2 Substantive Requirements 116
2.1 Novelty; The Grace Period 116
2.1.a *Dos and Don'ts* 123

2.2 Nonobviousness (Sufficient Inventive Step) 123

CHAPTER 5
Amending the Application 127
1 Amendments by the Applicant's Initiative 127
2 Continuation and Continuation-in-Part Applications 135
3 Amendments Submitted in Response to the Patent Examiner's Action, or as a Consequence of the Division of Applications, or in the Course of Invalidation Proceedings 135
4 *Dos and Don'ts* 136

CHAPTER 6
Pre-grant and Post-grant Challenges, Third-Party Observations, Invalidation, Revocation 139

CHAPTER 7
On the Rights Conferred by the Patent: Setting and Calibration 145
1 Compulsory Licenses: Effective Tools or Mirages? 145
1.1 Definition and Essential Points 145
1.1.a Compulsory Licenses Must Take the Individual Circumstances of Each Case into Account 147
1.1.b Infringers Should Not Be Allowed to Benefit from Compulsory Licenses 148
1.1.c The Scope and Duration of a Compulsory License Should Be Adapted to Its Purpose 149
1.1.d Compulsory Licenses Shall Be Nonexclusive and Nonassignable (with One Exception) 150
1.1.e The Rights Conferred by the Compulsory License to the Beneficiaries Shall Not Include Exporting the Patented Product or the Product Made with the Patented Process (Except Where the Law Provides Otherwise) 150
1.1.f Remuneration 153
1.2 Circumstances That May Trigger the Grant of a Compulsory License 154
1.2.a Compulsory Licenses to Remedy Anticompetitive Acts 154
1.2.b Compulsory Licenses of Dependent Patents 156
1.2.c Compulsory Licenses on Grounds of Lack of (Sufficient) Exploitation (or Suppression) 156
1.2.c.1 Dos and Don'ts of Requiring the Working of the Patent 160
1.3 Drafting the Provisions Dealing with Compulsory Licenses 162
2 On Exhaustion: Neither National nor International—Alternatives Are Available 168
2.1 Advantages and Disadvantages of National and International Exhaustion 168

2.2 Conditioned Exhaustion 170
2.3 Other Approaches to Exhaustion 173
2.4 Discussion 175
3 About the Prior User Exception 176
3.1 *Dos and Don'ts* Concerning the Prior User Exception 182
4 Licenses of Right 183

CHAPTER 8
On the Independence of Patents and of the Rights They Confer 185

CHAPTER 9
On the Terms of Patents and Their Extension 189
1 The Extension of the Term of Patents: Dos and Don'ts 189
1.1 Compensating for Unreasonable Delays in Examining Patent Applications 190
1.2 Compensating for Delays in Obtaining Marketing Approval for (Regulated) Patented Products 197
1.3 Compensating for the Insufficient or Late Recognition by Society of the Inventors' Efforts and/or for the Invention's High Social and Technical Value 200

CHAPTER 10
On the Use of Patent Rights: Licensing and Enforcement 203
1 Patent Licensing and the Role of Patent Offices and Competition Authorities 203
2 On Infringement 209
2.1 The Various Modalities of Infringement 209
2.2 On Remedies (and the Relative Freedom of WTO Members to Adopt Their Own Rules, Including Making Injunctions Dependent on the Protection of Public Interest) 214
2.3 Other Matters 219

CHAPTER 11
Other Issues 225
1 Should the Country Have One Single Office for All Intellectual Property-Related Areas? 225
2 Should the Patent Law Deal with the Profession of Patent Attorneys? 226
3 On Employees' Inventions 226
3.1 Inventions Made by Employees Hired for Inventing 227
3.2 Inventions Made by Employees Not Hired for Inventing 229
3.3 Observations 230
3.4 Inventions Made by Civil Servants 232
4 Secret Inventions 233
5 Ensuring Compliance with International Obligations 238

Index 241

Preamble

This book is the result of my 12-year-or-so-long experience in providing legislative assistance to a large number of Member States of WIPO (World Intellectual Property Organization) during my 16-year tenure with the Secretariat of that Organization, in Geneva.

When I joined WIPO, in 1999, I started working with Traditional Knowledge (TK) and Genetic Resources (GRs). In that capacity, I accompanied and assisted in the installation and preliminary work of the WIPO Intergovernmental Committee on Intellectual Property and Genetic Resources, Traditional Knowledge and Folklore (known as the IGC). I also helped draft some of the documents prepared by the Secretariat for the first meetings of the Committee and undertook a few missions to Member States to discuss legal options on the protection of TK with local communities and government officials.

Three years later, I was transferred to the then-called IP Law Division, which was in charge of helping WIPO Member States transpose to national laws the obligations they had recently acquired under the TRIPS Agreement. In addition, the Division also helped those Members to implement obligations under other WIPO Treaties, such as the so-called Internet Treaties and the PLT (Patent Law Treaty).

The work of the Division was never triggered by the Secretariat's own initiative. Without exception, the Division worked on demand by Member States. The work consisted of drafting statutes and regulations, or of proposing amendments to existing statutes and regulations. In several instances, our assistance was required by Member States that were engaged in negotiations concerning free trade agreements (FTAs). In addition, the Division's staff participated in numerous meetings and seminars with Members' government officials, when ideas and suggestions on implementing TRIPS (and FTAs) obligations were exchanged.

This book is about the experience I have acquired in providing legislative assistance to WIPO developing Member States in the period 2002-2015, first as a senior staff member of the IP Law Division, and later as the Director of the IP and Competition Division. The book focuses on patents, but my work covered all other areas of Industrial Property, when required by Member States. These would be mostly, if not exclusively, developing countries.

The Division's work consisted basically of three phases: (1) it received a written request from a Member State; that request could be in the sense of providing a draft statute or regulation; or it could be accompanied by a copy of the national laws, so that the Division could give advice on how to make them compatible with the country's international obligations; (2) the Division provided the requested advice, in writing; when the work had implications on other specialized sectors of the Secretariat (e.g., matters involving the Patent Cooperation Treaty (the PCT), or the Madrid or Lisbon systems (concerning international trademark and geographical indication registrations, etc.)), the Division would coordinate with them; eventually, when confronted with sensitive issues, the Division's staff would consult and obtain clearance from supervisors; and (3) subsequently, meetings and seminars, either in Geneva or in the capitals of the concerned countries, would be organized to discuss the implementation of our recommendations, as well as providing training and agree on future work (such as the preparation of implementing regulations).

This book reflects the nature of my work on legislative assistance concerning patent law. For each topic, several options, where available, were presented and discussed with Member States. Preferences for one or another solution, when expressed, were based on the concrete situation of the Member State in question. Therefore, not always one single solution would be proposed. Moreover, as the Introduction of the book will show, public policies vary from country to country, and therefore solutions adopted should vary accordingly. WIPO had abandoned the "Model Law" approach many years before.[1] Instead, during my tenure there, the IP Law Division used a sort of legislative templates that, depending on the specific requests and concerns expressed by Member States, were adapted and modified on a case-by-case basis.

A few notes are important at this point.

First, not all staff members of the IP Law Division would provide the same assistance. In many instances, exactly because of the abandonment of the Model Law approach, our recommendations would follow our personal views and understanding of IP. So, the comments made through this book correspond specifically to my way of interpreting the Paris Convention and the TRIPS Agreement, and not that of the Secretariat. In many ways, I tried to resort to creative thinking to find solutions that would better match the interests of the particular country I was working with, without breaching that country's international obligations.

Second, eventually, not all suggestions presented to Member States were adopted. In some cases, the country would not agree with my recommendations, or they feared the reaction of their trading partners, when the proposals seemed to them too creative. In other cases, government officials would simply not agree.

1. Between the 60s and the 80s of last century, WIPO developed and adopted model laws on inventions, on trademarks, and on unfair competition. These models were discussed with and approved by Member States. In spite of their consensual nature, the models became obsolete in the face of the advent of the TRIPS Agreement. Moreover, because they were written as if they were statutes, they did not offer alternative means for implementing international obligations.

At this point, it should be emphasized that there is a general understanding that the role of WIPO is to promote the strongest protection of IP, in accordance with its own mandate. For that reason, it was not rare that WIPO's legislative advice was received in some countries with suspicion, and sometimes even with outright hostility. Some areas of government, such as the sectors dealing with public health, tended to be more hostile than others. However, that was (and is) a misperception. The WIPO Convention does not speak of WIPO's role of promoting *stronger* IP protection. In fact, Article 3(i) of the Convention provides that the objectives of the Organization are "to promote the protection of intellectual property," i.e., without any qualification or quantification. This point has already been made by the WIPO Secretariat in a public document delivered in the context of the debate concerning patents for human stem cells. Justifying the Secretariat's view that they had no stance as regards the patenting of human stem cells, the document reads:

> It should be clarified at the outset that WIPO's role is not to increase intellectual property protection at any cost, but to develop ways to facilitate its efficient protection. Efficient protection of intellectual property, it goes without saying, is not necessarily the same as increasing and expanding protection to areas where protection is not socially useful or necessary. This is why, despite WIPO's treaties silence on ethical issues, it is so important for WIPO and its Member States to engage in a constructive discussion on possible social constraints on the expansion of intellectual property protection. A precise and correct identification of those constraints may indeed be a powerful tool to assist WIPO and its Member States to draw a line between efficient and inefficient intellectual property protection.[2]

The statement above was read by me on behalf of WIPO. But I drafted it only in part. A good deal of the text was drafted and/or revised by Francis Gurry (then WIPO Deputy Director General and subsequently, Director General). So, the statement is not my personal opinion, but the position of the Secretariat on the real meaning of Article 3 of the WIPO Convention.

In this token, I have always strived to maintain neutrality and impartiality, as many references included through this book will show.

And yet, as said, there has been a general misperception that WIPO officials, like me, in providing legislative assistance, did not look at the specific needs and interests of particular countries, and instead followed a general template that was blind to those needs and interests. It is that misperception that explains the language of part of the Agenda for Development that, in 2007, WIPO Member States approved (upon the pressure of a group of active developing countries, which wanted to stop the negotiations on the SPLT (Substantive Patent Law Treaty) at all costs).[3] The suspicion on the

2. European Group on Ethics in Science and New Technologies to the European Commission, Opinion on the ethical aspects of patenting inventions involving human stem cells, Opinion No. 16, of May 7, 2002, accompanying document, at 97, *The WIPO Approach to Ethical Issues* (WIPO statement), at 101, available at <op.europa.eu/en/publication-detail/-/publication/687b0402-32b8-4b1a-905e-b7885d2a3eac> [access January 2025].
3. The negotiations on the SPLT were running very smoothly in WIPO during the first years of this century. After the entry into force of the TRIPS Agreement, with its harmonizing effects, and the approval of the Patent Law Treaty, in 2002, disciplining the formalities around the filing of patent applications, some WIPO Member States understood that the moment had come to set some

lack of impartiality in WIPO's legislative assistance is reflected in various passages of the Agenda's 45 recommendations, in particular:

> "13. WIPO's legislative assistance shall be, *inter alia*, development-oriented and demand-driven, taking into account the priorities and the special needs of developing countries, especially LDCs, as well as the different levels of development of Member States and activities should include time frames for completion."
> "14. Within the framework of the agreement between WIPO and the WTO,[4] WIPO shall make available advice to developing countries and LDCs, on the implementation and operation of the rights and obligations and the understanding and use of flexibilities contained in the TRIPS Agreement."
> "17. In its activities, including norm-setting, WIPO should take into account the flexibilities in international intellectual property agreements, especially those which are of interest to developing countries and LDCs."
> "19. To initiate discussions on how, within WIPO's mandate, to further facilitate access to knowledge and technology for developing countries and LDCs to foster creativity and innovation and to strengthen such existing activities within WIPO."[5]

The repeated reference to the need for a special attention to be paid to least-developed and developing countries' needs reflected the view of a number of delegates that the WIPO Secretariat provided the same advice to all WIPO Member States, regardless of their specific level of development and special interests. The fear was that we were pushing for the adoption of "TRIPS plus" levels of protection, thereby serving the interests of a number of developed countries and of their companies, namely in the pharmaceutical sector.

Actually, it was not the level of countries' development that dictated WIPO's advice, but the special concerns manifested by their government officials. The irony—and the evidence that the Development Agenda was motivated by politics, not by facts—was that delegates of some of the developing countries that supported the proposal for the Agenda were very well aware of the nature and content—and

---

common rules on the definitions of the conditions of patentability, including the grace period (which is an exception to novelty). But later, when the negotiations were already in a developed stage, some developing countries started feeling uncomfortable with the idea of the SPLT. A few governments feared that the harmonization of the conditions of patentability was a first step in the setting of a global patent mechanism, which the WIPO International Bureau had proposed in 2001. *See* WO/GA/26/4, Annex II, WIPO Industry Advisory Commission, *Report of the Third Meeting* [to the General Assembly of September 25 to October 3, 2000], Geneva, May 4 and 5, 2000, at 2. Other governments were misled by the term "Substantive" and believed that the SPLT, once approved, would impose new and higher substantive standards of protection. For a discussion on the idea of the global patent, from the PCT to the Global Dossier Initiative, *see* Nuno Pires de Carvalho, The TRIPS Regime of Patents and Test Data, at 21 et seq. (5th ed., Wolters Kluwer, 2018). The latest version of the draft SPLT can be found in document SCP/10/2, of September 30, 2003, Standing Committee on the Law of Patents, Tenth Session, Geneva, May 10 to 14, 2004, *Draft Substantive Patent Law Treaty*, prepared by the International Bureau.

4. Even if it did not mention legislative assistance expressly, the agreement between the two Organizations, of 1995, in addition to other commitments, was understood as meaning that WIPO's International Bureau of WIPO would provide legislative assistance to WTO Members regardless of their being WIPO Member States or not.
5. *See* <www.wipo.int/ip-development/en/agenda/>.

eventually of the attendant risks—of the legislative advice provided by the WIPO Secretariat.

An element that is frequently forgotten by the critics of WIPO's legislative advice is that the legal provisions that require and give guidance on the quality of drafting a patent application and determine that inventors be treated fairly by the patent office contribute to the implementation of public policies as much as those provisions that determine the rights and the manners of using them. Tolerance with poorly drafted patents hurts small inventors because they will lack the means to enforce the rights that result from them. The same is not true for holders of large patent portfolios, who can benefit from mistaken patents, in particular when the mistakes consist in the broadening of the scope of exclusivity.

It is also important to note that this book does not provide any recommendation on the techniques of legal drafting. The drafting of laws may be very tricky. In the first place, legal drafting requires a full domain of national language(s), and in particular of legal language, in order to avoid as much ambiguity and obscurity as possible. And, in the second place, the drafter should be aware of national jurisprudence and the existing links that form the interactions between the various branches of law and IP. Usually, the drafts prepared by me and submitted to governments would be sent to a national specialized committee in charge of legal drafting. That committee would then make the necessary adaptations to local legal traditions and techniques.[6] Poorly written laws may give rise to serious problems of construction and lead to frivolous or unjustified litigation, even when the adopted language mirrors legal texts transposed from international treaties or is imported from foreign legal texts.

And yet one should not forget how important it is to have a well-drafted statute as opposed to one that contains ambiguities and language imprecisions. Of the many stories in this regard with which I was confronted during my tenure at WIPO, I may invoke one particular experience that illustrates well the negative consequences of a poorly drafted statute. The story (a real one, I insist) is about a country that, in the first years of this century, with the objective of opening its economy to international trade and investment, decided to join the WTO. One of the conditions that country had to obey was the updating of its patent law, then very dated and rarely used (and containing IP standards that were significantly below the minimum levels of protection imposed by the TRIPS Agreement). In preparation for the accession, the government announced publicly that it had the intention of undertaking a complete modification of its IP laws. And suddenly, the country's tiny, frozen, almost nonexistent patent office was flooded with tens of thousands of patent applications of foreign origin, all claiming old priorities, many resulting from thirty, forty, even fifty-year-old filing dates. The reason was that the patent statute that at that time was in force in that country provided that patent applications of foreign origin could benefit from a right of priority—but without defining what priority meant, and without even making an explicit reference to

6. It is in this sense that para. 1 of Art. 1 of the TRIPS Agreement refers to the freedom of Members "to determine the legal method of implementing the provisions of this Agreement within their own legal system and practice."

the Paris Convention.[7] Therefore, in the (ambiguous, poorly drafted) language of the law, the right of priority was time-unlimited. In that event, foreign companies and their local patent attorneys saw an opportunity: before the entry into force of the new statute, drafted in compliance of TRIPS rules, including those provisions of the Paris Convention incorporated through Article 2.1—thus limiting the right of priority to one year from the date of the first regular filing—the local patent office could not reject patent applications on the ground of their having exceeded the time limit assigned to the claim of priority, for the simple reason that the lawmaker had not set any limit whatsoever.

I am personally aware of this story (and many others) because the filing of those tens of thousands of patent applications (the figure cited by government officials was of around 40,000 patent applications, a significant number of them concerning chemical and pharmaceutical inventions) coincided with one mission I undertook to the country's capital, in preparation for the future negotiations the country wished to launch aiming at celebrating a free trade agreement with one of its trading partners. In that context, the government wished to discuss several matters of IP law that might arise in those negotiations. It was in one of the meetings with the head negotiator of the Ministry of Commerce that he mentioned the kind of flash flood of patent applications of foreign origin. He told me that the authorities did not know what to do. My answer was the following: "give instructions to the person in charge of the patent office to reject all those 40,000 patent applications, for lack of novelty." The reason, as I explained, was not a problem of exceeding the priority time limit (because there was none, as said), but because the fundamental notion behind priority, as adopted in the Paris Convention, was to give some time—a limited, short period—to patent applicants to take the necessary measures to prepare for applying for protection in other countries.[8] Even though the patent statute of that country, as said, did not mention the right of priority as granted by the Paris Convention, it was obvious that the lawmaker had obtained inspiration from Article 4 of the Convention. In other words, buttressing the concept of priority, there is a notion of hurry, of haste. Patent applications claiming

7. At that time the country in question was not a Contracting Party to the Paris Convention.
8. Initially, the idea of the priority was to give inventors the possibility of filing a first patent application (eventually, in their home country) and verifying whether its commercial exploitation was feasible—it being understood that starting the commercial exploitation would take no longer than one year. After learning about the possibility of a successful commercial exploitation, then the inventor could seek protection in other countries without losing the right to obtain a patent because of lack of novelty. This was the explanation given by Chair of the first Diplomatic Conference, in 1880, that led to the approval of the text of the Paris Convention (the second and successful conference was held, also in Paris, in 1883):

> As regards the interest of industry, the concerns of several delegates appear to him to be exaggerated. The normal period for putting an invention into exploitation is one year, and it seems fair not to impose on the inventor the expense of taking out a patent abroad until he is in a position to know whether his invention can be exploited fully. In summary, he considers that the one-year period presents few disadvantages and many advantages.

Ministère des Affaires Etrangères, Conférence Internationale pour la Protection de la Propriété Industrielle, at 54 (Imprimerie Nationale, 1880).

the right of priority based on a filing date that was 5, 10, 20 years old (and more) did not match that concept. So, those patent applications could not benefit from priority and, therefore, failed to comply with the novelty requirement. In this manner, the burden of proof was reversed: patent applicants would need to give evidence that as soon as they applied for a patent abroad, they had started taking the measures to file the same application in the country in question (translating, hiring a patent attorney, etc.); otherwise, the publication of the applications in other countries constituted per se a factor destroying patentability.

The title of this book refers to developing countries. Actually, comments are included that concern developed countries as well, but the book is especially oriented toward the former. The reason is that suggestions and recommendations have been elaborated having developing countries as targets.

However, when I mention legislative advice given to developing countries and their governments, it is important not to forget that I am referring to giving advice to people, human beings, who work for their governments and countries. Human beings are motivated by their beliefs and interests. So, although statutes may express collective efforts of countries' parliaments and executive branches (and eventually, the judiciary), it is the belief, the interests, and the hopes of the persons who intervene in the political process of drafting and approving laws that are expressed in those statutes. Statutes may set rules of conduct in an abstract, impersonal manner, but they reveal concrete intentions of those who draft them.

I emphasize this at the outset in order to clarify why we can see expressed in patent statutes a wide variety of public policies that their makers would wish to pursue through their enactment, and yet those statutes have to conform to the templates that exist in multilateral agreements and cannot be, therefore, very different from each other in their essence, that is, in setting how patent rights are acquired, how they are used, and how they are lost.

The objective of this book is not to cover all aspects of a patent statute, but only those that address public policies. For example, to discuss the introduction into a patent statute of the requirement that patented objects be identified with the symbol Ⓟ may be useful in a country that has a particular concern with compliance with IP rights. But it is not essential. In many countries, actually, such a requirement has been dropped, for it does not constitute sufficient notice of infringement, particularly when the patent covers a process or part of a complex product. Eventually, the opposite may be more helpful, that is, to sanction the undue use of that symbol by someone who has no patent or whose patent has been invalidated or has otherwise expired. Another topic that patent laws, both of developed and developing countries, cannot be passed without dealing with in detail is the claim of priority, the formalities needed for its acceptance, and the consequences of abandoned, unpublished applications. Priority is a matter of essence for the international patent system, and yet it does not reflect any public policy of particular interest for development, either technical or economic.

As noted above, legal assistance is provided by the WIPO Secretariat on a bilateral and confidential basis. In order to keep that confidentiality, this book does not reveal the many discussions I have had with government officials of many countries throughout the world. Most of those conversations were deeply interesting, and some touched upon philosophical ways of looking at law and, in particular, at patent law. It has been fascinating to me to realize that so drastically different views could be expressed by government officials of different countries on exactly the same international obligations. However, due to a duty of confidentiality, some of those amazing stories and episodes cannot be revealed.

Finally, it is important to note that in identifying the *dos* and the *don'ts* in drafting a patent statute, I am expressing my personal views, which, as said, I shared with the governments of many developing countries during my tenure in the WIPO Secretariat. They are my personal views, I repeat, not necessarily those of the Secretariat.

Belo Horizonte, Brazil, August 15, 2025

Introduction

ARE THERE PATENT STATUTES THAT ARE PROPER FOR DEVELOPING COUNTRIES?

We have to admit: patents are not a tool of development, in the sense that, alone, they do not contribute to a country's development. The clear proof of this is that many poor countries have adopted patent systems without those systems showing any impact on those countries' pace of development.

And yet, the question that forms the heading of this section is a relevant one. According to the title of this book, the answer is "yes"—the drafting of a patent law should indeed take the developing status of a country into consideration. But once that question is answered, another question springs to mind: in what *should* a patent statute for a developing country differ from one that has been adopted in a developed country? Before providing the answer, it should be noted that the modal verb *should* was highlighted on purpose. In effect, one thing is thinking and discussing the peculiarities of a patent statute that is adapted to the economic and social structure of a developing country, and another is perusing existing laws and trying to perceive in them those provisions that are the result of a matching with the country's economic status. The reason is that, in the face of the various international agreements that in the last decades have been negotiated and accepted worldwide with the aim of harmonizing the standards of intellectual property protection, it has become increasingly difficult to identify the legal elements that distinguish a patent law drafted by a developing country's lawmaker from one drafted by the lawmaker of a developed country.

At the outset, it should be emphasized that the patent system performs the same function in developed and developing countries: to secure new functionalities and technical features that entrepreneurs introduce in products and services in order to differentiate them from those that are made and sold by their rivals, so as to keep and to lure the clientele. The patent system is about commercial rivalry. Patents are tools of free entrepreneurship. They bring legal security, thus motivating creative entrepreneurs to invest in new products, and reducing transaction costs in technology transfer.[9]

Once this is said, developing countries are under the pressure of a large variety of elements that lead them to face the patent system under a perspective that, although not forgetting the fundamentals of patent law, is different from the way in which developed countries consider it. In developing countries, legal institutions are not as secure and predictable as they are in developed countries, and because of their lower educational level, the population of developing countries tend to believe in the merits of a strong and constant interference of government in individual lives and in the economy in general.

As far as patent protection is concerned, developing countries would prefer not to share with the societies of developed countries the burden of paying the costs of inventions in some important fields where the national scientific and technological networks do not have enough knowledge and do not possess the tools for inventing new solutions adapted to national needs, such as in the pharmaceutical and telecommunication areas. Developing countries would prefer to use the mechanism that the Paris Convention has made available to them in the sense of allowing the denial of patent protection to foreign inventors, provided they denied the same protection to their own nationals. By resorting to that dimension of national treatment, developing countries could either reproduce inventions patented abroad or import the corresponding products, without worrying about the necessity of covering the resources spent by the inventors in inventing and testing the inventions. This avenue was closed with the advent of the TRIPS Agreement, which adds to the national treatment principle the imposition of compliance with minimum standards of protection, in particular the prohibition of discriminatory treatment of technological fields under patent laws.

Under this significant constraint, a patent law for a developing country must provide for adequate protection for inventions in all fields of technology, this necessarily meaning that foreign inventors will be entitled to seek opportunities for commercially exploiting their inventions in its territory under effective security. This is the price that developing countries accepted to pay during the Uruguay Round of GATT negotiations in exchange for obtaining facilitated access (in terms of tariffs and sanitary and phytosanitary measures) for the commodities they produce in the markets of developed countries. However, once this methodological base is set, the patent lawmaker of a developing country keeps two major concerns in mind:

(1) the law should reduce the burden of sharing the costs of invention with developed countries to a minimum possible; and
(2) the law should provide for a mechanism of granting patents that is efficient but simple and cost-effective, this meaning a system the operation of which

9. A detailed discussion of the function of IP as a mechanism that leads to and encourages product differentiation can be found in Nuno Pires de Carvalho, The Intellectual Property of the Poor and Other Essays on the Economic and Social Function of IP (self-publication, KDP 2024), in particular in Chapter 1, *Product Differentiation: The Core Function of IP*, at 15-57.

does not impose a heavy burden on the country's public administration and still provides legal security to inventors.

The first concern is about the so-called and frequently mentioned *flexibilities*—measures that, without infringing international obligations, seek creative solutions that respect the national interests in terms of reducing the exclusionary impact of foreign patents.[10] In this field, limits are determined, on the one hand, by the rules imposed under international law, and, on the other, by lawmakers' creative thinking. In this book, we will see many examples of flexible approaches that the patent laws of developing countries have, or might have, taken.

The second concern relates to the sound management of the administrative, bureaucratic component of the patent system. Patents are public documents that express public faith. They should not be granted lightly, therefore. But the granting of patents should not require from the country's civil administration a disproportionately high amount of human, technical, and financial resources. The TRIPS Agreement has a provision that explicitly deals with the need for developing countries to adequately measure the quantity of resources made available to enforcing patent rights—it is Article 41.5.[11] The provision is, actually, about enforcement, but it could very well be analogically read as dealing with the prosecution of those IP rights that depend on the formalities of registration. In this particular regard, the only mandatory requirements mentioned by the Agreement are that procedures and formalities be "reasonable" and sufficiently expeditious so as to "permit the granting or registration of the right within a reasonable period of time so as to avoid unwarranted curtailment of the period of protection"—in other words, procedures and formalities concerning the grant of patents (as well as of other industrial property titles) should allow for a reasonably expeditious outcome (paragraphs 1 and 2 of Article 62).

So, the answer to the initial question is a firm "yes": there are, indeed, patent statutes that are proper to developing countries. The World Trade Organization (WTO) itself, whose legal framework includes the TRIPS Agreement, answers that question affirmatively. First, developing countries (which, in the WTO, are not designated as such, but as territories, given that in order to be a WTO Member, the requirement is

10. However, we should not forget that WTO Members can also adopt flexible approaches that lead to an increase in the protection of inventors' rights, such as those that result from free trade agreements. Those are flexibilities "upwards," which are authorized by Art. 1.1 of the TRIPS Agreement, whereas flexibilities "downwards" are authorized under Arts 30 and 31, among other provisions. Both upwards and downwards flexibilities are conditioned to the compliance with a number of requirements.
11. Article 41.5 of the TRIPS Agreement reads:

> *It is understood that this Part does not create any obligation to put in place a judicial system for the enforcement of intellectual property rights distinct from that for the enforcement of law in general, nor does it affect the capacity of Members to enforce their law in general. Nothing in this Part creates any obligation with respect to the distribution of resources as between enforcement of intellectual property rights and the enforcement of law in general.*

that a territory enjoys autonomy in the matter of customs) have been granted special and longer transitional periods for the implementation of most TRIPS obligations. Second, decisions adopted by the WTO Membership after the TRIPS Agreement entered into force present certain particular aspects that concern developing economies exclusively (such as allowing developed and large developing countries to grant compulsory licenses with the purpose of exporting pharmaceutical products to those countries). And, more evidently, the successive extensions of transitional periods granted to the least-developed countries (LDCs) for implementing patent and test data protection in the area of pharmaceuticals and agrochemicals correspond to the very low level of interest that developed economies have in the importing markets of those countries.

One additional aspect is that the distinction between a developing country and a developed one can be extremely blurred. The economies of many developing countries include sectors that are sophisticated and productive (and inventive), in tandem with sectors that are underdeveloped and inefficient, and thus require some insulation from foreign competition. Actually, the same can be said of some countries considered to be developed. This is the reason that has led the WTO to rely on the self-designation by its Members of the developing or developed status (by contrast, the LDC status is provided by a list prepared by the United Nations).

Anyway, this book deals with aspects of patent statutes that, although concerning both developed and developing countries, contain solutions that are especially adequate for the latter.

Among the many statutes that I have had the opportunity to read and to whose drafting I have contributed, in one way or another, I would single out the Industrial Property Act of the Sultanate of Oman, of 2007, as that which, although following the same standards of protection as those of all other WTO Members, contains a significant number of very creative solutions that are particularly adapted to the status of a developing country. The reason is that, in spite of that law having been drafted under the constraints of a free trade agreement that the Sultanate had signed with the United States, the Omani lawmaker was able to introduce new and creative solutions to ensure that the law successfully pursues a number of significant public policies. Of particular relevance in that statute are the provisions that deal with plant patents, exhaustion of patent rights, and the conditions for the granting of injunctions in enforcement procedures.[12] These particular elements will be commented on later in the book.

12. The number of patent applications in Oman has grown significantly since the FTA's entry into force. From almost zero applications filed directly in the country (Oman being part of the Gulf Cooperation Council, patent applications designating Oman can also be filed through the GCC patent office), in the first decade of this century, patent applications increased to 346, in 2015, and to 874, in 2023. This growth reflects the confidence of national and international innovative companies in Oman's initiative toward evolving from an oil-and-gas-based economy to a diversified one, as well as in the importance the country is gaining in the international scenario, independently from the larger economies of the other GCC Member States (Bahrain, Kuwait, Qatar, Saudi Arabia, and the United Arab Emirates).

WHAT OBJECTIVES SHOULD A DEVELOPING COUNTRY'S PATENT STATUTE PURSUE?

Patent statutes, like all laws, serve collective interests. Attendance to those interests is pursued through the implementation of objectives, which in general aim at fulfilling public policies. Not all patent laws designate the objectives they are aimed at achieving, but a significant number of them do, for a very practical reason: their explicit expression in the text of the statute has a significant influence on the way courts construe its provisions. In some countries, those objectives, or, at least, those that are deemed more important—because there may be collective objectives that in one country are deemed more important than others—are given the deference of being set in the Constitution. This is not common, however, because the general view is that the protection of inventions through patents mostly seeks utilitarian purposes, which are not deemed to deserve the dignity of becoming part of a text such as the Constitution, which expresses the fundamental organization of a country's society. And yet, in some countries, Constitutions have expressed the major goals of granting patents, e.g.: to promote the progress of science (United States, since 1789[13]), and to ensure the inviolability of property rights (Brazil, since 1824[14]).

Another important introductory point is that the identification of the objectives that one country wishes to achieve through its patent law may imply the trading-off of certain of those objectives for the sake of giving preeminence to other, eventually conflicting, goals. We will see through this book numerous examples of those exercises of trading-off. After all, in making decisions concerning the drafting of the provisions of a patent statute, it is of the essence that the lawmaker fully understands the implications of the decisions he/she makes. One particular case of trade-off in patent laws can be seen in the option for national or international exhaustion of patent rights—both options with their conveniences and inconveniences. Below, we will discuss possible solutions for keeping the conveniences and avoiding the inconveniences of both types of exhaustion.

1 THE FIRST PUBLIC POLICY: TO PROTECT INVENTORS' RIGHTS AS HUMAN RIGHTS

Paragraph 2 of Article 27 of the Universal Declaration of Human Rights reads:

> *Everyone has the right to the protection of the moral and material interests resulting from any scientific, literary or artistic production of which he is the author.*[15]

13. *See* < www.senate.gov/about/origins-foundations/senate-and-constitution/constitution.htm > .
14. The Portuguese version of the Brazilian Constitution of 1824 is available at < www.planalto.gov.br/ccivil_03/constituicao/constituicao24.htm > . The Constitution of 1988, which is in force today, keeps in the Preamble to Art. 5 a very similar text to that of the Preamble to Art. 179 of the Constitution of 1824 (adopted two years after the independence of the country), both texts emphasizing the inviolability of the right to property, and enunciating the rights of inventors as an expression of that superior, fundamental right.
15. The full text of the Declaration is available at < www.un.org/en/about-us/universal-declaration-of-human-rights > .

In view of the explicit language of the Universal Declaration, countries might feel obliged to enact patent laws in respect for human rights. Indeed, inventors' proprietary interests in their creations are a natural right, the same way in which the property in the fruits of labor is naturally attributed to laborers. Such an attribution corresponds to the third of the three precepts of Law, as they were enunciated by Ulpianus, a Roman jurist of the third century AD: "*Iuris praecepta sunt haec: honeste vivere, alterum non laedere, suum cuique tribuere*" ["The precepts of law are these: to live honorably, not to harm others, to give to each his own]"[16] (Inst. 1,1,3-4).

In this sense, a country may feel inclined toward protecting inventions through patents as an expression of human rights. In doing so, that country not only professes a philosophical adherence to the protection of inventions as a superior value but also wards off eventual attacks and criticisms by opponents of the system.

One example can be found in the Industrial Property Act of Guatemala. In its Preamble, the Act reads (in part):

> *The Congress of the Republic of Guatemala,*
> *Considering:*
> *That the Political Constitution of the Republic recognizes and protects the right to freedom of industry and commerce, as well as the right of inventors, as rights inherent to the human person, guaranteeing their holders the enjoyment of exclusive ownership of their creations, in accordance with the law and international treaties of which the Republic of Guatemala is a party; . . .*[17]

The same inclination, but with a different perspective, is expressed in the patent law of Cuba. In its Preamble, the law enunciates two basic justifications for the protection of inventions through patents:

> *Whereas: The Constitution of the Republic of Cuba establishes in its article 9, paragraph a), that the State protects the creative work of the people and the property and wealth of the socialist nation.*
> *Whereas: Inventions and industrial designs and models constitute valuable results of man's intellectual activity, insofar as they contribute to satisfying his material and spiritual needs and to the development of society.*[18]

The major difference between Guatemala's and Cuba's objectives in protecting inventions is that the former emphasizes the private nature of the rights granted to inventors, whereas Cuba places those rights within the rationale of socialism. Actually, Guatemala's law is more faithful to the letter and spirit of the TRIPS Agreement, which,

16. These precepts of law were cited in one of the most fundamental and influential compendia of legal rules—the INSTITUTA, of Emperor Justinian, completed in the sixth century AD, and which provided for the legal basis for the empires of Roma and Byzantium during several centuries. *See* < www.britannica.com/biography/Ulpian > [accessed January 20, 2025].
17. Decree nr. 57-2000. Most statutes mentioned and quoted throughout this book are available at WIPO Lex (< www.wipo.int/en/web/wipolex >). When obtained from other sources, an explicit reference will be made. Individual references to national statutes and regulations will appear in this book only once, in order to avoid useless repetition of references. In the event the law of a country is quoted more than once, the first reference that will appear in the Index will guide the reader to the numbering of the law and, eventually, to its source (if it is not WIPO Lex).
18. Decree-Law nr. 290, of 2012.

in paragraph four of the Preamble, states that, while agreeing on a set of principles and rules on IP, WTO Members recognized that "intellectual property rights are private rights."[19] This means that the enforcement of private proprietary rights in inventions in Cuba might lead to some tension between private interests and public objectives, particularly when those inventions concern some areas of collective interest, such as health and the production of sugar cane. But the absence of a private industrial sector and a consumers' market in that country reduces the probability of those conflicts to zero.

2 THE MOST FREQUENTLY MENTIONED PUBLIC POLICY UNDERGIRDING PATENT STATUTES: TO PROMOTE ECONOMIC AND TECHNOLOGICAL DEVELOPMENT, IN GENERAL, AND INVENTION, IN PARTICULAR

Recognizing the human being's inherent, natural right to ownership in his/her intellectual work may be an obvious objective of any national patent system. But the vast majority of countries envisage the enactment of patent laws with more utilitarian goals, in search of economic effects that will result in an improvement in the lives of citizens, namely by means of technical progress. This objective has been recognized by the WTO Membership, and is reflected in the fifth paragraph of the Preamble of the TRIPS Agreement:

19. The analysis of how Cuba can conciliate its socialist objectives with a TRIPS-consistent IP scheme would permit a fascinating discussion, but this book is not the place for that. During my tenure at WIPO, I have undertaken various missions to Cuba, and more than once I have discussed that topic with Cuban civil servants. The last time was before my retirement, in 2015, when Cuba was softening its stance against private property, in order to permit a commercial and political approach to the U.S. administration, then under the Presidency of Barack Obama. The major concern of Cuban authorities was with the awakening of commercial rivalry among the Cuban businesses oriented to provide services related to tourism, such as B&Bs and restaurants, which had recently been allowed to be privately owned. Some practices of unfair competition started to emerge, which left the authorities baffled, given their lack of familiarity with competition. At that time, I served the WIPO Secretariat as Director of the IP and Competition Policy Division. The purpose of my mission was to help the Cuban government consider and eventually adopt a statute on the repression of unfair competition in order to address those practices, such as the aggressive approach by the employees of some restaurants located near the Cathedral of Havana, who invited tourists to prefer the restaurant they worked for—a practice of tortious interference, which has been deemed illegal since the adoption of the by-laws of the guild of cooks of Paris, in the end of the thirteenth century. *See* Nuno Pires de Carvalho, The Intellectual Property of Food and Hospitality: From Sybaris' Banquets to NASA's Deep Space Food Challenge, at 13-14 (Wolters Kluwer, 2024). Another sort of unfair practice was the registration by Cuban citizens of trademarks of foreign origin. The objective of those dishonest persons was "to bank" on foreign trademarks, so that when, if the opening of the Cuban economy progressed, their legitimate owners came to Cuba, they had to negotiate with them. The trademark law of Cuba Decree-Law nr. 203, of 1999, had a provision that could be used to address the problem. It is Art. 17.1(j), which provides that when "the registration of the sign has been applied for with the purpose of doing, facilitating or consolidating in an obvious manner an act of unfair competition" is prohibited, but its language could make its application difficult, namely the reference to the obviousness of the intention. Later, in 2016, Cuba enacted a statute repressing unfair competition, which repeats the text of Art. 10*bis* of the Paris Convention and, in addition, dedicates extensive attention to trade secrets and regulatory data.

Members,

. . .

Recognizing the underlying public policy objectives of national systems for the protection of intellectual property, including developmental and technological objectives; . . .

This same objective is stated in the Preamble of the Patent Cooperation Treaty (PCT), of 1978:

The Contracting States,

. . .

Desiring to foster and accelerate the economic development of developing countries through the adoption of measures designed to increase the efficiency of their legal systems, whether national or regional, instituted for the protection of inventions by providing easily accessible information on the availability of technological solutions applicable to their special needs and by facilitating access to the ever-expanding volume of modern technology, ...

Interestingly, this Recital does not state that the Treaty supports economic and technical development as a consequence of its facilitating the filing of patent applications in Contracting States. What the Recital says is that the disclosure of technology provided by patent applications makes a broad technological database available to developing countries, and thus it helps their development. But that is not necessarily true. As we will discuss below, when analyzing the patent law provisions that concern the enabling disclosure, the description of inventions does not necessarily mean that patent documents can be used as instruments of teaching.

Actually, we find this same approach in the majority of patent laws that state their own objectives. In some countries, those objectives are found in their Constitution. That is the case, for example, of Brazil, whose Constitution (of 1988), as said above, declares the patent system a matter of protection of fundamental property rights. But subsequently, the same provision (Article 5), and to some extent in a contradictory sense,[20] provides that:

20. The (apparent) contradiction is that the *caput* of Art. 5 of Brazilian Constitution seems to designate patent rights as a matter of superior value, in association with the framework of a free economy based on private property. To that extent, the very existence of patent rights serves the collective interest of a society that has organized itself around a fundamental concept of private property rights. However, its proviso nr. XXIX follows a utilitarian approach: patent rights are useful only as far as they serve the social interest—as if there were a social interest that is not the same as that of setting the foundations of a free economy—and promote technological and economic development. Therefore, Brazilian courts may very well be tempted to filter the rights of those who rely on them for delivering justice and enforcing their patents against infringers. The filter could be the modulation of patent rights in conformity with the "social interest." This has happened already, when the Supreme Court of Brazil, in deciding that the legal provision that granted automatic extension of the terms of patents whose prosecution had taken longer than ten years (for reasons not attributable to the applicant) was unconstitutional, and, consequently, cancelled with immediate effect all pharmaceutical patents. In doing so, the court preserved all other patents the terms of which had been extended. The main reason invoked for the discriminatory treatment against pharmaceutical patents was the alleged prejudice they caused to the cheap access to medicines by the Brazilian poor. *See infra*, Chapter 9, section 1.2.

XXIX. The law will ensure to authors of industrial inventions the temporary privilege for their use, [...] taking into account the social interest and the technological and economic development of the country.

This objective is often mentioned in national patent laws. For example, Article 1 of the Patent Act of Japan reads:

The purpose of this Act is to encourage inventions by protecting and utilizing them, thereby contributing to the development of industry.[21]

Guatemala, whose law was quoted above, because it qualifies inventors' rights as fundamental rights, additionally identifies a utilitarian value to the granting of patents. In other words, as in Brazil, Guatemala's legal system attributes a double dimension to the objectives of the national patent system. Article 1 of the law of Guatemala reads:

The purpose of this law is to protect, stimulate and encourage intellectual creativity that has applicability in the field of industry and commerce and, in particular, [...] patents for inventions and utility models [...].

In the same direction, the patent law of Angola states in its Preamble:

With Angola's economy currently undergoing radical change, now is an opportune time to define the legislative framework applicable to industrial property, a tool capable of stimulating innovation and inventive activity at the national level, encouraging investment, and promoting the expansion of trade and the widespread dissemination of technology.[22]

In a somewhat more complex language, but with the same meaning, the introductory recitals of the patent law of Andorra say the same:

In the current context of expansion of innovative activities, it is important and necessary for the Principality of Andorra to promote productive activities that, because they are based on sectors such as research, development, and innovation, bring high added value and have a positive impact on the competitiveness of our country. Considering this, it is important to promote innovation and technological development, taking into account the challenges and opportunities that this development creates, facilitating access to knowledge and its dissemination, particularly with regard to inventive activities.[23]

Australian law has taken the same approach:

2A. Object of this Act. The object of this Act is to provide a patent system in Australia that promotes economic wellbeing through technological innovation and the transfer and dissemination of technology. In doing so, the patent system balances over time the interests of producers, owners and users of technology and the public.[24]

21. Act No. 121 of 1959, amended up to April 1, 2024.
22. Law No. 3/92 of February 28, 1992.
23. Law nr. 26/2014, of October 30, 2014.
24. Patents Act 1990, updated as of 2021.

Interestingly, this provision expresses an idea that is generally formulated as a wishful result, not as a statement of fact. Indeed, Article 7 of the TRIPS Agreement reads, in part, that:

> *The protection and enforcement of intellectual property rights* should contribute *[...], to the mutual advantage of producers and users of technological knowledge and in a manner conducive to social and economic warfare, and to a balance of rights and obligations* (emphasis added).

By contrast with the wishful tone of Article 7 of the TRIPS Agreement, the way the Australian statute is phrased seems to imply that national courts have no room left for looking at certain provisions of the statute and weigh their applicability in terms of the search for the desired equilibrium of rights and interests of patent owners and the users of patented inventions. It seems that the Australian lawmaker understands that the desired balance has already been obtained through the way in which the rights and obligations have been designed in the statute. In terms of balance, therefore, there is nothing more for the lawmaker to be concerned about: the executive branch of government and the courts will apply and enforce patent rights, and inventors and society will use inventions as provided in the law, and the balance is automatically reached.

Significantly, the same statement-of-fact approach appears in the "law on inventions" (not "law on patents") of the Democratic People's Republic of Korea. Article 1 of that law reads:

> *The Invention Law of the Democratic People's Republic of Korea, establishing the rules and orders in the application and examination for registration of inventor's certificate or patent and in its protection, thereby encouraging the creation of invention and promoting its use, shall contribute to the development of science, technology and the national economy.*[25]

The use of the verb form "shall" instead of "should" seems to reflect that the objective of the law is not a matter of desire, but of fact.[26] Apparently, simply by implementing the system of inventors' certificates (inherited from the model created in the Soviet Union) cumulated with utility patents causes those objectives to be achieved, even if at some later stage.

Language that is very compelling in terms of associating the protection of patents with technological development can be found in the Patent Act of Ethiopia, which has

25. Law on Inventions of the Democratic People's Republic of Korea (amended up to Decree No. 507 of 2021 of the Presidium of the Supreme People's Assembly).
26. As a matter of course, one should always be aware of eventual, if not expected, errors of translation in IP laws. Given that there is a specific legal jargon for IP, and taking into consideration that multilateral IP commitments include the obligation to notify foreign laws in the accepted languages, during my careers at the WTO and WIPO Secretariats I heard many complaints concerning misinterpretations and mistakes made by interpreters and translators. At some point, there was inside the WIPO Secretariat a discussion on setting organized courses on the basic notions and terminology of WIPO for translators. Due to the high costs, the idea was abandoned. Ensuring the quality of translations is, actually, the responsibility of Member States.

adopted a tone that is very hopeful of the benefits that such protection can bring to the country. The text goes as follows:

> *WHEREAS, it is necessary to create favourable conditions in order to encourage local inventive and related activities thereby building up national technological capability.*
>
> *WHEREAS, it has been found essential to encourage the transfer and adoption of foreign technology by creating conducive environment to assist the national development efforts of the country.*
>
> *WHEREAS, the task of fulfilling the nation's multidimensional demand for a harmonious scientific and technological progress, to be used for the public benefits, shall be most effectively served when there exists an appropriate legal framework. . . .*[27]

In the same token, the law of Cape Verde emphasizes industrial property's general goals of ensuring fair competition and the promotion of wealth. In explicitly mentioning "technical processes," Cape Verde takes a reductionist view, assimilating industrial property with its components that cover technical ideas, such as patents (and similar titles, like utility models and plant variety certificates), trade secrets of a technical nature, and industrial designs. But that is a conceptual mistake that is found in many other laws. Cape Verde's text goes as follows:

> *Article 4 Function of industrial property*
>
> *Industrial property shall have the social function of guaranteeing fair competition, by conferring private rights in various technical processes for production and development of wealth.*[28]

The association of patent protection with development can be seen in the Preambles and introductory provisions of many other national laws, as a sort of a mantra. The same understanding of the patent system as a factor for development was also the main foundation that buttressed the proposal by Argentina and Brazil for a WIPO Agenda for Development, in 2004. But it should be obvious that patent protection, as strong as it may be, does not promote development by itself. Development—of an economic, or technological, or other nature—requires a combination of multiple political, legal, economic, and social factors, patent protection being just a small fraction of the total. Indeed, a country cannot engage in development without an operating patent system. But a country may be deeply underdeveloped even with a patent system in full force. WTO Members have understood this when they suspended the least-developed-country (LDC) Members' obligation to implement the TRIPS minimum standards of protection.[29]

27. Inventions, Minor Inventions and Industrial Designs Proclamation No. 123/1995.
28. Legislative Decree No. 4/2007, of August 20.
29. The extension started with the TRIPS Agreement itself (Art. 66.1) and has been extended since. The last extension was decided in 2021, and is effective until July 1, 2034. *See* IP/C/88, of June 29, 2021. Until then, or until the extension is terminated, LDCs only have to comply with the TRIPS fundamental principles, of national treatment and most-favored-nation treatment.

3 A RARELY ADMITTED BUT FREQUENTLY PRESENT GOAL OF NATIONAL PATENT STATUTES: TO ATTEND TO TRADE COMMITMENTS

Let us be realistic: in a significant number of developing country WTO Members, the patent system—at least, a system that follows the minimum standards as set by Section 5 of Part II of the TRIPS Agreement—is seen as a burden, which national authorities would prefer not to implement.[30]

Actually, between 1986 and 1991, the Members of the Paris Union had engaged in discussions on a draft treaty that, if approved, would introduce in the Paris Convention a number of new provisions that would increase the standards of patent protection (in particular, by prohibiting discrimination against pharmaceutical inventions).[31] It is a fact that negotiations on this draft treaty ran in WIPO in parallel with the GATT Uruguay Round, and yet it was not that coincidence that led to their failure, but rather the resistance of developing countries against higher standards of patent protection, which, in their view, would defeat the possibility of putting patent law at the service of national industrial policies. The reason that led to the acceptance of those same higher standards in the Uruguay Round was the overall bargaining trade-off that was behind the acceptance of the TRIPS Agreement: concessions in a number of fields, such as tariffs, subsidies, sanitary and phytosanitary measures, were promised by developed countries, in exchange for concessions in the field of intellectual property by developing country trading partners. This means that, in the Uruguay Round, developing countries abandoned the use of intellectual property, and in particular of the patent system (with which they were particularly concerned) as a tool of industrial policy, and accepted it as a tool of market access.

---

30. As a matter of course, this idea should never be generalized. Depending on the ideological inclination of the government in place, views on the convenience of fowling higher, standardized patent standards may vary. For example, at the time of the entry into force of the TRIPS Agreement, in January 1995, Brazil was ruled by a center-left party that promoted privatization and respect for property rights. Brazil's President, a distinguished politician and academic, Fernando Henrique Cardoso, really believed in the perspective of the country becoming a center for the generation of technology and industrialized goods. In the ceremony of signature of Brazil's Industrial Property Law of 1996, which anticipated the implementation of most of TRIPS obligations (which were due by 2000), Brazil's President made the following statement:

> No country grows based on buccaneering. What we are doing now, by signing the Patent Act, is to put an end to the colonialist mentality—the mentality of those who think that Brazil has no competence, of those who still think that foreigners know everything and that they will dominate us. Neither do foreigners know everything nor are they going to dominate us. Our country needed to be in a position of being able to debate, in the WTO, without being always assumed that we were cheaters. Worse: cheaters and dull, because cheating has never led us anywhere.

Speech by President Cardoso, on May 14, 1996. This speech was kept for some time on the website of the Presidency of Brazil, but later it was deleted.

31. Draft Treaty Supplementing the Paris Convention as far as Patents are Concerned. *See* Actes de la Conférence Diplomatique pour la Conclusion d'un Traité Complétant la Convention de Paris en ce qui concerne les Brevets, vol. I, Première Partie de la Conférence Diplomatique, La Haye, 1991 (WIPO, 1993).

This objective, as the heading of this section states, is not very frequently expressed in legal texts. But here and there, one can find language that reflects that the primary purpose of the Patent Act is not to protect inventions and promote their exploitation and dissemination but to comply with international trade commitments for the sake of securing exports of commodities. In few cases where the law itself "confesses" that complying with international trade-related obligations is its primary objective, eventually the country is not even a WTO Member, but aspires to become one. This is the case of Cape Verde, which, when its national law passed, was still in the process of acceding to the WTO.[32] The Preamble to the patent law of Cape Verde reads (in part):

> *7. In addition, in order to enable the free circulation of new technologies, knowledge, goods, and services, the forthcoming and inevitable accession by Cape Verde to the World Trade Organization (WTO), requires the elimination of some incompatibilities and restrictions established by current legislation (or which result from the absence of law), and the adaptation of existing legislation regulating industrial property to that new reality. This requires the adoption of principles, concepts and the creation of institutions, today enshrined worldwide, and in particular the taking of some rules derived from the existing agreements at the level of that International Organization.*

Actually, one has to admit the possibility that a small, poor economy does not care about patent protection, admitting thereby that securing the rights and interests of national inventors is less important than allowing for the possibility of copying and importing off-patent products. Such country would be giving preference to free riding in opposition to enacting a legal regime supporting proprietary rights in inventions. Of course, that country would ignore that the transaction costs generated by a patent system, provided it is fair and balanced, are lower than those that result from not having the system (in terms of the difficulties of enforcing trade secrets as well as of the legal insecurity overriding unprotected inventions).

However, in view of the barriers to exportation created by tariffs and phytosanitary measures imposed by foreign markets, which negatively affect the exportation of commodities, and eventually of some industrialized goods, produced by that hypothetical developing country, the government is persuaded to decide to adopt patent protection as a negotiated deal, or as a trade-off. In the terms set by the TRIPS Agreement, that country is not even required to grant patent protection to its own nationals—the obligation, as mentioned above, is to provide for the levels of protection to the nationals and residents of the other WTO Members. Securing protection for nationals and residents may then become a matter of constitutional rules, which usually prohibit to accord more rights to foreigners than to nationals.

This objective is not exclusive to developing countries. Even a strong and developed economy, such as that of Spain, acknowledges that changes to its patent system have been made in accordance with trade commitments. One of the recitals to Spain's patent statute reads:

32. Cape Verde joined the WTO in 2008.

> *Another factor of change [of the law], associated with the decisive role of innovation as a support for international trade in an increasingly globalized economy, was the integration of Industrial Property, through the Agreement on Trade-Related Aspects of Intellectual Property Rights (TRIPS), within the framework of the Agreement establishing the World Trade Organization (WTO), signed in Marrakech on April 15, 1994, to which Spain joined on January 1, 1995.*[33]

Countries' objective of attending trade commitments as a justification for patent protection should not be underestimated. Not only developing countries had to raise their levels of protection to bring their national systems up to the minimum standards required by the TRIPS Agreement but also a significant number of them, subsequently, saw themselves under the obligation to raise those levels of protection even further as an expression of commitments made in bilateral (or regional) free trade agreements. Throughout this book, we will see several examples of this.

Today, this point has gained relevance in the face of the weakening of multilateralism, as a result of unilateral measures that some large trading partners have been taking, namely in the fields of tariffs and sanitary measures, and the diminution of the impact of the WTO Dispute Settlement Mechanism. This means that in the near future we may see a rise in the adoption of bilateral agreements concerning trade-related matters, including intellectual property. That happened in the first decades of the nineteenth century, and led to a high level of inconsistency among national trademark and industrial design regimes, in spite of the fact that some of those bilateral agreements included a most-favored-nation clause.[34] The world had to wait for the acceptance of globally harmonized standards under the Paris Convention and its several revisions through the end of the nineteenth and the first decades of the twentieth century.

Anyway, developing countries may see themselves confronted with difficult choices, between adopting a patent system that would better match national concerns and objectives and a patent system that attends to the interests of their trading partners (which are willing to exchange trade-related favors). The decision has to be made by national governments. When they cannot avoid bowing to the interests of their exporters, strategically (although eventually) associated with the interests of foreign inventors and investors, those countries can nevertheless search through the range of options offered by the TRIPS Agreement and pick those that are less strange to national interests. It is in that search that we can identify the "flexibilities" that are provided by the TRIPS Agreement, which, as noted above, can operate both downwards—in the sense of diminishing the rights of patent owners (compulsory licenses and other exceptions)—and upwards—in the sense of augmenting those same rights.

33. Law No. 24/2015, of July 24, 2015, on Patents (amended by Law No. 6/2018, of July 3, 2018).
34. The principle of the most-favored-nation determines that every trade-related concession that one country makes to another shall be immediately and unconditionally extended to all other countries that engage in trade relations with the former. In the TRIPS Agreement, the most-favored-nation principle is expressed in Art. 4 in the following terms:

> *With regard to the protection of intellectual property, any advantage, favour, privilege or immunity granted by a Member to the nationals of any other country shall be accorded immediately and unconditionally to the nationals of all other Members.*

4 ANOTHER OBJECTIVE: TO PROMOTE THE COUNTRY'S COMPETITIVENESS AND CAPACITY OF LURING FOREIGN DIRECT INVESTMENT (FDI)

Patents, depending on their quality,[35] permit to a significant extent the recovery of sunken costs in research and development (R&D), as well as of the investments in equipment and capacity building that permit their commercial exploitation. The availability of effective patent protection, therefore, may serve as bait for foreign direct investors (FDI) to bring their businesses to the country—if other conditions are present that encourage those investors. In other words, patent protection alone is not sufficient to lure FDI, but its absence or its ineffectiveness may be a significant factor that scares investors.

So, patent protection may constitute a powerful element for attributing competitiveness to a country. But it should be noted that competitiveness here means the comparative capacity of that country to attract FDI, not the creation of a procompetitive environment for businesses. Patent protection is undeniably an important factor for this latter kind of competitiveness, to the extent that its primary function is to protect inventions that serve as elements of differentiation of products that compete with similar products on the market. But the concept that most developing countries wish to retain when drafting a patent act is basically the former. This means that most of those laws that in their introductory provisions refer, implicitly or explicitly, to competitiveness are actually referring to the competitiveness of countries vis-à-vis other countries, rather than to the competitiveness of undertakings vis-à-vis their rivals.

The identification of the objective ensuring the country's competitiveness is present in the laws of many countries. One example is the patent law of the United Arab Emirates, of 2021:

> *Article (2) Objectives*
>
> *This Law is aimed at the following:*
>
> . . .
>
> 2. *The reinforcement of the State's competitiveness in the field of industrial right protection in line with the international best practices.*[36]

Another example is found in Article 2 of the law of Cambodia:

> *The objective of the Law is:*
>
> . . .
>
> *(iii) to encourage innovation and scientific and technological research and development; to stimulate and promote increased internal and external commerce and investment; to promote the transfer of technology to the Kingdom of*

35. The quality of patents is evaluated in accordance with their capacity of resisting challenges regarding their validity. Thorough and rigorous examination of patent applications leads to patents with a higher quality—hence, with a higher value.

36. Law No. 11, of 2021.

Cambodia in order to facilitate industrial activity and the development of the economy; . . .[37]

Significantly, a statute that, instead of referring to the competitiveness of the country, mentions the strengthening of commercial rivalry among undertakings (as a result of the adoption of a new patent law) is the already mentioned Industrial Property Law of Cape Verde. Very wisely, its law makes a special reference to the primary function of patents (and other IP assets) of ensuring product differentiation as a tool that undertakings use in their struggle against commercial rivals:

The new international stage has made [of] competitiveness an unquestionable element for the survival of companies. The change in worldwide behavior has prompted measures to facilitate the accelerated changes experienced by some countries, including Cape Verde. In this context, industrial property represents a strategic competitive instrument, working decisively alongside the industrial and scientific community.

5 STATING A WIDE RANGE OF OBJECTIVES

The lawmaker may not be sure of which objective the patent law that he/she is drafting will specifically pursue. Or he/she may believe that the impact of patent law on the country's economy will depend on the operation of market's dynamic forces, and therefore it is not advisable to emphasize one objective over the other. In this token, a number of national patent statutes, in their Preambles, cite a vast array of objectives and public policies, without any preference or emphasis for one or another.

Following this line of legal reasoning, one can quote from the Patent Act of the Philippines, which, in its section 2, reads:

Declaration of State Policy.—The State recognizes that an effective intellectual and industrial property system is vital to the development of domestic and creative activity, facilitates transfer of technology, attracts foreign investments, and ensures market access for our products. It shall protect and secure the exclusive rights of scientists, inventors, artists and other gifted citizens to their intellectual property and creations, particularly when beneficial to the people, for such periods as provided in this Act. The use of intellectual property bears a social function. To this end, the State shall promote the diffusion of knowledge and information for the promotion of national development and progress and the common good.[38]

The patent law of China also states its objectives in broad language:

Article 1. This Law is enacted to protect the lawful rights and interests of patentees, to encourage invention-creation, to promote the exploitation of invention-creation, to enhance innovation capability, and to promote the advancement of science and technology and the development of economy and society.[39]

37. Law on Patents, Utility Model Certificates and Industrial Designs, of 2003.
38. Intellectual Property Code, Republic Act No. 8293 (2015 Edition).
39. Patent Law of the People's Republic of China, of 1984, amended up to 2020.

6 CONCLUSION

The statement of the objectives of the patent law is not a matter of necessity. WIPO's legislative advice would not suggest any particular approach to this matter. After all, an international organization may recommend a Member State to pursue a number of guidelines concerning patent protection, but it is not its business to influence as regards the policy or objective to which the Member in question should give priority, to the point of mentioning it in the introductory recitals or articles. The perspective that WIPO Member States prefer in considering a law on patents lies entirely within their sovereignty.

Anyway, the lawmaker eventually understands that mentioning one or two particular objectives of the patent law may be useful in providing guidance to those national bodies in charge of implementing it, such as the national patent office and the courts. But, at the same time, that lawmaker should also be aware that doing so means according preeminence to the identified objectives, which may somehow limit the leeway of courts in their role of construing the provisions, given that a teleological approach will necessarily confine them to pursue those specific objectives, and not others. Moreover, particularly when the law refers to specific trade commitments as the trigger of the new provisions, courts will tend to identify the legal provisions of those trade agreements as binding legal sources.

However, associating the law with societal objectives, as Article 7 of the TRIPS Agreement does, may invite judges to shift the weighs of the balance toward consumers, or users of the patented inventions, in detriment of the legitimate interests and expectations of inventors. This shift introduces an imbalance where a balance should be found, and ends up undermining other public objectives of the law, such as technology transfer and attraction of FDI. This imbalance has been used against pharmaceutical patents, as will be described later.

In conclusion, a recital identifying the presiding objectives of the law may not be an idea as useful as it seems, in the sense that it may generate more problems than solutions, unless it is drafted in very broad and flexible terms, so as to accept eventual changes in the inclination of authorities and courts in securing the protection of inventions through patents.

CHAPTER 1

On the Right to Apply for (and Obtain) the Patent

1 THE PROBLEM(S)

Usually, the first provisions of a patent statute that follow the Preamble (when one is included) cover the crucial issue of the entitlement to the patent (as well as to the right to apply for it).

A person less familiarized with patent-related issues may believe that the entitlement to the patent is obvious: the patent goes to the inventor. And that the right to apply for the patent is likewise a question of obviousness: only the inventor can apply for the patent.

However, the designation of the inventor(s) and his/her (their) right to apply for the patent may become a complex issue, which a patent statute should handle carefully. Four kinds of questions may arise in this context:

(1) Who is (are) the inventor(s)? This question gains particular significance in companies' research departments, where invention is often the work of groups of researchers and assistants. The problem is not only one of legal precision and recognition of the inventive merits of certain employees but also a topic of entitlement to remuneration under the Patent Act, or under labor laws (including the internal company's regulations).

(2) The same question can be asked not in terms of entitlement to inventors' moral or material rights, but, more basically, in terms of the human or nonhuman nature of the inventor. This may seem a sort of a thoughtless question, but it arose recently in association with the use of generative artificial intelligence (AI) in creating/developing technical solutions with a *modicum* of nonobviousness, such as computer programs and methods of collecting and organizing data.

(3) Does the right to the patent always belong to the inventor? When and under what conditions is the right to the patent assigned to a third party?
(4) In the case of assignment of the right to obtain the patent, should the patent office require the applicant to submit a written authorization from the inventor? What happens if the inventor denies to sign the authorization?

Before discussing these four questions, let us see how the statutes of several countries deal with the issue of the designation of the inventor and the right to the patent.

2 EXAMPLES OF ANSWERS GIVEN BY NATIONAL STATUTES

In general, national patent statutes address the four topics mentioned above in a straightforward manner, as if lawmakers failed to foresee that in the future they might become controversial. The laconism of statutes may be an easy solution for lawmakers, but it tends to lead to litigation, which sometimes may inspire judicial constructions contrary to what the lawmakers had in mind.

The first example comes from the Patents Act of Antigua and Barbuda, which provides in section 2 (on Interpretation) that:

In this Act, unless the context otherwise requires—

> . . .
> *"inventor" means the actual deviser of an invention and "joint inventor" shall be construed accordingly.*

Section 11 of the same Act (on the Right to a patent) reads (in part):

(1) The right to a patent shall belong to the inventor.
(2) If two or more persons have made an invention jointly, the right to the invention shall belong to them jointly. . . .
(4) The inventor shall be named as such in the patent unless in a special written declaration signed by him and addressed to the Registrar, he indicates that he does not wish to be so named. . . .
(6) The right to a patent may be assigned or transferred by succession.

And section 12 (on "Invention by employee or person commissioned") provides (in part):

(1) Where an invention is made in execution of a contract of employment or for the execution of work, the right to the patent shall, in the absence of any agreement to the contrary, belong to the employer or the person who commissioned the work, as the case may be.[40]

Therefore, these are the answers that the statute of Antigua and Barbuda gives to the four questions raised above:

40. The Patents Act, No. 22 of 2018. On employees' inventions, *see infra* Chapter 11, section 3.

(a) The inventor is the person who "actually devises the invention." This means that, if the matter is raised before a court, the court will need to assert the meaning of the verb "to devise." A definition of "To devise" extracted by Google from the *Oxford Dictionary* says that it means "plan or invent (a complex procedure, system, or mechanism) by careful thought." It seems, therefore, that the definition provided by Antigua and Barbuda's Patents Act is tautological: the inventor is one who invents.

(b) The explicit reference to the inventor's moral rights—which are set, but not explicitly mentioned in Article 4*ter* of the Paris Convention[41]—implies that the statute of Antigua and Barbuda establishes that the inventor is a human being because only persons, not machines, own moral rights. Section 13(1) of the statute (on "Judicial assignment of patent application or patent") could not be more explicit in its reference to persons as being the inventors:

> *Where the idea of the invention claimed in a patent or application for a patent has been unlawfully derived from an invention for which the right to the patent belongs to another person, such other person may apply to the Court for an order that the said patent application or patent be assigned to him.*

(c) The third question is clearly answered: the right to apply for the patent as well as the right to obtain it belong to the inventor originally, but the inventor may assign both rights, by contract or by succession.[42]

(d) The fourth question has also deserved an unambiguous response from Antigua and Barbuda's lawmaker: where the patent application is not filed by the inventor (or by one or more of the inventors, in the case of collective invention), the request must be accompanied by "a written statement justifying the applicant's right to the patent" (section 14(1)(2) and (3)). That written statement does not consist necessarily in an authorization signed by the inventor. If the inventor is willing to sign it, that makes things easier for the applicant. Otherwise, the applicant may justify his/her right to the patent by identifying the inventor(s) and showing the relevant document that justifies the assignment—namely, a labor or service contract, or a certificate of legal succession, such as a will or a death certificate.

Now, let us look at the example of Argentina's patent law and corresponding regulations:

41. Article 4*ter* of the Paris Convention provides that:

> *The inventor shall have the right to be mentioned as such in the patent.*

This is what is known as the "moral right" of inventors.

42. Incidentally, it should be noted that the right *to apply* for the patent and the right *to obtain* it are different rights, even if they tend to be closely associated. It is possible—actually, it is frequent—that the inventor, after filing the patent application, assigns the right to obtain the patent to a third party. This is the case of some countries, where the right to apply for the patent cannot be assigned, except in rare circumstances.

Article 1—Inventions in all technological fields and areas of production shall confer upon their authors the rights and obligations specified in this law.

. . .

Article 8—The right to the patent shall belong to the inventor or his or her successors in title, who shall have the right to assign or transfer it by any lawful means and enter into license agreements.

Article 9—Unless proven otherwise, the inventor shall be presumed to be the individual or individuals designated as such in the patent application or utility model certificate. The inventor or inventors shall have the right to be mentioned in the corresponding title.

Article 10—Inventions made during an employment relationship:

(a) Those made by the worker during the course of their contract or employment relationship with the employer, which are wholly or partially intended to carry out inventive activities, shall belong to the employer.

. . .

Article 13.—The patent may be applied for directly by the inventor or by his/her successors in title . . . .

Regulations

Article 9—The inventor or inventors who have assigned their rights may intervene at any time during the procedure and request to be mentioned in the corresponding title, providing reliable proof of their status as such.

Article 12—In order to obtain a patent, the applicant must complete . . . the following information and documentation:

a) A patent application that must include:

. . .

5) Full name of the inventor or inventors . . .;
6) Actual address of the inventor or inventors . . .; . . .[43]

The law of Argentina provides for useful hints to answer the four questions enunciated above, but here and there, it would require some clarification. For example, the first question (who is the inventor?) is answered in a tautological manner: the inventor is the author of the invention. This response, of course, does not give a straight answer to the problem that not infrequently arises in the context of collective inventions made in large research centers where the final inventive result is the product of a group of researchers.

The moral rights of the inventor are clearly identified in Argentina's statute. This implies that inventors are persons, human beings, not machines. This conclusion is strengthened by the wording of Article 9, which mentions "the individual or individuals." Individuals are persons. Machines cannot be individualized, as much sophisticated as they may be. Machines can be exactly replicated; hence, they possess no individuality.

43. Law No. 24,481, of September 20, 1995, on Patents for Inventions and Utility Models (amended by Law No. 27,444, of June 18, 2018) and Regulation, with the amendments introduced by Law No. 24,572.

In Argentina, the right to apply for patent does not necessarily originate from the inventor. It may be assigned by a service or employment contract (Article 10).

As regards the fourth question (concerning an eventual request for the submission of the inventor's authorization when the application is filed on someone else's behalf), the law of Argentina follows a line of solution that is common to other national statutes: the designation of the application serves as a presumption of the applicant's entitlement to the right to the patent. That is not, of course, a presumption *de juris*, this meaning that the presumption can be rebutted. However, the presumption operates in favor of the applicant (eventually, an assignee), which implies that the inventor, when he/she understands that the applicant was not entitled to the patent, has to intervene in the procedure at a later stage.

When the inventor is an employee, conflicts over the entitlement to the patent (as well as over the remuneration, when due) shall be settled by the national patent office, whose findings may be appealed to the civil courts (Article 10, paragraphs 3 through 5, of the law). The authority of the patent office is limited by the law to the conflicts between the *trabajador en relación de dependencia* (worker in a relationship of dependency), thus apparently excluding conflicts between civil (or service) Contracting Parties, which are left to civil courts (or arbitration, when it is available).

Another national statute that makes explicit reference to inventors' moral rights is the Industrial Property Act of North Macedonia, as follows:

> *Article 6*
>
> (1) *The inventor of a patent and the author of industrial design shall have moral and exclusive rights to their creative works laid down by law.*
>
> . . .
>
> *Article 7*
>
> (1) *It shall be the moral right of the inventor and the author to be stated in the application and documents relating to the patent and the industrial design.*[44]

Under the law of North Macedonia, therefore, only human beings can be inventors, not machines. This is confirmed by Article 32(1), which reads (in part): "An inventor shall be a natural person . . ." We will come back to this provision.

Now let us have a brief look at the provisions of the Bangui Agreement, which operates as supranational patent law for the Members of the African Intellectual Property Organization (OAPI is its original acronym, in French):

> *Article 9 Right to the patent*
>
> (1) *The right to the patent shall belong to the inventor or his successor in title; the applicant shall be deemed to be the owner of the right.*
>
> (2) *If and where several persons have created the same invention independently of one another, the right to the patent shall belong to the person who filed the application whose filing date or, in the event of a priority claim, whose validly*

44. Law on Industrial Property, of 2009.

claimed priority date is earliest, provided the application is not withdrawn, abandoned or refused.

(3) Where several persons have made an invention jointly, the right to the patent shall belong to them jointly; the title shall be issued to them as joint owners.

Article 11 Employees' inventions and commissioned inventions

(1) Where the inventor is an employee, the right to the patent shall be governed by the following provisions in the absence of contractual provisions more favorable to the employee:

(a) Inventions made by employees in performance either of an employment contract encompassing an inventive task consistent with their actual functions, or of studies and research expressly assigned to them, shall belong to the employer. . . .[45]

Like the vast majority of patent statutes, the Bangui Agreement answers the first question in a sort of a tautological manner: inventor is the person who creates the invention. However, the Agreement answers with clarity two of the other (three) questions: inventors are persons, and the right to apply for a patent and the right to obtain the patent do not necessarily belong to the inventor. By contrast, there is no clarity as to the documents that must accompany the filing proving the applicant's entitlement to claim ownership. The Agreement does provide for procedural steps in the event the person who believes to hold the right to the patent (including the inventor) wishes to file an opposition (Article 21). The authority to settle that opposition is the Organization. However, matters concerning the remuneration of employees are to be settled by national courts (Article 11(1)). And any disagreement on OAPI's decisions concerning the entitlement to the patent may be brought to the consideration of national courts (Article 4).

The relevant provisions in the patent law of Ethiopia are the following:

1. *The right to a patent shall belong to the inventor.*

. . .

3. *In the absence of an agreement to the contrary, the right to a patent for an invention made in the execution of a contract of service or employment shall belong to the person having commissioned the work or the employer.*
4. *The inventor shall be named as such in the application and the patent unless in a special written declaration dressed to the commission he indicates that he wishes not to be named, and any promise or undertaking by the inventor made to any person to the effect that he will make such declaration shall be without legal effect. . . .*

9.1 *The person having the right to a patent for an invention . . . may, upon payment of the prescribed fees, apply to the commission for the grant of a patent for that invention.*

. . .

45. Bangui Agreement Instituting an African Intellectual Property Organization, of 1977, revised on December 14, 2015. OAPI has 17 Members from Sub-Saharan West African, mostly of which are French-speaking: Benin, Burkina Faso, Cameroon, the Central African Republic, Chad, the Comoros, the Congo, Côte d'Ivoire, Equatorial Guinea, Gabon, Guinea, Guinea-Bissau, Mali, Mauritania, Niger, Senegal, and Togo.

Ethiopia's patent statute, like many others, does not provide for a definition of what an inventor is. Also, like many other statutes, the law makes it clear that only persons may be designated as inventors. Article 9.1 establishes that the person (or entity) that is entitled to the patent (a service contractor, an employer) is also entitled to apply for the title. Following the same solution of Antigua and Barbuda, as mentioned above, when the applicant is not the inventor, the applicant shall submit a statement justifying his/her right to the patent. As said above, this seems to indicate that there is no need for an authorization from the inventor.

In the same token, the Patent Act of Indonesia unequivocally defines the inventor as a person or a collective of persons, as follows:

> *Article 1.*
>
> . . .
>
> 3. *Inventor means the person or persons collectively executing an idea in an activity to produce an Invention.*
>
> . . .
>
> *Article 11.*
>
> *Unless proven otherwise, party deemed to be the Inventor is a person or persons firstly declared as the Inventor of the Application.*[46]

As one example of a patent law that expressly mentions the moral rights of inventors—thus, explicitly acknowledging their human dimension—we can mention the statute of Uruguay, which reads:

> *Article 2*
>
> *The moral right of inventors and designers to be recognized as authors of their inventions and creations is inalienable and imprescriptible and is transferred to their heirs.*[47]

The law of the United States of America in this regard is particularly worth noticing, as the original right to apply for the patent is inherently attributed to the inventor. These are the relevant provisions in U.S. patent law that address the four questions asked above:

> *§100 When used in this title unless the context otherwise indicates—*
>
> . . .
>
> (f) *The term "inventor" means the individual or, if a joint invention, the individuals collectively who invented or discovered the subject matter of the invention.*

46. Law of the Republic of Indonesia No. 13, of 2016, on Patents.
47. Law No. 17.164 of September 2, 1999, on Patents (as amended up to Law No. 19.924 of December 18, 2020). It seems there is here a drafting problem, in the sense that moral rights are never transferable. What heirs receive and can exercise is the right to impose that the name of their predecessors be mentioned in the patent letter—obviously, they cannot have their name mentioned in the document instead.

This provision is followed by the following Historical and Revision Note:

Paragraph (f) indicates the necessity for the inventor as the party applying for patent. Subsequent sections permit certain persons to apply in place of the inventor under special circumstances.

§115. Inventor's oath or declaration

(a) Naming the inventor; inventor's oath or declaration.—An application for patent that is filed under section 111(a) . . . shall include, or be amended to include, the name of the inventor for any invention claimed in the application. Except as otherwise provided in this section, each individual who is the inventor or a joint inventor of a claimed invention in an application for patent shall execute an oath or declaration in connection with the application.
(b) Required statements.—An oath or declaration under subsection (a) shall contain statements that—
 (1) the application was made or was authorized to be made by the affiant or declarant; and
 (2) such individual believes himself or herself to be the original inventor or an original joint inventor of a claimed invention in the application.[48]

The U.S. lawmaker has adopted the tautological approach to defining the inventor: he/she is the individual (i.e., the person) who has invented or discovered the matter that is claimed in the patent application.[49]

The US Patent Act identifies the inventor as an individual, i.e., as a human being. Only the inventor can apply for a patent. Otherwise, in the event the right to the patent is assigned, the applicant needs to submit an oath or declaration that the inventor has authorized the application to be filed. In other words, the U.S. patent statute does not admit the presumption that the applicant, whoever he/she may be, is legitimately entitled to the patent.

As a final—but no less relevant—example, let us now give a look at how the 1979 version of the WIPO Model Law for Developing Countries for Inventions responds to the four questions:

Section 119: Right to Patent

(1) The right to the patent shall belong to the inventor.
(2) If two or more persons have jointly made an invention, the right to the patent shall belong to them jointly.
(3) The right to the patent may be assigned, and it may be transferred by succession.

. . .

48. United States Code, Title 35—Patents (35 U.S.C., amended up to Public Law No. 117-328).
49. A caveat is necessary here. The U.S. patent statute employs the term "discovery" with the same meaning as "invention," which does not correspond to the usual distinction that is usually made of the two words. In current language, invention is the result of human ingenuity, be it as a result of intelligent contrivance, or chance, or luck. By contrast, discovery is the finding of something that existed before, usually in Nature. If the activity of searching and finding the natural thing or phenomenon has somehow required some level of inventiveness, then the invention may lie in the method or process of finding, but never in the result or product. The synonymity of invention and discovery in the U.S. patent law was settled a long time ago by the Circuit Court of the District of Columbia in *In Re Kemper*, [1 MacA. Pat. Cas. 1; Cranch, Pat. Dec. 89.], May 1841.

Section 122: Naming of Inventor

The inventor shall be named as such in the patent, unless in a special written declaration addressed to the Patent Office he indicates that he wishes not to be named. Any promise or undertaking by the inventor made to any person to the effect that he will make such a declaration shall be without legal effect.

Section 123: Application

...

(2) (a) The request shall contain a petition to the effect that a patent be granted, the name of and other prescribed data concerning the applicant, the inventor and the agent, if any, and the title of the invention.

(b) Where the applicant is not the inventor, the request shall be accompanied by a statement justifying the applicant's right to the patent.

...

Section 130: Filing Date; Examination as to Form

...

(2) Where the request is accompanied by the statement referred to in Section 123 (2)(b), the Patent Office shall send a copy of the statement to the inventor. The inventor shall have the right to inspect the application and to receive, for strictly personal purposes, a copy thereof at his own expense. [50]

The Model is accompanied by a commentary that clarifies a large number of its provisions. The relevant comments to the provisions quoted above are the following:

> *Section 123. d. Subsection (2)(b)*: The most frequent case in which the applicant will have to furnish the statement referred to in this provision is where the inventor is his employee. In such a case, it will be sufficient if the statement simply mentions that the right of the applicant to the patent is based on the existence of an employment contract.
>
> *Section 130, Paragraph (d), Subsection (2)*: Where the applicant is not the inventor, the latter must receive a copy of the statement justifying the applicant's right to the patent, in order that he may satisfy himself that he has not been the victim of any abuse. For the same purpose, the inventor must be able to see the contents of the application (as the statement does not give an exact indication of the invention to which the application relates): this he can do by inspecting the application at the Patent Office or by receiving a copy of it at his own expense, but with the obligation to respect the confidentiality of the application (as indicated by the words "for strictly personal purposes"). If the inventor considers that the statement is unfounded and that the right to the patent does not belong to the applicant, he must bring an action before the court under Section 121; if a final decision has not yet been taken at the time of the grant of the patent, the Gazette and the patent will mention the fact that an action is in progress (see Rules 132 and 132ter).

50. This model was elaborated in 1965 under the auspices of the Bureaux Internationaux Réunis pour la Protection de la Propriété Intellectuelle (BIRPI), which gathered the secretariats that administered the Paris and the Berne Conventions. The model was updated several times, and the 1979 version, which is used throughout this book, was the last one. *See* WIPO MODEL LAW FOR DEVELOPING COUNTRIES ON INVENTIONS—VOL. I—PATENTS (Geneva 1979).

The WIPO Model Law does not respond to the first question on who qualifies as the inventor. But it makes it clear that the right to the patent belongs to the inventor, who may assign it. The language used by the WIPO Secretariat does not make it explicit that only human beings may be designated as inventors, and yet the relevant provisions and the corresponding comments lead to that conclusion. Indeed, it is not acceptable—at least, in the face of the current status of technological development—that a machine can receive from a third party (its owner, probably) a statement justifying the filing of the application by a third party "*in order that he [the computer] may satisfy himself that he has not been the victim of any abuse.*" We can see here a clear reference to a human being: only human beings, not machines, can be the victims of abuses.

On the provision that the inventor may initiate judicial proceedings concerning his/her legitimate entitlement to the patent, the Model Law omits the fact that sometimes, although less frequently, the abuse may be practiced by the employee (or former employee).

On the last question, the Model assigns the authority to settle disputes to courts. The Model adds an important clarification: a dispute involving the right to the patent should not lead to a suspension of the prosecution of the application.

3 *DOS AND DON'TS*

Lawmakers tend to not pay much attention to the matter of identifying the inventor and attributing the rights to apply for and to obtain the patent. After all, as already noted, this is a question inherently associated with human rights, and thus it may be assumed that there is no need for special provisions dealing with it. This is what explains why the patent laws of a vast majority of countries do not go beyond attributing to the inventor the right to obtain the patent (and stating that the inventor may assign his/her right to apply for the patent as well as his/her right to the patent).

And yet, eventually, problems may arise concerning the precise identification of the inventor and, eventually, of the legitimacy of the applicant's entitlement to the patent.

The inventor is the person who directly contributes to finding the inventive solution for a technical problem. Thus, in a team formed by several persons, only those within that team who have really proposed or found the inventive solution are to be treated as inventors. If a pleonasm is allowed, in a team, only inventive contributors are inventors. Any member of the team who has not done more than helping in the research and in making experiments may have significantly helped the generation of the inventive result, but he/she is not an inventor.[51]

In this regard, the statute of Saudi Arabia has a provision that is highly commendable, in the sense that it may avoid long and complex disputes about

51. One of the most difficult and sensitive issues that may result from collective invention is the identification of those who have contributed to the invention and in what proportion their contributions may have been. This is a matter to be discussed in Chapter 11, section 3, where we will very briefly deal with employees' inventions.

authorship of inventions, in particular in the context of teams of researchers. It is paragraph (c) of Article 5, which reads:

> *No one shall be deemed a partner [coinventor] unless he contributes to the subject matter of protection, and his efforts are only confined to assistance in its execution.*[52]

Provisions in the same direction can be found in the Industrial Property Law of North Macedonia, as follows:

> *Inventor*
>
> *Article 32*
>
> *(1) An inventor shall be a natural person that has created the invention in the course of his creative work.*
> *(2) An inventor shall not be considered the one who in the creation of the invention has provided only technical assistance.*

So, in principle, the application should be filed by the inventor(s). This is the regime adopted by the United States and which more closely conforms to the very rationale of the patent system. However, when the invention is made for hire, under a service or an employment contract, the contractor/employer should not be required to wait for the patent application to be submitted to the patent office by the inventors before he/she can claim the right to the patent. This possibility may give rise to conflicts between employers and employees and leave significant economic interests of innovative companies in the hands of the latter. The U.S. mechanism, although ethically more appropriate, as said, has been bypassed by the practice: employers usually file the patent applications on behalf of their employees-inventors and, once the filing is completed, they submit immediately an assignment request. When one discontent employee refuses to execute the filing or to assign the application, then regulation *37 CFR 1.64*, on the *Substitute statement in lieu of an oath or declaration*, applies: "If the inventor is deceased, is under a legal incapacity, has refused to execute the oath or declaration . . . or cannot be found or reached after diligent effort," the applicant executes a substitute statement in lieu of an oath or declaration.

Therefore, in order to avoid this sort of encumbrance, the best option is to attribute the right to patent to the inventor or his/her assignees. In other terms, the service contractor or employer is entitled to apply for the patent. However, this apparently simple equation leads to other questions: when the applicant is not the inventor, should the application be accompanied with an authorization by the inventor?; or, is a simple statement by the contractor/employer disclosing his/her entitlement to the patent enough?; or, alternatively, should the law simply provide that the applicant is presumed to hold the right to the patent (thus leaving all conflicts over legitimate entitlement to subsequent stages in the prosecution or after the patent is granted)?

---

52. Law on Patents, Layout-Designs of Integrated Circuits, Plant Varieties, and Industrial Designs (issued by Royal Decree No. M/27 of 29 Jumada al-awwal 1425H (July 17, 2004), and amended by Decision of the Council of Ministers No. 536 of 19 Shawwel 1439 (July 3, 2018)).

A combination of affirmative answers to the last two questions sounds the best option: as a presumption, when the employer files the patent application and designates an employee as an inventor, the employer is entitled to obtain the patent. But if some divergence arises, the submission of a copy of the contract should serve as sufficient proof of such an entitlement.

Here, a note, although brief, on the human nature of the inventor is required, in view of the recent debate on whether a machine operating generative AI can be designated as an inventor in the patent.

The answer is "no." A couple of years ago an inventor who has been assisted by a computer asked for a patent on a computer software and designated the machine, named DABUS, as the inventor.[53] The application was filed in several countries, and the designation of the machine was rejected in all of them, except in South Africa (where the patent application is not submitted to a substantive examination). In the United States, Australia, and Germany, the applicant brought the dispute to courts and was defeated in the three countries.

In the United States, the Court of Appeals for the Federal Circuit, in *Thaler v. Vidal*, No. 21-2347 (Fed. Cir. 2022), decided on a dispute initiated by Stephen Thaler, the owner of DABUS, an intelligent computer, eventually capable of making a certain kind of incremental inventions, against the USPTO, which had rejected the designation of the machine as the sole inventor. The court held: "Here, there is no ambiguity: the Patent Act requires that inventors must be natural persons; that is, human beings." The same conclusion was reached in Australia's Federal Court[54] and Germany's Federal Court of Justice.[55,56]

The understanding that there is no alternative to the inventor's human nature could not be different—at least in the present time. Generative AI can, indeed, make some minor, incremental inventions, provided the patent office does not fix the threshold for nonobviousness at a high level. And yet the machine cannot be designated as such in the patent application for two major reasons: (i) because the right to the patent is primarily attributed to the inventor, a third party can only file for the patent as a result of an assignment; however, machines have no legal ability to assign rights or execute any other sort of contract; therefore, there would be no justification for the machine owner to file a patent application on behalf of a computer; and (ii) patent laws have been devised to encourage inventors to invent by warranting them the legal security of a title of property, so that they can seek the interest of consumers

53. DABUS stands for "Device for the Autonomous Bootstrapping of Unified Sentience." This was the title of the invention that resulted in U.S. patent No. US7454388B2. The applicant, Stephen Thaler, filed other patent applications for inventions associated with neural networks, likewise mentioning DABUS as the sole inventor.
54. The "Court found that each of the people mentioned in the later subsections had to derive their title from the person in (a), which meant that the owner of a patent could only be a human inventor, or a person who derived their title to the patent from that human inventor." *Commissioner of Patents v. Thaler* [2022] FCAFC 62.
55. "Only a natural person can be an inventor within the meaning of section 37(1) of the Patent Act. A mechanical system consisting of hardware or software cannot be designated as an inventor, even if it has artificial intelligence functions." June, 11 2024, X ZB 5/22—DABUS.
56. These opinions are available in WIPO Lex Judgements Collection.

on the market; by contrast, a machine only needs a push on a button and an electric wire or a battery to connect them to a source of energy; these are the two only "incentives" for a generative AI-operating computer to invent.

We saw above that a number of national laws adopt a presumption of the applicant's entitlement to the patent. That is undoubtedly an easy solution, because it clarifies that the very beginning of the prosecution procedure will not be hampered by discussions on who is entitled to the patent. However, it does not provide any guidance on how the discussions will be addressed or whether the grant of the patent, if ever, is to be stayed upon the settlement of eventual conflicts over ownership.

The solution that national lawmakers tend to prefer is that the applicant, if he/she is not inventor, submits a statement along with the request for the patent. In that statement, the applicant will clarify why he/she and not the inventor is applying. There should be no need to attach copies of contracts because the patent office has no qualifications to look at those documents, let alone to find in them any leads on the attribution of the right to the patent. But the applicant in that statement must declare that the inventors are fully aware of and have granted their consent to the request for the application and that they have stated their wish to be nominated in the application (or that they have rejected the nomination). In this manner, the applicant becomes responsible for the exactitude of his/her statement. In the event that, later, the inventors prove that the statement was not truthful, legal consequences will result, which may consist in the assignment of the patent to those inventors or its invalidation on grounds of fraud.

If a conflict arises, the patent office should not be involved in settling it, even if experts may be called as arbitrators or witnesses. The job of patent offices is to prosecute patent applications (and provide for associated services of public interest, such as making patent information widely available). Conflicts concerning the right to the patent should be left to courts or to alternative dispute settlement mechanisms, when available, such as in Germany.[57] In some countries, disputes involving employees' inventions can be settled by specialized labor courts only.

In any event, conflicts concerning the entitlement to the patent should not obstruct the prosecution of the patent. Patent applicants are already sufficiently prejudiced with patent offices' backlogs; they can dispense with giving rise to an additional reason for the delaying of the examination of the patent. But one may wonder whether the solution provided by the WIPO Model Law of suspending the grant of the patent (but not the prosecution) until the dispute is settled is a good one. It seems to be. If the patent is granted to the wrong person or entity, its subsequent assignment may not be sufficient to repair any harm done to the legitimate right holder. Indeed, once the patent is granted, the patentee may assign it. The profits unjustly captured by the illegitimate patentee may eventually be recovered by the right holder, but profits made by third parties may be extremely hard to assess and recover.

57. *See* Employee Inventions Act of July 25, 1957, as last amended by the Act of June 24, 1994, last amended by Art. 7 of the Act of July 31, 2009, Art. 5 (judicial proceedings can be launched only after arbitration has been exploited). An English version of this Act is available at < www.dpma.de/docs/dpma/schiedsstelle/employee_inventions_act.pdf > .

In a nutshell, the following are the *do's* as regards the legal identification of the person who is entitled to the patent:

1. *Inventor is the person who directly contributes to finding the solution for a technical problem that complies with Section . . .* [this will be the Section defining the conditions of patentability] *of the present act.*
2. *The inventor is entitled to the patent.*
3. *The inventor may assign the right to file as well as the right to obtain the patent. When the invention is made in the context of a relationship of employment, the assignment shall observe the conditions and requirements set in Sections . . .* [these Sections are those that establish the rights of employers and employees as regards inventions made during the contract of employment].
4. *The request for a patent that is not filed by the inventor shall be accompanied by a statement, in which the applicant shall justify his/her right to the patent and declare that the inventor has been informed of the application and that*
   (i) he/she has given his/her consent; and that
   (ii) he/she has manifested his/her will in being nominated in the patent, if granted, or that he/she has expressed his/her will not to be nominated in the patent.
5. *In the event a conflict between the inventor and third parties concerning the right to the patent arises, the patent shall be issued by the patent office with a declaration that the settlement of the dispute is pending.*
6. *(a) These provisions shall apply mutatis mutandis to inventions made by persons who are bound by a service contract.*
   (b) Inventions made by civil servants shall follow a special regime, to be determined by . . . [the laws that preside over public service].[58]

58. In Chapter 11, section 3, we will come back to this point, but discussing it under the perspective of the payment of remuneration.

CHAPTER 2

On the Examination of Patent Applications

1 SUBSTANTIVE VERSUS MERELY FORMAL EXAMINATION PRIOR TO THE GRANT OF THE PATENT: THE DILEMMA OF SMALL PATENT OFFICES

In accordance with Article 12 of the Paris Convention, all 180 Members of the Paris Union are under the obligation of having a patent office:

> *Article 12*
>
> *[Special National Industrial Property Services]*
>
> *(1) Each country of the Union undertakes to establish a special industrial property service and a central office for the communication to the public of patents, utility models, industrial designs, and trademarks.*

This provision has been in force since the approval of the Convention, in 1883. The national patent office may be replaced by a regional office, in the event the country associates with others under a common, supranational law,[59] such as the *Organisation Africaine de la Propriété Intellectuelle (OAPI)*, which, as noted above, gathers seventeen Western French-speaking African Countries. Indeed, for those countries, with the exception of the few that are less underdeveloped, such as Cameroon, Senegal, and Ivory Coast, to maintain a national patent office would be unjustifiable. In 2017, OAPI received three patent applications from residents in Benin; two from Mauritania; and no patent application at all from Niger.[60] The number of filings by foreign residents is also very low. Because of the unified patent regime, there is no way to know which specific national territories are targeted by foreign patent applicants, but the low overall figures indicate that those applications would not justify the opening of a patent office in each country.

---

59. *See* G.H.C. Bodenhausen, GUIDE TO THE APPLICATION OF THE CONVENTION FOR THE INTERNATIONAL PROTECTION OF INDUSTRIAL PROPERTY AS REVISED IN STOCKHOLM IN 1967, at 153 (BIRPI, 1968).
60. *See* OAPI, ANNUAIRE STATISTIQUE 2017, at 18, available at <www.oapi.int/annuaire/>.

The same can be said of other countries that receive a very low number of patent applications, by both residents and nonresidents. For example, in 2023, Albania received ten filings; Antigua and Barbuda, Dominica, 2; and Vanuatu, 4. Djibouti, an LDC WTO Member, did not receive any patent application in 2023.[61]

So, once established that countries that are Members of the Paris Union are obliged to maintain a patent office, the question comes: are those countries obliged to confer to that office the task of performing the substantive examination of patent applications—i.e., the examination of the conditions of patentability (novelty, nonobviousness, utility, enabling disclosure, and exclusions from patentability)—prior to granting the patent? And, if not, is it possible to identify an objective criterion for determining when it would be convenient for a country to establish the mandatory prior examination as to the invention's merit?

Resorting to a concrete example, the patent law of Mozambique determines that the patent office shall proceed to the substantive examination of applications and that the submission of oppositions is possible:

> *Article 69*
>
> *Substantive examination*
>
> 1. *On expiry of the time period referred to in paragraph 1 of the preceding article and within 36 months from the date of filing of the application, or at the conclusion of argument in the event of opposition, at the request of the applicant and against payment of the prescribed fee, the [patent office] shall proceed with the examination of the process.*
> 2. *The examination shall consist, primarily and obligatorily, in examining the patent, the patent title, abstract, description, claims and drawings of the invention in respect of which registration is sought and checking the patentability requirements established in Article 32.*
> 3. *Should it be deemed necessary, the IPI may request technical assistance or for a substantive examination to be undertaken by national or international technical entities or experts.*[62]

Mozambique, in 2023, received a total of twenty-six patent applications, eighteen of which were filed by residents and eight by nonresidents.

Antigua and Barbuda is another country whose patent law requires the pre-grant substantive examination of patent applications,[63] in spite of having received, in 2023, four patent applications only, all filed from nonresidents.

In view of these very small numbers, is a system of pre-grant substantive examination useful for those two countries?

The answer should be an unequivocal "no"—but this does not mean that the examination of patent applications as to their merit is not required at all. What may change from one country to another is the opportunity for the examination—prior to or after the grant—not its execution. It follows then, in view of the language of the TRIPS Agreement (Article 27.1), that the patent law of all WTO Members, even of those that do not wish to have their patent offices engaged in pre-grant patent examination, must

61. These figures have been obtained in WIPO's Statistics Database.
62. Industrial Property Code (approved by Decree No. 47/2015 of December 31, 2015).
63. Patents Act, 2018 (Act No. 22 of 2018), section 24.

define the conditions of patentability, both formal and material, and make compliance with the conditions of novelty, inventiveness, utility, enabling disclosure, and exclusions from patentability, mandatory. Given the fact that these conditions are of mandatory observation, it also follows that, at some point, substantive examination must be performed or, at least, must be available, in the case of invalidation proceedings.

In multilateral treaties, we find different solutions for this dilemma.

The Paris Convention does not impose or even imply the need for either the pre-grant or post-grant substantive examination of patent applications. The examination that the Convention mentions in Article 4(5)(G)(1) ("If *the examination* reveals that an application [...]" [emphasis added]) is a *formal* one, this meaning an examination as to accessory aspects of the patent application. Formal requirements are those that do not concern the invention itself, but the manner in which the application is submitted. For example, the unity of invention requirement is formal in the sense that it concerns the number of inventions that can be presented to the patent office in a single application.[64] The PCT apparently distinguishes between the form and the contents of the patent application, but both are accessory to the essence of the invention. So, in relation to the substance (or essence) of the invention, both elements may be qualified as formalities.

However, one may suggest that the mere reference to the right of priority in the Paris Convention, as an exception to novelty, implies that patent applications filed in Paris Union Member countries should be scrutinized at least as regards that condition. But the Paris Convention does not contain language in that sense.

By contrast, both the PCT and the TRIPS Agreement express the need for a substantive examination of patent applications. The PCT, in Article 15, concerning the international search, provides that "Each international application shall be the subject of international search" and that "The objective of the international search is to discover relevant prior art." As a matter of course, the purpose of discovering prior art is to subsidize the scrutiny of a claimed invention as to its novelty and nonobviousness. However, the PCT does not enter into the matter of patentability. On the contrary, the Treaty is explicit in the sense that its provisions do not go beyond the procedure before the International Authority and the designated office(s). This clarification is made in Article 27(5).[65]

64. The unity of invention requirement was introduced in France, in the beginning of the nineteenth century, as a manner of increasing the fees to be paid by applicants. It has no other purpose whatsoever if the inventions are well defined and delimited in the claims. A good example is the application of a single patent for a product and the process of its making. Patent offices tend to admit that sort of application, without requiring the applicant to divide it. And yet, the patent can be enforced separately against those who infringe the claims concerning the process and the product.

65. Article 27(5) of the PCT reads:

> *Nothing in this Treaty and the Regulations is intended to be construed as prescribing anything that would limit the freedom of each Contracting State to prescribe such substantive conditions of patentability as it desires. In particular, any provision in this Treaty and the Regulations concerning the definition of prior art is exclusively for the purposes of the international procedure and, consequently, any Contracting State is free*

The TRIPS Agreement, in Article 27.1, establishes that patents "shall be available for any inventions, [...] provided that they are new, involve an inventive step and are capable of industrial application." Thus, as noted above, WTO Members are required to assess whether inventions meet those three requirements in order to be eligible for patenting. Even more explicitly, Article 32 provides that "An opportunity for judicial review of any decision to revoke or forfeit a patent shall be available." Revocation, here, does not mean the cancelling of the patent for reasons of mere convenience—which is arguably prohibited by the Agreement[66]—but its cancelling on grounds of failure to meet the conditions of patentability. Article 32, therefore, implies that an examination concerning those conditions should be carried out by WTO Members.

However, neither the PCT nor the TRIPS Agreement requires that the substantive examination be carried out by national patent offices *prior* to the grant of the patents. One may see in the international search report, which precedes the entry of the international application into the national phase, a component of the prior substantive examination. The same goes for those countries that have opted for the mechanism of the international preliminary examination report, under the PCT (Article 31). However, nothing prevents a country that is a PCT Contracting Party from receiving those reports and keep them as evidence of patentability (or of lack of patentability) in the case the patent, after being granted, is challenged. That is the case of the patent law of France, where a "research report" is established on the conditions of patentability of a given invention. But, regardless of the conclusions of that report on patentability, the patent will be granted anyway (Article 612-7). The merits of the invention may be reviewed only after its grant, by means of an administrative challenge (Article 613-23).[67]

So, for WTO Members, the question arises: Should their patent offices perform a pre-grant examination of patentability? The answer is not obvious, given the absence of objective criteria to determine the need for the prior examination. On the one hand, prior examination increases legal security because it avoids the granting of frivolous patents.[68] But, on the other hand, pre-grant substantive examination demands significant administrative, financial, and human resources, which may not be justifiable in

---

to apply, when determining the patentability of an invention claimed in an international application, the criteria of its national law in respect of prior art and other conditions of patentability not constituting requirements as to the form and contents of applications.

66. *See* in Chapter 6, *infra*, a discussion about this topic.
67. The French system, which is of a peculiar nature, particularly if we consider the highly innovative level of its industry, has deep historical roots in the social movement that led to the Revolution of 1789. One of the libertarian fundamentals of the Revolution was the struggle against the corporatist organization of industry and trade, which was seen as an instrument of social immobilism, in view of the strict rules on labor and companionship, and their anticompetitive inclination. The examination of patent applications, first established by the by-laws of the Royal Academy of Sciences, in 1699, was understood by the revolutionaries as an expression of that hateful regime. Since 1791, French patent laws have not required more than a formal examination prior to the grant. But the patent, if granted, is accompanied with a detailed and thorough report on the merits of the invention as regards its compliance (or lack thereof) with the substantive conditions of patentability.
68. A well-known story of a petty patent granted in Australia for the invention of the wheel illustrates the need for avoiding that kind of patents. Not only are patents of that sort completely useless but they also undermine the system's reputation (and it seems that was exactly the intent

view of the fact that not all—in fact, only a relatively few—patents give rise to challenges and litigation.

The answer, therefore, is that patent offices that receive a small number of patent applications—say, less than fifty per year—should not waste their time and resources with prior substantive examination. Substantive examination, if necessary—in the case of a challenge as to the validity of the patent, or in the case of enforcement-related litigation—should be carried *post*-grant, by court order or under a patentee's request, in preparation of the filing of an enforcement lawsuit. Alternatively, the lawmaker could establish a mechanism of pre-grant oppositions, and that substantive examination should be carried out only in the event an opposition is filed.

This latter option corresponds to the commendable solution provided by the patent law of Guyana, a country that in 2023 received thirty-five patent applications, all filed by nonresidents:

> *Section 16*
>
> (1) *If there is no opposition, or, in case of opposition, if the determination is in favour of the grant of a patent, a patent shall, on payment of the prescribed fee, be granted to the applicant, or in case of a joint application to the applicants jointly, or in the case of a joint application to the applicants jointly, and the Registrar shall cause the patent to be sealed in duplicate with the seal of the Patent Office and one duplicate shall be retained and filed in the Patent Office:*
>
> . . .[69]

A similar solution is found in the law of Botswana, which authorizes the Registrar to exclude certain categories of inventions to be excluded from substantive examination, except where a third person files "an observation or objection against the application for a patent." In this event, an *inter partes* procedure is established, and the Registrar shall decide on the grant (or denial) of the patent:

> *Section 21.*
>
> . . .
>
> (5) *Any interested person may, within the prescribed period and in the prescribed manner, submit to the Registrar, an observation or objection against the application for a patent on grounds that—*
>
> . . .
>
> (8) *Where an observation or objection is submitted, the Registrar shall send a copy to the applicant who may, within the prescribed period and in the prescribed manner, send to the Registrar his or her counter-statement.*
>
> (9) *If the applicant sends a counter-statement, the Registrar shall provide a copy to the person who submitted the observation or objection and the Registrar may, at his or her discretion, hear the parties if either or both wish to be heard.*

---

of the applicant). *See* BBC News, *Lawyer Moves to Patent Wheel*, July 2, 2001, available at < news.bbc.co.uk/2/hi/asia-pacific/1418165.stm > [access February 2025]. *See also*, New Scientist, *Wheel patented in Australia*, July 3, 2001, available at < www.newscientist.com/article/dn965-wheel-patented-in-australia/ > [access May 2025]. It is true, as the story goes, that the patentee was sued on grounds of ideological falsehood, but the damage to the system's reputation was irreversible, up to the point that Australia has abandoned that particular system of granting petty patents without examination.

69. Patents and Designs Act, Chapter 90:03, Act No. 9 of 1937, amended up to Act No. 13 of 1992.

(10) The Registrar shall consider the observation or objection made under subsection (5) before deciding on the application for a patent.

Section 22.

. . .

(2) The Minister may, by regulations, prescribe the categories of inventions in respect of which an examination under this section shall not cover the requirements of novelty and inventive step.[70]

Although phrased in a different manner, the patent statute of the Gambia also provides that only certain categories of inventions will be the subject of pre-grant substantive examination, as follows:

Section 10.

. . .

(5) The regulations may prescribe that, in respect of some categories of inventions, the examination shall not cover the requirements of novelty and inventive step under subsections (2) and (3) of section 4 of this Act.[71]

The problem with this differentiated treatment of patent applications according to the categories of technology may have negative implications as far as the prohibition of discriminatory treatment established by Article 27.1 of the TRIPS Agreement is concerned. The reason is that, although the provisions neither make those categories of inventions less patentable nor do they cause patent rights less enjoyable, they make the availability of certain patents more difficult, costly, and delay their grant. The question would be different if the provisions made reference to certain inventions as opposed to certain categories of inventions.

However, it should be emphasized that not submitting a patent application to a pre-grant substantive examination should not mean a total absence of examination before the grant concerning some of the substantive conditions of patentability. These conditions are those that determine that the invention be compliant with deep social values, such as morality and *ordre public*. Indeed, there are inventions that are so repulsive in their very concept and in their possible use that the patent office should not allow their authors to receive a certificate of inventive merit, even if preliminary. So, even in those countries where patent offices do not carry out a substantive examination of applications prior to the grant of the patent, there should be, in addition to the common formal examination, a pre-grant examination as to whether the claimed inventions offend collective moral values and whether they are outside the admitted technological fields of patentability.[72,73] Another important point is that the same

70. Industrial Property Act, Act No. 8 of 2010.
71. Industrial Property Act, Act No. 12 of 1989, as amended by Act No. 5, of 2015.
72. Apparently, the TRIPS Agreement has made the analysis of exclusions from patentability on moral grounds easier, given that it has made those exclusions dependent on the exclusion of the patented goods (or of the goods made with the patented processes) from commercialization. *See* Art. 27.2:

Members may exclude from patentability inventions the prevention within their territory of the commercialization of which is necessary to protect ordre public or morality ... .

pre-grant partial substantive examination should also look at the quality of the description. Again, there is no practical use in granting patents, even if they are not fully examined, that fail to give an adequate description of the invention.

Like the analysis of compliance with the provisions dealing with exclusions from patentability, the examination of the quality of the description does not require a deep, time-consuming study by the patent examiner.

Therefore, in those countries where a decision is made not to submit patent applications to a substantive examination before the grant, the Patent Act still should determine that patent offices have the duty to analyze whether the claimed inventions are not excluded from patentability and are described in a manner that complies with the relevant requirements of enabling disclosure.

This is the solution found in the patent law of Lebanon, as follows:

Article 12

a. *If the invention is among the inventions mentioned in Articles 3 and 4 of the Law herein stated[,] the Head of the Intellectual Property Protection Authority shall inform the applicant of such findings within a period of thirty days from the date of the recording, otherwise the filing application shall be deemed*

So, once the patent examiner is confronted with an invention that in his/her view offends public morality, he/she should check whether there is some rule prohibiting the commercialization of the results of its use. If yes, the patent examiner has to consider whether there is necessity to deny the patent in order to keep the product off-market. In the absence of such a rule, or in the absence of such necessity, the patent could be granted. However, things are not that easy because there may be inventions that offend public morality so blatantly that no law maker has even bothered to exclude them from commercialization. Just imagine the invention of a pathogen that is aimed at infecting anti-racism activists. In this regard, *see, e.g.*, Jerome Amir Singh, *Project Coast: Eugenics in Apartheid South Africa*, April 2008, available at <www.researchgate.net/publication/> [access February 2025]. Of course, there is no need for a law excluding such an invention from commercialization as a condition for the denial of protecting it through a patent. So, the patent examiner would need to rely on his/her common sense to deny the patent. Actually, the absence of a specific rule prohibiting the commercialization of that invention would not cause the rejection of the patent application to be a breach of the TRIPS Agreement, given that Art. 27.2 does not say that the prohibition should be expressed in a law or regulation.

73. The Industrial Property Act of Brazil, of 1996, adopts this solution as far as industrial designs are concerned. Article 106 of the Act says that, once it is verified that the conditions set in Arts. 100, 101, and 104 have been observed, the design shall be published and the respective certificate shall be issued. Article 101 concerns the contents of the application and the documents to be presented. Article 104 is about unity (which is mandatory, admitting until twenty variations of the object). Article 100 is about subject matter that is excluded from protection:

The following is not registrable as industrial designs:

I— *anything that is contrary to morality and good customs or that offends the honor or image of people, or violates freedom of conscience, belief, religious worship or ideas and feelings worthy of respect and veneration;*

II— *the necessary common or vulgar form of the object or, even, that determined essentially by technical or functional considerations.*

Law on Industrial Property No. 9,279, of May 14, 1996, as amended up to Law No. 14.200 of September 2, 2021. These two topics, and, in particular, the first one, can be easily checked out by a patent examiner without the need for a very thorough and time-consuming exercise.

> *accepted. The applicant may present his remarks of such findings within sixty days of being officially informed of such.*[74]

Article 3 identifies technical creations that are excluded from patentability, and Article 4 prohibits the grant of patents for inventions that violate "the public order and morality." Unfortunately, the Lebanese lawmaker failed to include in Article 12 a reference to Article 8, which requires the submission of a description of the invention (although without imposing its enabling capacity). This means that the Lebanese patent office may issue patents that do not describe the inventions in a precise and useful manner.

Anyway, this discussion does not imply that, in countries where the substantive examination is not carried out before the patent is granted, a full examination may not be required later. Indeed, if the validity of the patent is challenged, the patent office may be requested by a court to carry it out. Or, in preparation of the filing of an enforcement lawsuit, the patentee should be allowed to request the full examination of his/her invention.[75] Additionally, this possibility could also be admitted in the case the patent owner wishes to start negotiations concerning the licensing or the assignment of the patent.

In conclusion, lawmakers should be aware that the problem of denying patents that should have been granted may be worse than granting patents that should not have been granted. Good quality patents are the basis of inventors' reliance on the system. And a patent office that is too strict in its handling of claimed inventions ends up scaring individual and small inventors away, to the loss of the overall system's credibility and the risk that valuable inventions are brushed away from prospective market entry. Furthermore, lawmakers should never forget that a patent office that deals efficiently and fairly with substantive examination is a component of democracy. When a patent office starts forming a significant backlog, those who are the first to avoid entering its facilities in search for the protection of their inventions are the small inventors, who cannot afford to wait an indefinite and large number of years for being granted a patent. Inefficient patent offices are antidemocratic because only large companies have to gain from administrative inefficiency. Some large companies even gain from delaying the procedures and use the pendency of patent applications as a threat against competitors. That is not, as a matter of course, the case of individual

74. Law No. 240/2000 of August 7, 2000, on Patents.
75. It should be noted that, in the course of patent enforcement procedures, when their validity is challenged, courts may tend to rely on their own experts. Even though this is not a matter of patent law, but of civil procedure law, and therefore it is not a topic for this book, it is worth noticing that courts should rely as much as they can on the patent office's technical opinions. After all, patent examiners are usually very experienced professionals and, in view of their following the guidelines prepared by their organizations, they tend to issue consistent opinions. Court experts should be involved only when the patent office's decisions on patentability, based on pre-grant examination, are questioned. As it will be discussed below, here a problem of conflict of interests may arise. Moreover, as it will be discussed below, when they have not the due expertise, patent offices may rely on the expertise of outsiders for carrying out the substantive examination of patent applications.

inventors, whose financial success or whose possibility of gaining access to venture capital depends on the speedily acquisition of a reliable patent.

Therefore, those countries that opt for the adoption of pre-grant substantive examination must be aware of the responsibility that comes attached to patent offices' duties. Of course, one can say that it is a matter of administrative management, not of patent law. That is true, and yet the patent law should be drafted in a way that clearly draws the line between discretion and arbitrariness in the exercise of authority by patent examiners. And, importantly, the requirements for a patent application to be accepted should be clearly established, so as to avoid ambiguity and uncertainty in the meaning of the patent claims. We should never forget that patent specifications, including the claims, which define the scope of the rights, are made of language. And language, although it does not have the same precision as mathematical formula, should be used with as much exactitude as possible.

Even patent offices that do not carry out pre-grant substantive examination should be aware of that and should not allow patents to be granted that do not describe and claim inventions precisely and unequivocally.

It is in this regard that a number of developing country lawmakers have taken the important decision of admitting that the examination of patent applications be carried out by experts who are not civil servants with the patent office. This is the case of the laws of Botswana, Costa Rica, and Uruguay, among others.

The relevant language of the law of Botswana reads:

Section 22.

(1) The Registrar shall cause the application to be examined for compliance with the requirements of the Act.

(2) The Minister may, by regulations, prescribe the categories of inventions in respect of which an examination under this section shall not cover the requirements of novelty and inventive step.

(3) An examination under this section may be undertaken by persons or institutions appointed by the Registrar, including any designated foreign, national or regional industrial property authorities.

In the same sense, the law of Costa Rica provides:

Article 13

...

(2) The Industrial Property Registry shall rely on professional examiners to conduct the substantive examination of patents, the cost of which shall be fixed by tariffs set for this purpose by the Administrative Board of the National Registry. Likewise, the Registry may request an opinion from official, higher education, scientific, technological or professional establishments, national or foreign, or, failing this, from independent experts in the field, as to the novelty, inventive step and industrial applicability of the invention. In all cases, the appointed examiner shall be independent, honest and not have a conflict of interest. He shall also respect the confidentiality of the information being examined. The abovementioned centers that depend on or are funded by the State and the professional bodies shall be obliged to provide the required advice. Any person signing reports shall be held responsible for their content, as the case may be, in

accordance with the provisions of Article 199 of the General Law of Public Administration.[76]

And the statute of Uruguay provides:

Article 32

The purpose of the substantive examination of the application will be to determine whether the claimed invention meets the patentability requirements and conditions set forth in this law. To this end, the following shall be permitted:

. . .

B) To request advice from institutions that carry out scientific and technological activities.

This is, actually, a commendable directive that may prove to be very cost-effective, to the extent it does not oblige the patent office to keep a large structure of specialized workforce, particularly in countries where filings are not abundant (and, therefore, the revenue obtained through the fees paid by patent applicants is not significant).

It should be noticed that the possibility of resorting to outside expertise can be confined to specific areas of technology, namely those that demand more specialized knowledge. The patent laws of several countries, for example, attribute the task of examining patent applications related to technology relevant for national security to the Ministry of Defense. The Industrial Property Law of North Macedonia goes further and establishes that patent applications for inventions relating to national defense shall be filed directly with the Minister for Defense (Article 71(1)).[77] Here, of course, two are the issues involved: the technical aspects of the claimed inventions and security-related concerns.

Other laws give the Ministry of Health the mandate of examining patent applications in the medical field. This was the case of Brazil, the patent law of which had a provision that said:

Article 229-C.

The granting of patents for pharmaceutical products and processes shall depend on the prior approval of the National Agency for Sanitary Vigilance—ANVISA.

This was a transitional provision inserted into the law of 1996, through an amendment, in 2001, and revoked in 2021. In those two decades, the conditioning of the patent grant to the prior approval of pharmaceutical-related inventions, which was supposed to apply to those applications included in the TRIPS Agreement mail-box mechanism only, was applied to all patent applications in that same field.[78] The

76. Law No. 6,867 of April 25, 1983, on Patents, Industrial Designs and Utility Models (as amended up to Law No. 8,686 of November 21, 2008).

77. In the case the inventor mistakenly files the application with the patent office, the latter will send it to the Ministry of Defense (Art. 71(5)). Reciprocity will take place when the Ministry of Defense, upon examining the application, decides that the invention is not of interest to national security (Art. 71(6)).

78. The mail-box mechanism was a temporary system introduced by Art. 70.8 of the TRIPS Agreement. According to the mechanism, those WTO Members that enjoyed a transitional

practical result was not only an institutional conflict between the patent office and the Ministry of Health, which for some time even maintained its own patent office, but also the origins of the huge backlog in patent applications that Brazil has endured (and still endures, even if the situation has improved in recent years). The reason for the backlog was that pharmaceutical-related inventions were submitted to a double substantive examination, with the two agencies following different understandings on the conditions of patentability.[79]

The use of specialized agencies in examining certain patent applications is found, articulated in a general manner, in the Patent Act of Egypt, as follows:

> *Article 17*
>
> *The Patent Office shall send to the Ministry of Defence, the Ministry of Military Production, the Ministry of Interior or the Ministry of Health, as required, copies of patent applications, with their annexes, that relate to defence, military production, security matters or that have a military, security or health significance, within 10 days from the examination of the application, notifying the applicant thereof within 7 days. The Minister of Defence, the Minister of Military Production, the Minister of Interior or the Minister of Health, as might be the case, may, within 90 days from the date of notification, oppose the publication of the application acceptance.*
>
> *Where the acceptance of the application is made public, the competent Minister may oppose the procedure to grant a patent within 90 days from the date of the publication, in the Patent Gazette, of the decision to accept the patent application, if it appears that the application relates to defence, military production, security or is of military, security or health significance.*
>
> *Opposition in the aforementioned cases shall stop the procedure of granting the patent.*[80]

It seems, however, that the law of Egypt reserves the decision of granting or denying the patent to the patent office, the specialized agencies mentioned in Article 17 having simply a role of providing subsidies for the substantive examination, not of deciding. The Brazilian provision had a different reading because it implied the sanitary agency's authority to deny the grant.

Whereas submitting patent applications to the specialized scrutiny of other governmental agencies and/or of individual experts should not be seen as a reason for concern, the idea of double examination is troublesome, in the sense it is counterproductive and discouraging to inventors. Indeed, besides infringing TRIPS obligations, in view of the discriminatory treatment as regards the technological field when it applies to certain inventions only, double examination introduces unreasonable delays in the grant of patents.

---

period for introducing patent protection without discrimination as to technological fields were required to accept the filing of applications concerning pharmaceutical and agrochemical inventions as from the date of the entry of the TRIPS Agreement into force (January 1, 1995), so that they could be examined (that same date applying to the criteria of patentability) once their laws were amended and patents granted.

79. For example, examiners in the Ministry of Health refused to grant patents for second uses, whereas the patent office had no objections to grant patents for those discoveries (yes, discoveries, literally, as it will be discussed below).
80. Law No. 82, of 2002, on the Protection of Intellectual Property Rights, amended up to Law No. 178, of 2020.

2 GETTING HELP IN THE EXAMINATION OF PATENT APPLICATIONS

Now that the case has been made for the absence of necessity for a patent office, under some circumstances, to engage in pre-grant substantive examination of patent applications—this not meaning, however, that such examination, either pre- or post-grant, is not required by international law, where necessary—the question comes of whether that office is obliged to carry out that examination by itself.

The answer is "no." The national patent office may very well accept and validate patents granted by patent offices of other countries.[81] This possibility is even explicitly contemplated by note 8 to the TRIPS Agreement, which reads:

> *It is understood that those Members which do not have a system of original grant may provide that the term of protection shall be computed from the filing date in the system of original grant.*

A country in which a very small number of patent applications is filed every year has three ways of approaching this solution: (i) the lawmaker can simply write in the Patent Act that it acknowledges the titles for inventions issued by country x; (ii) the country may celebrate an agreement with another country, under which patent applications filed in the former shall be sent to the latter, so that they can be substantively examined by the patent office of that other country; in this case the patents are still issued by the country in question; (iii) the country may replace the functions of a national patent office by those of a regional office—in which case the country must adhere to a regional agreement, which serves as supranational law.

Within these three options, there are still other possibilities available, such as combining the pre-grant examination of patent applications filed with the national office with accepting and revalidating patents granted by a foreign patent office,[82] or having a national patent system of filing and granting without prejudice to accepting and according enforceability to patents granted at a regional level (this is the case for the countries that have joined the European Patent Convention).

However, in agreeing with other patent offices on the examination or on the revalidation of patents granted by those offices, the country in question should be aware of a number of issues to be considered.

First, there may be cultural problems. One should never forget that a significant number of the technical reports issued by the patent examiner are of a subjective nature, namely those elements that concern the analysis of topics such as offense to morality and nonobviousness. What may be offensive to the examiner in one country may not be to the examiner in another country. What seems obvious to one examiner

81. A number of large and technically equipped patent offices do engage voluntarily in this sort of cooperation schemes with small, developing countries, such as the European Patent Office (EPO) and the Korean Intellectual Property Office (KIPO).

82. It was recently announced that Costa Rica and the European Patent Organization signed a patent validation agreement, *see* EPO, December 20, 2024, *Costa Rica signs historic validation agreement*, at <www.epo.org/en/news-events/news/> [access February 2024].

may be deemed significantly inventive to another. Thus, cultural and personal sensitivities have a great influence on the performance of examiners.

Second, there may be differences in the laws concerning what is and what is not patentable subject matter. Moreover, there may be differences in examiners' approaches to the exclusions from patentability.

Thresholds of sufficient inventiveness may also be significantly diverging.

This means that when one country wishes to rely in some manner on examinations carried out by foreign patent offices, it should be concerned with affinities in culture and in law.

For those countries that do not wish to lose their independence and sovereignty in deciding which patent applications should be accepted (and originate enforceable patents) and which ones should be denied, but lack the necessary (and costly) technical and human resources, there is always the alternative of obtaining technical assistance from a large patent office. Many are the modalities available for such assistance, but the most common is sending experienced patent examiners from large patent offices to spend a period in small offices, so that, for a given period, examiners from both offices perform searches and examinations jointly.

In recent years, a growing number of countries have joined schemes of cooperation between national and foreign patent offices. Those schemes are generally designated as PPH, from *Patent Prosecution Highway*. Under the PPH mechanism, the patent applicant, as soon as his/her patent application is accepted, entirely or partially, by an office that has joined the system, may bring that decision and accompanying documents (such as search and examination reports) from that office to another office that has likewise joined the system.[83]

The PPH mechanism has three main advantages:

(1) it significantly increases the quality of examination, given that, as the saying goes, two heads think better than one; through the PPH mechanism, less experienced patent examiners working in developing countries can benefit from the experience and acquired skills of patent examiners working for large patent offices; they can also benefit from the access to vast databases that large patent offices have at their disposal in order to perform thorough novelty and nonobviousness analyses;
(2) the mechanism also contributes to speeding the examination of patent applications, given that having access to a thorough examination report from a large patent office obviously alleviates the task of (re)examining the same invention in another (small) patent office; and
(3) to a large extent, it has the function of harmonizing the task of examining patent applications and ensuring that internationally consistent patents are granted in different countries.

83. A full explanation of work sharing by patent offices is available on WIPO's website, at < www.wipo.int/en/web/patents/topics/worksharing/index >.

It is this third advantage that actually justifies and explains the birth of the PPH mechanism, which, as explained elsewhere, was proposed by the five largest patent offices as a substitute to the idea of the global patent, which has been consistently rejected.[84]

Actually, the first examination reports issued by a PPH participating patent office have the same practical effects of the preliminary international examination reports issued under the Patent Cooperation Treaty (PCT) schedule. Those reports are not binding (a proposal by the WIPO Secretariat to give them binding effects failed in 2003[85]), but they are nevertheless very persuasive, given the high technical capacity and experience of those professionals that produce them.

3 FAST-TRACK PROCEDURES

Some inventions are more important than others. Some inventions are eagerly waited for by the market, while others can very well be left sleeping in inventors' drawers. Some inventions address urgent matters related to health and the environment, while others seek more trivial, if not futile, applications. Given the limitations of human resources available at patent offices, should not patent examiners give preference to the earlier examination of those more valuable inventions?

The answer is straightforward: yes, provided the preferential treatment is not accorded on a field-of-technology basis because in that event the matter would become one of technological discrimination, which is clearly prohibited by the TRIPS Agreement.

As explained elsewhere,[86] the main provision (and the reason of being of the TRIPS Agreement) is the prohibition of discriminatory treatment of technological fields under the patent system. The objective of TRIPS negotiators was to get rid once and for all of the exclusion of pharmaceutical inventions from patentability that was applied in some large economies. This important historical factor was briefly described above: such exclusion did not offend the provisions of the Paris Convention, given that the only substantive condition the Convention imposed on patents was the obligation for complying with the national treatment principle, under which Members of the Paris Union had to treat inventors based in other countries in the same manner they treated the inventors residing in their own territories. Therefore, if a country did not grant pharmaceutical patents to its own residents, it had no obligation to grant them to inventors residing in other countries. The TRIPS Agreement changed this and required that the residents in other territories received *at least* protection in accordance with the standards set in the Agreement—regardless of whether nationals are entitled to protection or not.

84. *See* Nuno Pires de Carvalho, The TRIPS Regime, *supra* note 3, at 27.
85. *Ibid.*, at 25.
86. *Ibid.*, at 233 et seq.

In this token, WTO Members are obliged to make:

> *. . . patents . . . available for any inventions, whether products or processes, in all fields of technology, and . . . patent rights enjoyable without discrimination as to . . . the field of technology.*

But the ban of discriminatory treatment by the TRIPS Agreement goes beyond Article 27.1. Indeed, the TRIPS Agreement prohibits not only negative discrimination but also *positive* discrimination. This prohibition is found in Article 1.1 of the Agreement, which provides that:

> *Members may, but shall not be obliged to, implement in their law more extensive protection than is required by this Agreement, provided that such protection does not contravene the provisions of this Agreement.*

In other words, where the patent law provides that, say, energy-saving inventions submitted to the patent office should receive the privilege of being examined with precedence, such provision would be contrary to Article 27.1, to the extent it discriminates against inventions in all other fields. Such positive discrimination contradicts, therefore, the letter and the spirit of the Agreement.

But patent lawmakers have a solution: they can allow for priority treatment in the substantive examination of patent applications on a case-by-case basis. The patent office, in that manner, is accorded authority to review requests from patent applicants for the expedited examination of their claims. The justification for such treatment can result from the specific nature of the invention—the cure for some illness, for example—or from special circumstances—the urgent need for the inventor to obtain seed money for establishing a new industry, for example. Even though this is not a matter for the statute, but for regulations, the patent office may express its inclination to rely on a declaration by a credited organization, such as an Association of Industries or a National Bank of Development, recommending an earlier examination of the patent application in question. Anyway, the justification for the application to jump the (invariably long) queue of applications waiting for the examination can never be that the invention belongs to a specific technological field.[87]

---

87. Provisions allowing for the prior examination of "green inventions" are found in some patent laws and regulations of WTO Members. They are all in conflict with Art. 27.1 in combination with Art. 1.1 of the TRIPS Agreement. The only exception that could be admitted concerns inventions in the field of defense and national security. This exception results from Art. 73 of the TRIPS Agreement, on "Security Exceptions," which reads (in part):

> *Nothing in this Agreement shall be construed:*
>
> . . .
>
> *(b) to prevent a Member from taking any action which it considers necessary for the protection of its essential security interests;*
> *(i) relating to fissionable materials or the materials from which they are derived;*
> *(ii) relating to the traffic in arms, ammunition and implements of war and to such traffic in other goods and materials as is carried on directly or indirectly for the purpose of supplying a military establishment;*
> *(iii) taken in time of war or other emergency in international relations; . . .*

A different but related issue that patent lawmakers may have to confront, to the extent it also deals with mechanisms tending to overcome long procedural delays in patent offices, is accepting provisional applications. By "provisional application," it is meant that, before finishing the build-up and the testing of the inventive concept, the inventor may have the urgent need to secure priority in claiming his/her invention. In such an event, the inventor has already an exact idea of the invention, and of how it will work when put into practice, but there may be some details, minor adjustments, and final improvements still in the process of being created, and therefore he/she is not yet at a point that would allow for the precise drafting of claims. That inventor may fear that some other inventive mind may be pursuing solutions for the same technical problem, and that those solutions may be the same as his/her own. In the event that other inventor completes the invention before he/she filed the application, he/she would lose the possibility of obtaining the patent, thereby losing all the sunk investments in terms of money and time.[88]

To address this issue, some laws admit provisional applications. The inventor files with the patent office a thorough description of the invention, but does not submit the claims. Such filing accords the invention a priority date. Consequently, that inventor is benefited with a given period—usually, of one year—for submitting the definitive application, with the claims. This new filing does not change the priority date. For the purposes of Article 4(2) of the Paris Convention, where the national patent statute considers that provisional application to be a regular filing (in the sense that it does not need to be replaced by a new application when the unfinished steps are completed), the provisional application is recognized as giving rise to the right of priority.[89]

Is this convenient? The reality is that provisional applications do not attend to deep policies and therefore patent lawmakers should look at them as a matter of convenience, rather than of necessity. Provisional applications, however, have the advantage of encouraging the early filing of patent applications. They may also serve as persuasive tokens of encouragement for small inventors to use the patent system. They are, therefore, of great convenience, particularly for a developing country that wishes to promote invention and innovation, on the one hand, and, on the other, reduce the possibility of complex conflicts between inventors of simultaneous inventions, under the rules available (the first-to-invent or the first-to-file rules).

88. Two systems are available to solve this conflict: the first-to-invent rule and the-first-to-file rule. Whenever possible, the inventor should avoid being in a situation where he/she needs to resort to one of those rules (depending on which rule the national lawmaker has preferred). That is where the utility of provisional applications lies as a tool that gives advantage to the first who finishes the invention.

89. Article 4(2) of the Paris Convention reads:

> *Any filing that is equivalent to a regular national filing under the domestic legislation of any country of the Union or under bilateral or multilateral treaties concluded between countries of the Union shall be recognized as giving rise to the right of priority.*

4 *DOS AND DON'TS*

In the matter of pre-grant substantive examination, let us start with the *don'ts*. They are two.

The first *don't* is that the patent law should not establish a complex patent examination procedure prior to the grant in those countries where the applications are scarce. The administrative efforts for ensuring a good quality examination may prove too burdensome for a small economy, and in the end, the examination may end up being of poor quality. In terms of legal security, it is better for a patent owner to have in his/her hands a non-examined patent that he/she can anytime, in the event of litigation, submit to the scrutiny of an examination (by the patent office or by a judicial expert), than a poorly examined patent, whose presumptive validity is close to zero.

The second *don't* is that in his/her wish to help particularly promising inventions to reach the market quickly, the lawmaker should not fall into the temptation of creating classes of preferred inventions according to their technological fields. Although commonly found in national patent laws as well as in patent offices' practices, that is a blatant infringement of the TRIPS Agreement.

The *dos* are also two.

The first *do* is that although the law does not require that patent offices engage in examination of patent applications as to novelty, inventiveness (or nonobviousness) and utility before granting the patents, it should nevertheless require that the claimed inventions be, albeit perfunctorily, scrutinized as to their conformity with deep national moral and religious values and as well as to their conformity to the statutory provisions on exclusions from patentability. A superficial analysis of the quality of the disclosure should also be performed.

The second *do* is that, when patents have not been previously examined, and their owners need to enforce the corresponding rights, or need to assert them in any possible manner (e.g., where the patent owner needs to use the patent as a collateral or as a title of security), the patent office must provide services for the post-grant patent examination of a good quality. It is better that this task be attributed to the patent office rather than to courts, in preliminary rulings, because although the judicial expert is by definition impartial (otherwise he/she would not have been hired by the court and/or accepted by the parties), the patent office stands, also by definition, away from the adversarial nature of court proceedings and can always resort to the assistance of expert organizations that can help it carry a good quality examination, such as foreign patent offices. When the country in question is a Contracting Party to the Patent Cooperation Treaty (PCT), there are even rules determining WIPO's assistance to Contracting Parties concerning the substantive examination of patent applications.

In conclusion, the presumption of validity that administrative law almost invariably attributes to legal titles issued by the public administration, such as patent letters, should only be admissible when the grant or the assertion of those patents has been preceded by a substantive examination.

CHAPTER 3

On Patentability

One matter that is of special concern for lawmakers is the scope of patentability. Here, a distinction should be made between creations of a technical nature that are not considered to be inventions, on the one hand, and, on the other, technical creations that qualify as inventions but, for one reason or another, lawmakers decide to place them outside the scope of patentable subject matter.

Let us look at these two categories of technical creations ("technical" meaning that they are aimed at solving practical problems) and the *dos* and *don'ts* in dealing with them in statutory language.

1 INVENTIONS THAT OFFEND MORALS OR THAT ARE CONTRARY TO PUBLIC POLICIES

Article 27.1 of the TRIPS Agreement allows WTO Members to exclude from patentability:

> *. . . inventions the prevention within their territory of the commercial exploitation of which is necessary to protect ordre public or morality, including to protect human, animal or plant life or health or to avoid serious prejudice to the environment.*[90]

90. Article 27.1 adds:

> *. . . provided that such exclusion is not made merely because the exploitation is prohibited by their law.*

In other words, the law cannot simply exclude a type of invention from patentability because the commercialization of the products that are made using (directly or indirectly) those inventions is prohibited. This caveat existed already in Art. 4*quater* of the Paris Convention, in the following terms:

> *The grant of a patent shall not be refused and a patent shall not be invalidated on the ground that the sale of the patented product or of a product obtained by means of a patented process is subject to restrictions or limitations resulting from the domestic law.*

The exclusion of inventions from patentability on grounds of morality was briefly discussed above. In note 72, *supra*, it was said that, as regards inventions whose exclusion from patentability results from fundamental social values of a morale or religious nature, the patent examiner may rely on his/her common sense, and, although a law prohibiting the commercialization of the inventions in question may have never been passed, he/she is still under the duty of denying the patent if, as much objectively as possible, he/she sees the invention as offensive to those fundamental values.

As a matter of course, one may find it difficult to find objectivity in the assessment of compliance with values that are components of culture and civilization, such as morality, but there is at least one patent statute that suggests that such a criterion is possible. It is the Patent Act of Costa Rica, which reads:

> *Article 1.—Inventions.*
>
> . . .
>
> 4.— *The following may not be patented:*
> (*a*) *inventions whose commercial exploitation must objectively and necessarily be prevented to protect public order, morality, the health or life of persons or animals or to preserve plants or prevent serious damage to the environment;* . . . (emphasis added).

Unfortunately, the Costa Rican lawmaker has not provided any clarification on how objectivity in the examination of this exclusion can be achieved by the patent examiner. Therefore, when the opportunity arrives, the examiner will need to rely on the criteria of objectivity to be defined by the examination guidelines prepared by the patent office.

It is worth emphasizing that, as said, Article 27.2 does not require that the legal norm prohibiting the commercial exploitation of the invention that is contrary to *ordre public* or morality be set in writing. That norm may very well be of a customary nature; i.e., the norm may consist in a nonwritten expression of society's beliefs and conduct.

But when it comes to reasons for exclusion that are not embedded in the deep social beliefs of a given society, such as those that concern public policies (like access to health and protection of the environment), their exclusion from commercial use must be explicit in legal, binding norms, regardless of their level, in order to justify the exclusion of those inventions from patentability. Therefore, an examiner should not deny the grant of a patent to an invention that, in his/her assessment, e.g., constitutes a highly pollutant product or device, without confirming that the commercial exploitation of the invention is legally prohibited.

The difference between the two provisions is that the TRIPS Agreement refers only to the exclusion from patentability, this meaning that, where an invention meets the conditions of patentability, the grant of the patent shall not be denied, unless the denial is necessary to prevent its exploitation. Article 4*quater* of the Paris Convention is more restrictive, in the sense that not only the patent has to be granted but also it cannot be cancelled afterward, where the law is changed and the making of the product falls under a new prohibition. However, because Art. 4*quater* of the Paris Convention is part of the TRIPS Agreement (as a result of Art. 2.1), the added restriction would not be strictly necessary. Important is the condition that the exclusion is to be adopted only when it is necessary in order to prevent the commercial exploitation of the invention in question.

However, when Article 27.2 says that the rejection of patentability must be necessary, in view of the application of the rule that prohibits the commercial use of the invention, an additional step is required for the examiner's analysis.

In fact, as explained elsewhere,[91] the identification by an examiner that a certain regulation or directive prohibits the use of a specific insecticide, for example, should not lead automatically to the rejection of an invention that concerns the mentioned product. It is required by Article 27.2 of the TRIPS Agreement that the rejection be *necessary* in order to avoid the product being commercialized.

In reality, the idea that the denial of a patent leads to the abandonment of the idea of exploiting an invention commercially is not self-evident. The predominant reason for an inventor to invent a new product is his/her expectation of putting it on the market and extracting profits therefrom. Once the commercial exploitation of that same product is prohibited or is permitted, but under severe restrictions, the inventor most probably will not spend time and money inventing around that product. The reason is that if he/she invents something related to that product, and gets a patent, the prohibition of commercial use of the invention remains in force. The patent is not an authorization for using but for excluding.

This means that the way in which Article 27.2 is drafted does not make it clear how the exclusion from patentability on those grounds will be effectively implemented.

And it is exactly in view of that lack of clarity that the advice to developing country patent lawmakers is that they should reproduce the text of Article 27.2 *ipsis verbis* and let the patent office put the exclusion into practice. This does not mean to add legal insecurity to that provision because, as said, the provision has already enough elements of legal insecurity and ambiguity. To try to overcome those elements by drafting a provision that explains, in objective terms, how refusing the grant of a patent leads, necessarily, to the nonexploitation of an invention seems to be an impossible task.

Indeed, a significant number of developing country WTO Members have followed this path of simply reproducing the provisions of Article 27.2. For example, the regional law that applies in Peru, Colombia, Bolivia, and Ecuador (countries that form the Andean Community) provides that:

> *The following shall not be patentable:*
>
> *a) inventions whose commercial exploitation in the territory of the Member Country concerned must necessarily be prevented in order to protect public order or morality. For these purposes, the commercial exploitation of an invention shall not be considered contrary to public order or morality solely because of the existence of a legal or administrative provision prohibiting or regulating such exploitation.* [92]

91. *See* Nuno Pires de Carvalho, The TRIPS Regime, *supra* note 3, at 294, explaining the two-step necessity test required by Art. 27.2.

92. Intriguing in the Andean Directive is the note that the mere existence of a legal or an administrative provision prohibiting or regulating the commercial exploitation of an invention that offends morality should not, in itself, justify the exclusion from patentability. This caveat, when in connection with inventions tainted by moral or religious objections, does not make any sense. That rule was included in Art. 4*quater* of the Paris Convention having in view that the

> b) *Inventions whose commercial exploitation in the Member Country in question must necessarily be prevented in order to protect the health or life of people or animals, or to preserve plants or the environment. For these purposes, the commercial exploitation of an invention shall not be considered contrary to the health or life of people, animals, or to the preservation of plants or the environment solely because there is a legal or administrative provision prohibiting or regulating such exploitation.* [93]

The same solution can be found in the Patent Act of Pakistan:

> *A Patent shall not be granted for invention the prevention of commercial exploitation of which would be necessary to protect the "ordre public" or morality, including to protect human, animal or plant life or health or to avoid serious prejudice to the environment, provided that such exclusion is not made merely because the exploitation is prohibited by any law for the time being in force.*[94]

However, there is also a significant number of countries the laws of which simply state that certain inventions shall not be patented, without setting the two-step test that is imposed by Article 27.2 of the TRIPS Agreement (i.e., without requiring that, first, it be verified by the patent examiner whether a law or regulation is in place that prohibits the commercial exploitation of the invention; and, second, without asking the examiner to assess whether the exclusion from patentability is necessary in order to ensure compliance with that same law).

This is, for example, the case of Brazil, whose Industrial Property Act reads:

> *Article 18. The following are not patentable:*
>
> *I— anything that is contrary to morality, good customs and public safety, order and health . . . .*

The Patent Act of the Philippines goes in the same direction:

> *Section 22. Non-Patentable Inventions. The following shall be excluded from patent protection: . . .*
>
> *6. Anything which is contrary to public order or morality.*[95]

---

prohibition of commercialization that is imposed on certain products may be temporary or provisional, such as pharmaceutical, agrochemical, and cosmetic products. Pending their approval by authorities, those products may not be commercialized—hence the caveat. It is difficult, however, to consider that commercial restrictions or bans resulting from moral and religious grounds may be provisional or temporary. Those grounds may evolve, and they do evolve indeed, but as a consequence of deep social changes, which take decades, if not centuries, to take place. Article 4*quater* of the Paris Convention (quoted in *supra* note 90) was, in this regard, much better drafted than Art. 27.2 because it simply mentions restrictions or limitations on the sale of a given product. In reality, it is probable that the drafters of the TRIPS Agreement wanted to confine this condition to inventions that harm "human, animal or plant life or health or [that cause] serious prejudice to the environment" and other inventions whose commercial exploitation may have a negative impact on public order—but not to inventions whose exploitation offends morality.

93. Decision No. 486 of the Commission of the Andean Community Establishing the Common Industrial Property Regime, of 2000, Art. 20.
94. Patents Ordinance, 2001 (as amended by Patents (Amendment) Ordinance, 2002), Art. 4(1).
95. Intellectual Property Code, Republic Act No. 8,293 (2015 Edition).

Further clarification, along the explanation given above, should be given by the patent office, through examination guidelines. Importantly, those guidelines may also serve as indications for the court experts, who may be called to give their advice in the context of the settlement of disputes involving the topic of exclusions from patentability.

2 DIAGNOSTIC, THERAPEUTIC AND SURGICAL METHODS FOR THE TREATMENT OF HUMANS OR ANIMALS

These methods, which are inventions for all purposes, may also be excluded from patentability by WTO Members, under Article 27.2. The reason for this permission is allegedly based on professional ethics—the novelty and utility of therapeutic methods have traditionally been scrutinized by peer review, not by patent offices, and it is generally accepted that the inventors' colleagues should be entitled to share the inventions. Actually, the true reason for the lack of patent protection in the field of therapeutic methods lies somewhere else. Therapeutic methods, as well as diagnostic and surgical methods, are, with a very few exceptions, procedures whose success depends much more on the individual skills of doctors or surgeons who use them than on the methods themselves. In other words, therapeutic methods are not to be massively applied (even where they are repeatedly applied), which confines their economic relevance to the extremely narrow market of the few patients of a given doctor or surgeon. Moreover, certain surgical methods are easily kept by their inventors under secrecy. Therefore, it is not necessary to patent those methods in order to appropriate them. Creative doctors and surgeons are paid through increased professional prestige and attendant higher fees.

In the light of the TRIPS Agreement, the exclusion of therapeutic methods from patentability does not stem from the lack of any of the substantive requirements. If it did, therapeutic methods would not be patentable subject matter under Article 27.1 and the language of Article 27.3(a) would be meaningless. In effect, methods, therapeutic or not, are processes that consist of a series of steps. They are inventions. The fact that therapeutic methods are used on human bodies does not eliminate their susceptibility to industrial application. Therapeutic, diagnostic, and surgical methods, directly or indirectly, manipulate the human body. They are as concrete as processes of manufacture. However, it is not the fact that a process manipulates concrete materials that makes it capable of industrial application. What characterizes the susceptibility of industrial application is the possibility of using the process repeatedly and consistently in the production of goods ("industry" for the purposes of "industrial property" means human labor).

In the United States and in Australia, therapeutic methods are patentable subject matter.[96] However, section 287 of the US Patents Act, which deals with limitations on

96. In *Apotex Pty Ltd v. Sanofi-Aventis Australia Pty Ltd* [2013] HCA 50, the High Court of Australia held that "methods of medical treatment are a 'manner of manufacture' and therefore represent a patentable invention in Australia." The opinion is available at <www.austlii.edu.au/cgi-bin/viewdoc/au/other/HCASum/2013/46.html> [access in May 2025].

damages and other remedies, was amended in 1996. Under subsection (c)(1), medical practitioners and health care entities have immunity against liability for the infringement of patents covering therapeutic methods whose applications were filed on or after September 30, 1996.[97,98]

A distinction must be made, however, between therapeutic methods and methods that are performed on the human or animal body but which are not therapeutic (or diagnostic or surgical) in nature. For example, methods for conserving human organs for later transplantation and reproduction-inducting methods are nontherapeutic and therefore are not excluded from patentability. Patent examiners, thus, must scrutinize those methods as to their compliance with the substantive conditions of patentability spelled out in Article 27.1.

If the patentability of therapeutic methods is not a very relevant issue, at least from an economic point of view,[99] that situation may change in the field of biotechnology, especially as far as regenerative medicine is concerned. Both gene therapies and therapeutic transplantation methods tend to become standardized and repetitive procedures, and, therefore, they tend to be no longer performed individually by doctors and surgeons in their private offices, but rather become mass-used methods. Therapies in the biotechnology field, therefore, tend to become as economically important as the biotechnological products themselves, and thus acquire an economic role stemming from their commercialization—rather than in the offices of individual doctors and surgeons. Inventors of massively used biotechnological therapeutic methods will no longer be able to internalize R&D costs through individual prestige and fees.

Should the developing country lawmaker be worried about this particular topic? The answer could be straightforwardly a "no," but it happens that a small number of

97. That amendment was introduced after an infuriated public debate caused by a lawsuit lodged by a certain Dr. Pallin, an ophthalmologist surgeon, who had obtained a patent (No. 5,080,111) on the shape and the location of the incision for cataract surgery. Dr. Pallin attempted to enforce his patent against a colleague and his clinic. The District Court of Vermont, in a consent order dated of March 28, 1996, dismissed the action on grounds of invalidity of the claims. This case outraged the medical community because Dr. Pallin had announced his intention to recover damages from all the surgeons who used his technique. Being a commonly used technique, virtually all the ophthalmologists in the U.S. felt they were threatened of a costly lawsuit. *See* Katherine J. Strandburg, *Legal but Unacceptable: Pallin v. Singer and Physician Patenting Norms*, published online by Cambridge University Press, May 5, 2014, available at <www.cambridge.org> [access in July 2025].
98. When the Senate Judiciary Committee was examining the bill that led to that amendment, the General Counsel of the United States Trade Representative's Office sent a letter to the Senate expressing her concern that, if adopted, that provision would violate the TRIPS obligations of the United States, specially Art. 27.1 (concerning the discriminatory treatment against a given technological field), in conjunction with Arts. 44 and 45 (which deal with remedies, including injunctions and damages, that must be available to address patent infringement), and Art. 30 (in accordance with which immunity against enforcement is not included in the exceptions to rights conferred). The provision was enacted nonetheless.
99. In the United States, where therapeutic methods are patentable subject matter, and therefore, patents for therapeutic methods are enforceable (with the limitations introduced in 1996), they have been invariably invalidated (including the famous Dr. Pallin's patent) whenever their validity has been challenged on grounds of lack of novelty, of obviousness, or of absence of utility. *See, e.g.*, *Morton v. New York Infirmary*, 17 F. Cas. 879, Case No. 9,865 (S.D.N.Y. 1862); *Martin v. Wyeth*, 193 F.2d 58 (4th Cir. 1951); *In re Stanley*, 1992 U.S. App. LEXIS 2361 (Fed. Cir. 1992).

developing countries have acquired and continue acquiring relevant knowledge and expertise in areas related to surgical methods, to the point that they have become regular providers of "health tourism," a new line of medical business that is defined by Google AI as follows:

> Several countries are popular destinations for health tourism due to a combination of factors like cost, quality of care, and specialized treatments. Some of the leading countries in this field include Thailand, India, Malaysia, Singapore, Turkey, Costa Rica, Mexico, South Korea, and the United Arab Emirates. These countries offer a range of specialized treatments and procedures, often at a lower cost compared to Western countries, while maintaining high standards of care.[100]

In Europe, it is common knowledge that a few North African countries, like Tunisia and Morocco, have also become the destiny of health tourists in search of good quality and low-priced services of esthetic surgery.

So, for the lawmakers of those countries, the idea of making patents available for surgical methods may not be entirely bad. The main criterion for adopting such measure should be the assessment of the real significance of the health tourism industry for the country.

3 PLANTS AND ANIMALS (OTHER THAN MICROORGANISMS) AND ESSENTIALLY BIOLOGICAL PROCESSES FOR THE PRODUCTION OF PLANTS AND ANIMALS (OTHER THAN NON-BIOLOGICAL AND MICROBIOLOGICAL PROCESSES)

Article 27.3(b) authorizes WTO Members to exclude from patentability the following biotechnological inventions:

- whole animals (including, obviously, human beings), animal varieties and parts of animals (including parts of human beings);
- whole plants, plant varieties (provided an alternative system of protection is provided) and parts of plants; and
- essentially biological processes.

As far as plant varieties are concerned, Article 27.3(b) authorizes Members to combine aspects of the patent system with those of a sui generis regime, such as UPOV (French acronym for the International Union for the Protection of New Varieties of Plants). A sui generis mechanism draws provisions and principles from existing regimes and adapts them to the specific characteristics of its subject matter. Under the TRIPS Agreement, protection of plant varieties can be ensured by one of three possible mechanisms: patents; or a sui generis system (provided it is effective); or a combination of both.

100. This was the response by Google's AI Overview in response to the entry "health tourism countries" (on August 16, 2025).

The regime set by the various versions of the UPOV Convention—and, in particular, of the 1991 version—is generally considered by WTO Members as sufficiently effective for the purposes of Article 27.3(b). Actually, the UPOV Convention, on the one hand, accords to breeders rights that are above those minimum standards ensured by the TRIPS Agreement, and, on the other, provides for some exceptions to those rights that a strict construction of Article 30 of the TRIPS Agreement might not accept. For example, the UPOV Convention imposes limits to the grounds on which plant variety certificates may be annulled and cancelled, which may be seen as a *TRIPS-plus* measure. Moreover, the UPOV Convention of 1991 prohibits governments from restricting the free exercise of the right accorded to breeders "otherwise than for reasons of public interest" and establishes that "all measures shall be taken to ensure that the breeder receives equitable remuneration" (Article 17). The provision that private rights may only be diminished on grounds of public interest, in principle, also applies to patents and compulsory licenses under the TRIPS Agreement, but the GATT negotiators unfortunately have failed to make that clarification. Furthermore, breeders are entitled to provisional protection in the period between the filing date and the date on which they obtain the certificate. Under the 1978 text, provisional protection is optional and applies to abusive acts of third parties only (Article 7(3)).[101] Article 28 of the TRIPS Agreement fails to provide for such an important measure.

In addition to these additional mechanisms of protection of breeders, the text of UPOV 1991, in addition to incorporating the 1978 provisions mentioned above, establishes a national exhaustion regime and extends protection to essentially derived varieties.

As far as exceptions to breeders' rights are concerned, the UPOV Convention provides two major exceptions: the farmers' exemption and the breeders' exemption.

The farmers' exception was implicit in the definition of breeders' rights under UPOV 1978, pursuant to Article 5, and made explicit in Article 15(2) of the 1991 version, which reads:

> *Article 15 Exceptions to the Breeder's Right*
>
> . . .
>
> *(2) [Optional exception] Notwithstanding Article 14, each Contracting Party may, within reasonable limits and subject to the safeguarding of the legitimate interests of the breeder, restrict the breeder's right in relation to any variety in order to permit farmers to use for propagating purposes, on their own holdings, the product of the harvest which they have obtained by planting, on their own holdings, the protected variety or a variety covered by Article 14(5)(a)(i) or (ii).*

Given that the UPOV Act of 1978, like the Act of 1991, is a minimum standards agreement, the adoption of the farmers' exception is optional (as the Convention explicitly states). In other words, UPOV Members can opt for not having it. What the Act of 1991 changed as regards the farmers' exception was to ensure some minimum protection for the breeders, so that the exception could not be used by UPOV Members

101. Under the text of 1991, provisional protection is mandatory; it applies to any act of infringement (or any act that requires the authorization of the rights holder); and it must entitle the right holder to equitable remuneration at least (Art. 13).

to make the rights of breeders meaningless. In this token, the exception must be confined within reasonable limits, and the legitimate interests of the breeder must be preserved. This language is not very different from the language adopted by Article 30 of the TRIPS Agreement, on exceptions to rights conferred by the patent. Furthermore, the exception only covers the use of the saved material: (i) that has been obtained by planting, (ii) on the own holdings of the farmers benefited by the exception and (iii) that can be used for propagating purposes only, (iv) on their own holdings (i.e., it cannot be used for bartering seeds or otherwise assigning them to others).

Many adversaries of the UPOV Convention have challenged the wisdom of following its standards because these might affect food security, given the risks that small and traditional farmers would no longer be able to save seeds and maintain their traditional crops and farming techniques. Of course, UPOV only applies to protected varieties. Farmers who buy unprotected seeds are free to do whatever they want to do with them, unless they are bound by contractual clauses to do otherwise. But, even as regards protected plant varieties, there is no mechanism that may prevent small farmers from continuing their traditional practices of saving and resowing seeds. Small farmers are not seed traders, and therefore they are not affected by the limits imposed by Article 15(2) of the UPOV Act of 1991.

Under the breeders' exemption, which was provided for in the UPOV Act of 1978 (Article 5(3)) and renewed in the UPOV Act of 1991 (Article 15(1)(iii) in conjunction with Article 14), there is no need to obtain the prior authorization of the breeder's right holder for the use of the protected variety as an initial source of other varieties. The exception reaches all acts for which, in principle, the prior authorization of the right holder should be requested, such as producing or reproducing the protected variety, conditioning it for the purposes of propagation, offering for sale, selling or other marketing, etc. In contrast with the farmers' exemption, which is optional, the breeder's exemption is mandatory.

As a result of the practice of implementing TRIPS obligations, both texts of UPOV are widely understood as *effective* protection for the purposes of Article 27.3(b).[102]

It goes without saying that WTO Members are not obliged to join UPOV in order to discharge themselves from the obligation of providing for an effective alternative system for the protection of plant varieties. Nor are they obliged to adopt UPOV standards. As noted, the UPOV provides, it is true, for standards of plant variety protection that are generally understood as being effective and thus TRIPS-compliant. But nothing would stand in the way of Members' designing different standards of protection—provided they are likewise effective. So far, no such different standards have been developed outside the UPOV or the patent system.[103] Some attempts of including in plant variety-related legislation some provisions on access to genetic

102. *See* IP/C/W/273, of June 5, 2001.
103. For example, the United States, besides making utility patents available for some inventions in the area of plants, and in addition to a UPOV 1991-consistent system, has established a different sort of patents (the so-called plant patents) that cover inventions or discoveries concerning asexually reproduced, distinct and new varieties of plants, including cultivated sports, mutants, hybrids, and newly found seedlings, other than a tuber propagated plant or a plant found in an uncultivated state (35 U.S.C. §161).

resources do not mean necessarily that a new system has been created. What those laws or model laws contain is a combination of UPOV-like provisions with some norms on how to share benefits with local governments and traditional communities derived from the use of plant genetic resources (which are either wild or non-stabilized varieties and, therefore, could not be protected under a UPOV-like system in the first place) and associated traditional knowledge.

As said, Article 27.3(b) admits that WTO Members adopt a combination of patent protection and of a sui generis system of protection for plant varieties. This means two things. WTO Members may adopt a single system under which they combine standards extracted from both the patent regime (as defined by section 5 of Part II of the TRIPS Agreement) and the UPOV (or another sui generis) regime. For example, the law of a WTO Member could protect plant varieties through patents with a twenty-year term, subject to the farmers' and breeders' exemptions. Therefore, it would be possible for WTO Members to combine those elements of the two systems that best fit the characteristics of plant varieties and protect these under a patent regime—which would have the advantage of making the PCT mechanism available to plant varieties.

But Article 27.3(b) also means that WTO Members may put more than one single regime in place for the protection of plant varieties at the same time and for the same species or genera. The second sentence of Article 27.3(b) was drafted in the form of alternatives—one of those is the protection of plant varieties exclusively by a sui generis regime (such as UPOV).

3.1 Some Examples of National Provisions Dealing with Plant and Animal-Related Inventions

In view of the broad leeway that results from the TRIPS Agreement, countries have adopted different approaches to the protection of new and invented plants and animals.

For example, the patent law of Bahrain excludes animals from patentability but not plants. Its Act on Plant Varieties provides:

> *Article 2—Scope of the Application of the Law*
>
> . . .
>
> *The genera, species, and plant varieties for which the patent has been granted are excluded from the provisions of this law.*[104]

The law of Oman, which also makes patents available for new varieties, in parallel with special plant variety protection, deals with particularities that apply to them only:

> *Article (5): Anyone submitting an application claiming patent right should abide by the following:*
>
> . . .

104. Law No. 1, of 2004, as amended in 2006.

5— The description of plant varieties shall be deemed sufficient when they are as complete as is reasonably possible.

. . .

Article (11): 1—A patent shall confer on its owner the right to prevent third parties from exploiting the patented invention in Oman.

2— Exploiting a patented invention means any of the following acts:

. . .

C— when the patent has been granted in respect of a plant or plant variety:

1— producing or reproducing (multiplying);
2— conditioning for the purpose of propagation;
3— offering for sale;
4— selling or other marketing;
5— exporting;
6— importing;
7— stocking for any of the purposes mentioned in (i) to (vi), above;

D— The provisions of the previous paragraph shall also apply in relation to:

1— varieties which are essentially derived from the protected variety, where the protected variety is not itself an essentially derived variety,
2— varieties which are not clearly distinguishable from the protected variety; and
3— varieties whose production requires the repeated use of the protected variety.
4— a variety shall be deemed to be essentially derived from another variety ("the initial variety") when:

A— it is predominantly derived from the initial variety, or from a variety that is itself predominantly derived from the initial variety, while retaining the expression of the essential characteristics that result from the genotype or combination of genotypes of the initial variety;
B— it is clearly distinguishable from the initial variety; and
C— except for the differences which result from the act of derivation, it conforms to the initial variety in the expression of the essential characteristics that result from the genotype or combination of genotypes of the initial variety.

. . .

4. . . .

E)

. . .

With respect of patents granted for plants and plant varieties, the rights under those patents shall not extend to:

a) acts done privately and for non-commercial purposes;
b) acts done for experimental purposes; and
c) acts done for the purpose of breeding other varieties, including essentially derived varieties;

. . .

F) subject to the safeguarding of the legitimate interests of the patent owner, any acts practiced by farmers to use for propagating purposes, the product of the harvest which they have obtained by planting the patented variety or an essentially derived variety.[105]

105. Law on Industrial Property Rights (promulgated by the Royal Decree No. 67/2008). This language is clearly inspired by the US Patent Act, which, in section 162, reads:

No plant patent shall be declared invalid for noncompliance with section 112 if the description is as complete as is reasonably possible.

The Patent Act of Switzerland, which admits the patentability of some plant and animal-related inventions, also reflects the farmers' exemption (but not the breeders' exemption), as follows:

Article 2

. . .

Also excluded from patentability are:

. . .

b. *plant varieties and animal varieties or essentially biological processes for the production of plants or animals; however, . . . inventions that concern plants or animals are patentable provided that their application is not technically confined to a single plant or animal variety.*

. . .

Article 35a

1 *Farmers who have acquired plant reproduction material placed on the market by the proprietor of the patent or with his consent may reproduce, on their own farm, the product from this material cultivated on their own farm.*
2 *Farmers who have acquired animal reproductive material or animals placed on the market by the proprietor of the patent or with his consent may reproduce, on their own farm, the animals obtained through reproduction of this material or these animals on their own farm.*
3 *Farmers are required to obtain the consent of the proprietor of the patent when they wish to give the product of their harvest or the animal or animal reproductive material obtained to third parties for reproduction purposes.*
4 *Contractual agreements which limit or revoke the farmers' privilege in the area of food and feed production are null and void.*

The Industrial Property Act of Brazil follows the general trend of excluding animals and plants, and their parts, from patentability:

Art. 18. The following are not patentable:

. . .

III— all or part of living beings, except transgenic microorganisms that meet the three patentability requirements—novelty, inventive step and industrial application—provided for in art. 8, and that are not mere discoveries.

Of course, there is a redundancy in this particular language: where an invention for a new microorganism has met the inventive step requirement, it cannot be a discovery. However, one understands the concern of the Brazilian lawmaker, in the sense of not accepting lower standards of nonobviousness as far as microorganisms are concerned.

The statute of the Dominican Republic repeats very closely the language of Article 27.3(b) of the TRIPS Agreement:

Article 2.—The following are excluded from protection by patent of invention;

. . .

2) *The following inventions shall not be patented nor shall they be published.*

. . .

(c) *Plants and animals, except for microorganisms, and essentially biological procedures for the production of plants or animals that are not non-biological or microbiological procedures. Plant varieties will be regulated by a special law, in compliance with article 27.3(b) of the TRIPS Agreement.*[106]

3.2 *Dos and Don'ts*

The only recommendation that results from the various experiences in addressing the patentability of plants and animals is that, when a country opts for protecting new plant varieties through patents, some special provisions should be introduced, not only, as discussed, regarding the exceptions to the breeders' rights but also as regards the application and the conditions for patentability. As the statutes of the United States and Oman go, when it comes to the enabling description of a new plant, it is expected that the inventor will not be able to give a description as clear and precise as if it were a mechanical invention.

Should developing countries exclude nonhuman animals and their parts from patentability? The fact is that there is no objective reason to answer this question with a "no." One may think that admitting the patentability of animals and their parts would give rise to deep issues of an ethical and moral nature. But the reality is that, in search for increased production of animal-derived foodstuffs, genetic engineering is normally developed and applied to animals, without opposition.

Anyway, we would not be able to identify here any *dos* or *don'ts*. Developing countries have preferred to stay away from this debate and, with more or less words, have simply transposed to their national statutes the permission given by Article 27.3(b). The revision of the article four years after its entry into force has not produced any results that are worth noticing.

4 DISCOVERIES, SCIENTIFIC THEORIES AND MATHEMATICAL METHODS

This exclusion is present in the vast majority of national patent statutes, and its wording does not diverge significantly from the simple identification of the three types of human knowledge that, as per definition, are not the result of human inventive activity. No matter how sophisticated and how much research work those three sorts of knowledge may require, they are not inventions, and therefore they are outside the scope of patentability.

It is true that, in 1978, WIPO Member States approved the Geneva Treaty on the International Recording of Scientific Discoveries. The idea was to encourage the work of scientists by associating their names with significant discoveries. The Treaty was promoted by the former Soviet Union and was signed by two countries only: Bulgaria and Czechoslovakia. Eventually, the motivation behind the Treaty was the interest of

106. Law No. 42,406 on Implementation of the Dominican Republic—Central America—United States Free Trade Agreement (CAFTA-DR).

the Soviet Union and its political satellites to assert their scientific feats and glories on the international level. But the Treaty had no practical value whatsoever, and never entered into practice.

5 SECOND USES

Patents cover the new characteristics or components of a product (or steps of a process) and accord an exclusive right in any use whatsoever that is given to the product (or the process). Therefore, if, during the term of the patent, a third party identifies a new use of the patented substance or article, the patent owner may enforce his exclusive rights against that third party, even if the patentee was not aware of the possibility of such use. The reason is that exclusivity covers any use of the product, regardless of it being known or unknown to the patent owner at the time of filing the application or thereafter. Indeed, Article 28.1 of the TRIPS Agreement provides that:

> *A patent shall confer on its owner the following exclusive rights:*
>
> *(a) where the subject matter of a patent is a product, to prevent third parties not having the owner's consent from the acts of: . . . using . . . that product. . . .*

It is significant that the provision does not read "using in a manner that was known at the date of filing." The consequence is that new uses (or second uses), known and unknown at the date of filing, are reached by exclusivity, and, therefore, uses that are found subsequently are not, per se, inventions.

This topic is subject to controversy and affects the pharmaceutical and the agricultural-chemical industries, particularly. Finding new uses for known substances is generally the result of high and time-consuming investments in research, but they prolong the useful life of existing products in those two fields, where inventing new ones is an increasingly cost activity. However, regardless of the practical utility of new uses, a patent for a second use, actually, is nothing else than a disguised extension or a renewal of the term of the initial patent. This was the holding of an opinion issued by the Federal Court of Appeals, Second Region, of Brazil:

> [...] the grant of a new monopoly for the second use of already known substances would indefinitely extend the private rights of the patent holder in a matter that does not meet the internationally accepted requirements of patentability and, in return, would impair the public right of access to new knowledge by the Brazilian society, and would prevent national researchers from developing new formulations and new medicines.[107]

107. Civil Appeal 420502, 2nd Specialized Chamber, Federal Court of Appeals, Second Region, opinion of September 22, 2009, written by Appellate Federal Judge Messod Azulay Neto. This last argument only makes sense if the statute opts for granting patents for the known substance for which a new use is found, as the European Patent Convention does. But if the *Swiss claims* method is followed, there is no danger that the second use patent will prevent national (as well as foreign, for that matter) researchers from developing new medicines.

It is true that the prolongation of the term impacts the new use only, but it is no less a prolongation.

It is worth noticing that a number of laws take a different approach: instead of addressing new uses directly, they address the patentability of the known substances for which a new use has been found. In the first case, a patent may be issued (or refused) for the use itself; in the second case, a second patent is granted for the substance (which was new and has become known).

Second uses in the pharmaceutical field are of three types: (i) new dosages, leading to improved effects; (ii) new routes of administration; and (iii) administering the drug to new groups of patients.

A number of national and regional laws admit the patentability of second medical uses, this meaning that new uses found for previously approved (and commercialized) medicines that were previously unknown are deemed patentable subject matter.

5.1 Examples

We will now see a few examples of national and regional statutes dealing with the patentability of second uses.

The first example comes from the patent law of Indonesia, which, correctly, asserts that second or new uses of known substances do not constitute, in themselves, inventions, but discoveries. The relevant excerpt of that law reads:

> *Article 4*
>
> *Inventions do not include:*
>
> . . .
>
> *f. discovery in the form of:*
>
> *1. new use of existing and/or known product.*

This said, all the examples that follow admit the patentability of new uses, but, in order to eliminate the logical conflict between the notions of invention, on the one hand, and of a new use (which is a mere discovery or finding), on the other, those statutes make, in one way or the other, certain concessions as regards the core requirements of patentability. This suggests that lawmakers are aware of the primary inadequacy of patents for protecting second uses.

One of the most common of those concessions is that they usually apply only as far as second medical uses are concerned. Statutes allowing for the patentability of new uses of known substances in general, such as machines or other mechanical devices, are extremely rare. A second concession concerns the nonobviousness requirement. With different wordings, permissive patent statutes (as regards second medical uses) tend to diminish that requirement—or to eliminate it altogether.

For example, the European Patent Convention has provisions that deal very clearly with the availability of patent protection for second medical uses:

Article 53 Exceptions to patentability

European patents shall not be granted in respect of:

. . .

(c) *methods for treatment of the human or animal body by surgery or therapy and diagnostic methods practised on the human or animal body; this provision shall not apply to products, in particular substances or compositions, for use in any of these methods.*

Article 54 Novelty

(1) *An invention shall be considered to be new if it does not form part of the state of the art.*
(2) *The state of the art shall be held to comprise everything made available to the public by means of a written or oral description, by use, or in any other way, before the date of filing of the European patent application.*
(3) *Additionally, the content of European patent applications as filed, the dates of filing of which are prior to the date referred to in paragraph 2 and which were published on or after that date, shall be considered as comprised in the state of the art.*
(4) *Paragraphs 2 and 3 shall not exclude the patentability of any substance or composition, comprised in the state of the art, for use in a method referred to in Article 53(c), provided that its use for any such method is not comprised in the state of the art.*
(5) *Paragraphs 2 and 3 shall also not exclude the patentability of any substance or composition referred to in paragraph 4 for any specific use in a method referred to in Article 53(c), provided that such use is not comprised in the state of the art.*[108]

What is striking in the EPC is that Article 54 justifies the patentability of new uses of pharmaceutical substances on grounds of their novelty—but it omits the nonobviousness requirement entirely. The only conclusion possible is that the EPC has eliminated the condition of nonobviousness for second medical uses.

The same solution can be found in the patent law of a few other countries such as that of the Bahamas, as follows:

Article 8. Novelty

. . .

(4) *In the case of an invention consisting of a substance or composition for—*
   (a) *use in a method of treatment of the human or animal body by surgery or therapy;*
   (b) *the diagnosis practised on the human or animal body;*
   the fact that the substance or composition forms part of the state of the art shall not prevent the invention from being taken to be new if the use of the substance or composition in any such method does not form part of the state of the art.[109]

108. European Patent Convention (EPC), of October 5, 1973, as amended in 2000. Currently, the European Patent Organization has thirty-nine Member States.
109. Patents Act, 2015.

This approach implies two violations of TRIPS obligations: it omits the mandatory requirement of the inventive step, as set in Article 27.1, and it accords protection that is greater than the mandatory standards to one single field of technology (substances or compositions used in medical treatments), thereby discriminating against any other substances for which new uses are found (Article 1.1 in conjunction with Article 27.1).

Indeed, if the lawmaker believes in the usefulness of protecting second uses, it should extend it to uses of all kinds of products in all fields of technology. Granting positive discrimination is the same as according negative discrimination against the fields that are not covered.

The Patent Act of India, in this regard, reads:

> *Section 3. What are not inventions.—The following are not inventions within the meaning of this Act,—*
>
> . . .
>
> *[(d) . . . the mere discovery of any new property or new use for a known substance or of the mere use of a known process, machine or apparatus unless such known process results in a new product or employs at least one new reactant.*
> *Explanation.—For the purposes of this clause, salts, esters, ethers, polymorphs, metabolites, pure form, particle size, isomers, mixtures of isomers, complexes, combinations and other derivatives of known substance shall be considered to be the same substance, unless they differ significantly in properties with regard to efficacy;]* [110]

Like the EPC, the Indian statute requires that second uses of medicines be new in order to be patentable. Also like the EPC, the Indian Act does not require that second medical uses be inventive. But it replaces nonobviousness with significant efficiency. In other words, in India, second medical uses are patentable when they are new and present significant utility.

The statute of the Philippines contains a very similar provision, as follows:

> *Sec. 22. Non-Patentable Inventions.*
>
> *The following shall be excluded from patent protection:*
>
> *22.1. . . . in the case of drugs and medicines, the mere discovery of a new form or new property of a known substance which does not result in the enhancement of the known efficacy of that substance, or the mere discovery of any new property or new use for a known substance, or the mere use of a known process unless such known process results in a new product that employs at least one new reactant.*
>
> *For the purpose of this clause, salts, esters, ethers, polymorphs, metabolites, pure form, particle size, isomers, mixtures of isomers, metabolites, pure form, particle size, isomers, mixtures of isomers, complexes, combinations, and other*

110. The Patents Act, 1970, as amended by Act 15, of 2005.

derivatives of a known substance shall be considered to be the same substance, unless they differ significantly in properties with regard to efficacy; . . .[111]

The statute of the Philippines is worded in a different manner—by making reference to a new product employing at least one new reactant—but its meaning is very close to that of India: the nonobviousness requirement is replaced with a significant efficacy requirement.

A slightly different approach is found in section 4 of the Patent Act of Samoa, as follows:

(3) The following, even if they are inventions, are excluded from patentability:

. . .

(h) . . . the mere discovery of any new property or new use for a known substance or of the mere use of a known process, machine or apparatus unless such known process results in a new product or employs at least one (1) new reactant.[112]

Novelty becomes, therefore, the only substantive condition of patentability and results from the use either leading to a new product or employing at least one new reactant.

The same compromise with low (or inexistent) levels of inventiveness is, perhaps surprisingly, found in the patent law of Indonesia, which, in the same provision (quoted above) that excludes new uses from patentability because of their consisting of discoveries, admits the patentability of new forms of chemical (pharmaceutical) compounds, provided they present significant efficacy and have a certain level of novelty. As a matter of course, this specific provision should be in another place in the law, given that uses and forms are not similar concepts. Anyway, the relevant provision reads:

Article 4

Inventions do not include:

. . .

f. discovery in the form of:

. . .

2. new forms from existing compound which does not generate significantly enhanced efficacy and contains different relevant known chemical structures to compound.

Following a different trend, a number of developing countries admit the patentability of second uses without any qualification. That is the case, for example, of Bahrain, whose Patent Act reads:

111. Intellectual Property Code of the Philippines, Republic Act No. 8,293 (2015 Edition), as amended by Republic Act No. 9,502 or the Universally Accessible Cheaper and Quality Medicines Act of 2008.

112. Intellectual Property Act 2011 (Act No. 9 of 2011). It should be noted that the statute of Samoa does not confine the patentability of second uses to pharmaceutical inventions.

Article 3.

. . .

2. *Without prejudice to the provisions of the preceding Clause and Article (2) of this Law, a patent may be awarded for the use or manner of using a known product including the product that is used for certain medical cases.*

5.2 Discussion

The idea of extending patentability to second medical uses has many supporters both in industry and in the academy.

See, e.g., the following statement:

> *A priori*, there is no fundamental reason why an invention of this type should be less capable of patent protection than any other. The amount of work involved in the making of the invention, the potential benefit to the public, and the potential commercial importance may all be as great as for the invention of a new chemical entity having pharmaceutical utility. And, certainly, it is possible to obtain a patent for the dyeing of nylon with dyestuff previously known to be useful for dyeing wool. So, if new uses of dyestuffs can be patented (given that they are novel and non-obvious), why not new uses of pharmaceuticals?[113]

It is quite understandable and acceptable that one wishes to promote the augmentation of the utility of medicines that are already on the market. Bringing those medicines to new patients or through new ways of administration or to cure new diseases may be of great social utility. However—in spite of the acceptance of the economic significance of new medical uses—patents are granted regardless of the amount of work involved in inventing, or the benefits to the public. The purpose of patents is not to reward hard work or great results, but to acknowledge and protect invention, regardless of it having been made through hard experimentation, or great ingenuity, or mere luck.

Thus, when a lawmaker opts for making patents available for second uses, he/she is not only going beyond what is required by the TRIPS Agreement but also deviating from the sound fundamentals of patent law.

However, we should make it clear that new uses may indeed be new. In this regard, the EPC and the statutes of India, the Philippines, and Samoa are conceptually correct. Indeed, a second use of a medicine that was not previously known and that was found after experimental work is new for all purposes.

But, as already noted, such use was already covered by the original patent. A patent is not granted for a practical use, but for a product or a process, and it covers all uses—both known and unknown uses. If a third party uses the patented product for a purpose that was not known to the inventor and therefore is not described (let alone claimed) in the application, that third party is still liable for infringement.

113. Philip W. Grubb, PATENTS FOR CHEMICALS, PHARMACEUTICALS AND BIOTECHNOLOGY—FUNDAMENTALS OF GLOBAL LAW, PRACTICE AND STRATEGY, at 209, 213 (Oxford Univ. Press, 1999).

Moreover, the new use is not an improvement. If it were, there should be no problem in granting a new patent (or an additional patent) to the modified product. But the new use is a new use of the same invention.

Second, second medical uses are not, per se, methods of medical treatment. It is true that, following the "*Swiss claims* method,"[114] patents for second medical uses are formulated as if they consist of (new) methods of applying the known medicines in the treatment of illnesses. But this is not true. A second medical use is simply a new use, without the indication or description of the method (i.e., a sequence of several steps) for their administration to patients. Actually, many laws, in prohibiting the patenting of methods of medical treatment, exclude the products used in such treatment from the prohibition. *See*, for example, the patent statute of the Philippines:

> *Sec. 22. Non-Patentable Inventions.*
>
> *The following shall be excluded from patent protection:*
>
> . . .
>
> *22.3 Methods for treatment of the human or animal body by surgery or therapy and diagnostic methods practiced on the human or animal body. This provision shall not apply to products and composition for use in any of these methods; . . .*

A third problem that could eventually be identified in association with second medical uses is that they are already predicted (or predictable) in the patent. However, in some cases, this may prove to be a wrong view. The predictability of the new use does not necessarily correspond to reality. It may happen that the applicant did not know about possible new uses of his/her invention. The discovery of second uses may be the result of intense research and experimenting, and therefore, it would not appear as a logical banality to the inventor at the moment he/she conceived the creative solution. However, as it has been said already, the issue is not one of novelty, but of the real scope of patentability. Patents are not granted for uses, but for products and processes. The claiming of uses known to the inventor at the moment of filing should not even be claimed. Paraphrasing the text of Article 29.1 of the TRIPS Agreement, like the best mode, uses can be "indicated" in the specifications, but not claimed. Actually, where Article 29.1 reads that "Members . . . may require the applicant to indicate the best mode for carrying out the invention known to the inventor . . .," it is referring to a use. Carrying out the invention and using the invention are the same thing.

---

114. The "*Swiss claims* method" is a method of writing the claim(s) of an application for a patent for a second medical use that links the (new) use to the (known) product. Typically, a "Swiss claim" is formulated as follows:

> Use of substance [X] for the manufacture of a medicine used in the treatment of disease [Y].

This method was originated by a practice initially approved by the Swiss Federal Intellectual Property Office and later recognized by the Enlarged Board of Appeals of the EPO (Decision G 5/83, of December 5, 1984) as being compatible with the EPC. "Swiss claims" have been admitted by the EPO since then.

When the use implies the application of a new and inventive process, then a patent may be granted for the process itself (unless it is excluded from patentability, such as methods of medical treatment and diagnosis), but not for the use.

5.3 *Dos*

Does this mean that second uses, particularly in the medical field, should be entirely ignored by patent statutes? The answer is yes, when a country takes the three conditions of patentability seriously. Second medical uses (as well as second uses of agricultural-chemical products) may find adequate protection through the laws and regulations that cover those confidential data, the elaboration of which is mandatory in order to obtain marketing authorization for the corresponding products or chemical entities.

In countries that host a strong pharmaceutical industry, the lawmaker may feel tempted to attend to the legitimate interests of inventors and twist the foundations of the patent system in order to accommodate second medical uses as if they were inventions. And this is true not only as far as the research-based industry is concerned. Generic companies may also find, experiment and apply new uses for known substances.

But a lawmaker that is not under the pressure of those interests may very well adopt the solution of the Sultanate of Oman, whose patent law, as regards second medical uses, provides that:

> *Article (2):*
>
> *1— The following shall be excluded from patent protection:*
>
> . . .
>
> *D) Known substances for which a new use has been discovered; this provision shall not apply to the use itself, where it constitutes an invention.*

Correctly, the statute of Oman makes a distinction between the substance and its use. Significantly (and also correctly), the lawmaker of Oman has not narrowed the patentability of inventive uses to those of a medical purpose. Like the law of Samoa, the provision above applies to new uses of all known substances, regardless of their field of technology. Under the Omani law, those uses must be genuine inventions in order to be patentable, not mere discoveries or findings.

6 SCHEMES, RULES AND METHODS OF PERFORMING MENTAL ACTS, PLAYING GAMES OR DOING BUSINESS, AND PROGRAMS FOR COMPUTERS

The products of human creativity listed in this heading are generally viewed as corresponding to creations that do not qualify as inventions due to the fact that they do not handle tangible substances. They are usually understood as abstract ideas.

Elsewhere, it has been explained that this view is a major flaw of the current patent system, which fails to take today's economy of ideas into account.[115]

However, the lawmaker of a developing country may hold a legitimate reluctance in granting patents for services. The true reason would not be the fact that services are not inventions because of their lacking of tangibility. Tangibility or materiality is not a component of the notion of invention, but a condition of patentability. The creation of a new scheme of insurance or of a new financial tool may be as ingenious as the invention of a new mechanical device. The true reason for denying patents for abstract inventions, regardless of their practical utility, is that the vast majority of countries do not grant them. Therefore, the developing country that decides to start patenting business methods, insurance schemes, and financial tools will probably end up leaving those inventions in the hands of nonresidents, who, with very few exceptions, tend to outnumber national applicants. A situation of imbalance would necessarily follow: national entrepreneurs would not be able to reproduce foreign service inventions in their home country, but foreign entrepreneurs, in their countries, would be able to reproduce the inventions of those national entrepreneurs.

As it has happened with pharmaceutical inventions, the discriminatory treatment against which has been banned (to a certain extent) as a consequence of the TRIPS Agreement, patenting service inventions would require a global agreement, in order to avoid free riding.

Moreover, as explained in PATENTLY OUTDATED, the lawmaker would need to introduce some changes into the conditions of patentability, such as utility. The lawmaker should also pay serious attention to the drafting of claims in order to reflect the specificities of service inventions.[116]

6.1 Computer Software

Many national statutes exclude computer software per se from patentability. The reason is that, because computer software must be protected by copyright under Article 10.1 of the TRIPS Agreement, it is usually deemed not to constitute an invention unless it is embedded in hardware (the so-called *firmware*). However, the extension of copyright protection to software as a result of the Uruguay Round was (and still is) a conceptual mistake, which may have contributed considerably to the concentration of some markets of software products.

Actually, computer software is nothing more than a set of instructions for the operation of a machine. In this sense, software is not very different from a set of instructions used in the operation of a high-furnace. The only major difference is that the latter is read and applied by a human being, while computer software is read and applied directly by a machine. This fact alone does not justify applying a different set of laws to computer programs. At most, it could justify the establishment of a sui generis system of software protection, combining features of the patent and copyright

115. *See* Nuno Pires de Carvalho, PATENTLY OUTDATED: PATENTS IN THE POST-INDUSTRIAL ECONOMY—THE CASE FOR SERVICE PATENTS (Wolters Kluwer, 2012).
116. *Ibid.*, at 191 et seq.

regimes.[117] The practical result is that computer software (that generally becomes obsolete in a short period) receives protection during the life of the author plus fifty years.[118] Since computer software is protected as a literary work, its protection does not depend upon registration. There are no costs, therefore, in establishing the subject matter of protection or in keeping records for public inspection. This means that a longer term of protection for software does not raise social costs in a direct manner. However, as subject matter of copyright, computer software may not be reproduced by third parties—and it is this possibility of excluding others from copying software that frustrates inventing around by competitors. Of course, fair use exceptions, as established by Article 9(2) of the Berne Convention[119] and Article 13 of the TRIPS Agreement,[120] may assist in the development of competing software products. However, those exceptions have been allowed for the development of interoperable products, but not of competing products.[121] Patent protection—or, for that matter, a sui generis system combining features of the patent and the copyright regimes—in addition to better matching the technical characteristics of computer software, would permit the reproduction of the codes in order to develop competing inventions.

However, the combination of Articles 9.2 and 10.1 of the TRIPS Agreement may raise a problem as to the patentability of computer programs. Those two provisions, if read in conjunction, seem to indicate that computer programs are, as a matter of law, deemed to be expressions, and therefore they may not be perceived as ideas. It follows that, if computer programs are not ideas, but expressions, they may not be considered inventions. In other words, Articles 9.2 and 10.1 seem to exclude computer software from patentability per se, thus preventing WTO Members from applying Article 1.1 and resort to their national practices so as to identify computer programs as patentable inventions.[122] If they do, they must therefore provide for two combined mechanisms of

117. Between 1987 and 1998, Brazil adopted a sui generis regime for the protection of computer software, although based on copyright principles, the regime comprised some patent-related features, such as novelty and the prior user exception. In 1998, Brazil abrogated that regime and implemented a TRIPS-consistent statute.
118. Article 7.1 of the Berne Convention, in conjunction with Art. 10.1 of the TRIPS Agreement.
119. Article 9.2 of the Berne Convention provides:

> *It shall be a matter for legislation in the countries of the Union to permit the reproduction of such works in certain special cases, provided that such reproduction does not conflict with a normal exploitation of the work and does not unreasonably prejudice the legitimate interests of the author.*

120. The scope of Art. 13 of the TRIPS Agreement was examined by a WTO Panel in *United States—Section 110(5) of the U.S. Copyright Act*, WT/DS160/R, of June 15, 2000, adopted by the DSB on July 27, 2000.
121. *See* Charles R. McManis, *Intellectual Property Protection and Reverse Engineering of Computer Programs in the United States and the European Community*, 8 High Tech. L.J. 25 (1993).
122. This was the view expressed by Brazil in its answer to one question posed by the United States during the review of its TRIPS implementing legislation by the TRIPS Council:

> "Question: 'Article 27.1 of the TRIPS Agreement requires that, with specified exceptions, patents be available for any inventions, whether products or processes, in all fields of technology, if they are new, involve an inventive step and are capable of

protection, because, under Article 10.1 of the TRIPS Agreement, the copyright protection of computer software must be made available anyway.

6.2 *Dos and Don'ts*

In view of this last consideration, the suggestion is that developing countries leave computer programs out of the scope of patentable subject matter. This is not a correct solution, as explained, but the flaw can be corrected at the international level only.

And yet, a few developing countries have accepted the idea of not excluding computer software from patentability, in particular those that have entered into free trade deals with the United States. These are the cases, for example, of Oman and Bahrain.

But the vast majority of developing countries have followed the wiser trend of leaving computer software to be protected by copyright only, in order to avoid the traps of according double protection to the same subject matter (but, eventually, to different elements).

For example, the Patent Act of South Africa reads:

> *25—Patentable inventions*
>
> *(1) A patent may, subject to the provisions of this section, be granted for any new invention which involves an inventive step and which is capable of being used or applied in trade or industry or agriculture.*
>
> *(2) Anything which consists of—*
>
> . . .
>
> *(f) a program for a computer;*
>
> . . .
>
> *shall not be an invention for the purposes of this Act.* [123]

The Andean Community of Nations, in its industrial property statute, provides for the same exclusion from patentability, but adds a caveat:

> *Article 15. The following shall not be considered inventions:*
>
> . . .
>
> *(e) computer programs or software as such; . . .*[124]

---

industrial application. Please explain in detail how Article 10 of the Brazilian Industrial Property Law 9,279 of 1996, which makes computer programs unpatentable, is consistent with Article 27'."

"Answer: 'The correct provision of the TRIPS Agreement to be addressed in this question is not Article 27, but rather Article 10, which states that computer programs "shall be protected as literary works under the Berne Convention (1971)". This is the case in the Brazilian legislation. Article 2 of Law no. 9.609 of 1998 ("Software Law") states that computer programs are protected as literary works, as required by the TRIPS Agreement'."

See IP/Q3/BRA/1, of February 24, 2004, at 23.

123. Patents Act, 1978 (Act No. 57 of 1978, amended up to Act No. 58 of 2002).

124. Decision No. 486 of the Commission of the Cartagena Agreement Establishing the Common Industrial Property Regime, of September 14, 2000.

In the same sense, also with a caveat, the patent law of Honduras reads:

Article 5—The following are not considered inventions and will therefore be excluded from patent protection:

. . .

6) Computer programs considered in isolation; . . .[125]

The expressions "as such" and "considered in isolation" mean that when computer programs present some element of intangibility—such as when they are embedded in hardware, forming what is designated as *firmware*—a patent may be granted. The claims, however, have to refer to the physical elements of the device, not to the abstract information in itself.

7 BUSINESS METHODS

The so-called Internet bubble, which, at the end of the 1990s, generated intense speculation involving the shares of firms that exploited services connected with the worldwide network of computers, gave rise to a considerable number of patent applications (many of which were granted) related to methods of doing businesses in that particular environment.[126]

Business method patents have caused much anxiety because they could block the access of competitors to certain businesses, under the pretext that, in order to engage in those businesses, it was necessary to infringe those patents. Perhaps the most famous patent of that period was the *one-click patent*, owned by Amazon.com, the title of which was "Method and system for placing a purchase order via a communications network" (U.S. patent No. 5,960,411, of September 28, 1999). In its essence, Amazon.com's invention reduced the steps necessary for concluding a purchase on the Internet. Amazon.com's patent was challenged by Barnes and Noble in the course of a patent infringement lawsuit that the former filed against the latter. The discussion in the two courts that looked into the matter focused on the appropriateness of the preliminary injunction that Amazon.com has asked to be issued against the defendant. The Court of Appeals for the Federal Circuit analyzed the two elements that are necessary for an injunction to be granted: a prima facie infringement and the probability that, if challenged, the patent be maintained.[127] As regards the first element, the court found that the Barnes and Noble's website indeed infringed Amazon.com's patent. But, as regards the second element, the court held that the defendant had presented relevant elements that indicated the invalidity of the plaintiff's patent on grounds of lack of novelty. Therefore, the injunction was denied.

The court has not examined the essence of the matter, which is the patentability (or not) of business methods. This issue had been scrutinized in another case, *State*

125. Industrial Property Law (enacted by Decree No. 12-99-E and amended by Decree No. 16-2006).

126. Cf., e.g., to just mention two patents, *see* U.S. patent No. 5,983,199 (granted on November 9, 1999) ("On-line shopping system"); U.S. patent No. 5,937,390 (granted on August 10, 1999) ("On-line advertising system and its method").

127. *Amazon.com v. BarnesandNoble.com*, 239 F.3d 1343 (Fed. Cir. 2001).

Street Bank & Trust Co. v. Signature Financial Group, Inc. (1998).[128] The problem was that business methods were not, in general, deemed patentable subject matter because of their abstract nature. The court made an appropriate distinction between abstract business ideas and concrete processes and held that the so-called business method exception was ill-conceived, and it had never been established by case law.[129] Actually, the court quoted with approval a change in the USPTO Examination Guidelines for Computer Related Inventions ("Guidelines"), which in past editions read: "Though seemingly within the category of process or method, a method of doing business can be rejected within the statutory classes."[130] After modification, the Guidelines read: "Office personnel have had difficulty in properly treating claims directed to methods of doing business. Claims should not be categorized as methods of doing business. Instead, such claims should be treated like process claims."[131] The court said: "We agree that this is precisely the manner in which this type of claim should be treated."[132] As the Federal Circuit put it, business methods are processes. They consist of organizing production factors in a given way, theoretically more efficiently than the existing ways, so that an intended result is achieved. Thus, business methods are indeed processes that lead to the production of goods or services.[133]

Subsequently, the Court of Appeals for the Federal Circuit changed its position and adopted stricter requirements for business method patents, having eliminated the possibility of granting patents to ideas that are purely abstract.[134]

The problem of schemes, rules and methods of performing mental acts—which comprise business methods, financial schemes, insurance programs, and other services—is not one of lack of inventiveness in broad terms, but one of absence of materiality. The reluctance of WTO Members in making patent protection available for service inventions is just the expression of a bias against inventions in abstract, in spite of their consisting of economically valuable and practical ideas. Or, to put it more

128. *State Street Bank & Trust Co. v. Signature Financial Group, Inc.*, 149 F.3d 1368 (Fed. Cir. 1998).
129. *Ibid.*, at 1375.
130. *Ibid.*, at 1377 (quoting Manual of Patent Examining Procedures § 706.03(a) (1994)).
131. *Ibid.* (quoting US Patent and Trademark 1996 Examination Guidelines for Computer Related Inventions, 61 FED. REG. 7478, 7479 (1996)).
132. *Ibid.*
133. The problems with some business ideas that have been granted patents are not peculiar to business methods, but they rather concern all inventions: the problems of obviousness and utility. When an inventor reorganizes the factors of production in order to obtain a given result, there is an invention only where: (a) the factors of production are new and the method of organizing them is also new; or (b) the factors of production are known but the method of organizing them is new, and it does not appear to be obvious to a person with normal skills in that area. Most business ideas that are being patented in the United States fall within the second category, and thus their patentability depends upon the nonobviousness of the combination given to the existing elements. Therefore, the debate around those inventions should focus on the existence of real creativity in rearranging and recombining the required elements of hardware. Besides, it is a known rule of patent practice that where an invention consists of a combination of preexisting elements, its patentability depends upon an unexpected result. To put it simply, if the inventor seeks protection for an invention that adds two and two, he/she should get it only if the result is five, not four.
134. *See In Re Comiskey*, 554 F.3d 967 (CAFC 2009) and *In Re Nuijten*, 500 F.3d 1346 (CAFC 2007), certiorari denied, 129 S. Ct. 70 (2008).

crudely, it is the vestige of a mindset formed in the Industrial Revolution and that resists being adjusted to the Postindustrial Age we live in.

8 *DOS AND DON'TS* OF MAKING PATENTS AVAILABLE FOR ABSTRACT, YET USEFUL INVENTIONS

The suggestion here has to do with the assessment of the developing country's competitive advantages. If the country that is contemplating the idea of enacting a new patent law has a very competitive service sector, with a significant presence on the Internet, making patents available for services might not be a bad idea. But in doing this, the country has to realize that, because the vast majority of WTO and Paris Union Members do not grant those patents, the proprietary rights in those new, useful, and nonobvious types of abstract ideas would not be enforceable beyond its borders. Moreover, where a particular business method or financial scheme contains some secret features that contribute to its effectiveness and are not easily perceptible by outsiders, submitting them to a patent prosecution would necessarily lead to the disclosure of those features.

However, those patents would open the opportunity for global service providers to seek protection—and exclusivity—in the granting country, whereas in their country of origin, the patent owners would be subject to competition. In the absence of a multilateral agreement determining the patentability of services (and the corresponding conditions), large economies would have to gain more to promote and protect innovation in the area of services than small economies.

So, the suggestion is that, until international negotiations lead to a different orientation, the expansion of patentability to abstract ideas looks more like a *don't* than a *do*.

However, where the national lawmaker sees it as advantageous for the national service sector the grant of patents for certain services, it is mandatory that the statute takes into account the necessary adaptation of the three mandatory conditions of patentability to the peculiar characteristics of those inventions. After all, the notions of novelty, nonobviousness, and utility have evolved in the last three centuries around the concept of inventions that imply the handling of material substances. Patents for abstract ideas imply significantly different requirements—like, for example, plant varieties do.

9 UTILITY MODELS AND INNOVATION (OR PETTY) PATENTS; THE CASE OF HANDICRAFTS

Some developing countries, with the aim of promoting invention in traditional sectors of the economy, such as handicrafts, have extended (with adaptations) patent protection to minor inventions that require a lower level of inventiveness. Generally, those inventions correspond to less sophisticated sectors of industry, but they nevertheless lead to the introduction of technical improvements in products.

One of those mechanisms that is well known is the utility model system, which protects changes in the (internal or external) forms of known objects that increase the utility of those objects. Several large countries, and heavy users of the patent system, have resorted to the utility model mechanism, such as Germany, Japan, Brazil, and China. Statistical data show that those countries have had great success in luring small and traditional companies to apply for utility model protection.[135] In Brazil, litigation involving the enforcement of utility model certificates by small and medium companies is relatively frequent.[136] Usually, fees for (both for prosecuting and for maintaining) utility model models are lower than those that correspond to utility (or invention) patents. The nonobviousness requirement for utility models is also usually set at a less rigorous level. And a few statutes do not impose the pre-grant substantive examination for utility models.

It is in this sense that utility models may come close to the notion of innovation patents, adopted in a few countries. But the terms are not synonyms. By contrast with utility models, which cover products only, innovation patents may cover processes. The term "*innovation patents*" corresponds to titles granted to claimed inventions—no matter their field of technology—that are granted without any sort of substantive examination. The examination is carried on subsequently, in the case the patent owner wishes to enforce the patent rights against an alleged infringer (or if a third party seeks its invalidation).

The purpose of innovation patents was to persuade small inventors to use the system without the burdens and the costs of the traditional mechanism. But, as noted above, the idea suffered a major blow when, in 2001, in Australia, a practical joker applied for a petty patent for the wheel. Because of the lack of pre-grant substantive examination, the patent has been issued.[137]

Unfortunately, these approaches, which are generally recommended for addressing the needs of traditional sectors of the economy, are not entirely adequate for handicrafts. The reason is that genuine handicrafts are more than useful objects: they are also elements of identification of the community of crafters who design and make them. Usually, they are of a simple conception, but certain handicrafts may achieve high levels of ingenuity. Moreover, handicrafts, more often than not, combine visual with technical aspects—and frequently it is in their visual dimension that handicrafts are deemed expressions of cultural traditions.

Of course, a legal system that focuses on technical solutions is not fit to cover all the complex elements of handicrafts. For that, a sui generis intellectual property regime of a holistic nature is necessary. But a country that has not adopted such a specialized IP regime may start doing something in the sense of protecting handicrafts that goes beyond geographical indications and collective marks—the two IP regimes usually employed in association with handicrafts. Such solution can be found in utility models

135. In 2023, 9,704 utility model certificate (or patent) applications were filed in Germany; 4,949, in Japan; 3,063,928, in China; and 2,447, in Brazil. Date obtained in WIPO IP Statistics Data Center.
136. A search on Darts-IP website [in June 2025] concerning the enforcement of utility model patents in Brazil has produced 1,525 results between 2000 and 2025.
137. *See supra* note 68.

or in innovation patents, in spite of their shortcomings. However, as it will be suggested below, a special regime of patents for handicrafts could (and should) be envisaged, for the sake of protecting and promoting innovation in such an important sector of the economy, which, in many countries, can be a major source of job creation.

9.1 *Dos and Don'ts*

When it comes to the conditions of patentability, it should be clear that they are to be adapted to the nature of the invention. In the case of utility models, the lawmaker should put nonobviousness aside. The creation of a new shape that brings improved functionality to a known product implies per se the exercise of a certain level of inventiveness, but that should not be a separate requirement.

Utility models should be examined as to their formal and substantive conditions of patentability (except in those countries where the number of filings is very low, as discussed above). The grant of patent letters without examination runs against legal security—but, as explained above, reasons of public interest may determine that there will be no pre-grant substantive examination in a country that receives a very small number of applications. However, due to the special status of the vast majority of applicants of utility model patents, which are small and medium enterprises and individual artisans, the pre-grant substantive examination, in those countries where it is mandatory, must be carried out without delay. The suggestion is that the lawmaker should give the patent office a maximum period for carrying out that examination. If the patent office fails to observe the mandatory deadline, the patent shall be issued with losing the same presumption of validity as if it had been examined. This means that the utility model patent owner does not need to request that the patent be examined as to its validity prior to filing a lawsuit for infringement or prior to licensing it—if the law so requires. It will be the burden of the alleged infringer (or the licensee, if he/she has reasons to believe that the invention did not meet the conditions of patentability) to seek the invalidation of the patent through the channels approved by the patent statute. And if the fear arises that non-examined utility models are being used to harass competitors through groundless infringement lawsuits, when the certificate holders are necessarily and evidently aware of the failure of those models to comply with the conditions for protection (as in the case of the mentioned patent for the wheel), then courts can sanction the holders as frivolous litigators.

Moreover, the term of protection should be left to the economic interests of the creators, with a limit that is inferior to that accorded to utility patents—say, fifteen years from the date of filing. The ideal solution is to accord to utility model inventors a short initial term, with the possibility of extension(s), as it happens under many national statutes dealing with industrial designs. It will be up to the market to have a saying on those terms: in the case of products of commercial success, the inventors will tend to resort to the extensions (which will be automatic, if the inventor applies for them, depending only on the payment of the corresponding fee and, eventually, if the lawmaker so understands, the proof of effective commercial exploitation). It is expected that the commercial exploitation of the utility model will be carried out by the patent owner. But it may very well happen that the exploitation is carried out by one or more infringers. In such an event, it will belong to the patent owner to accompany the request for the extension of the term with evidence that he/she has already launched an infringement suit. If in the end the infringement has been proved as nonexistent and therefore it becomes evident that the utility model has not been exploited either by the infringer or by the patent owner—which causes the extension to be unjustified—the latter may be subject to legal proceedings based on allegations of fraud:

Article . . . Utility models

1. *An object of practical use, or part thereof, which presents a new form or arrangement, is patentable as a utility model, provided the new form or arrangement results in a functional improvement in the manufacture or the use of the object.* [138]
2. *The application for a utility model patent, after its formal examination, shall be immediately published in the Patent Office's Official Gazette.*
3. *The examination of utility model patent applications shall be carried out within a period of six months counted from the date of the publication.*
   (a) *In the event the application is not examined within that period, the patent shall be granted and will be treated for all purposes as having presumption of validity.*
4. *The patent for a utility model shall be valid for five years counted from the date of filing, renewable for additional periods of five years, up to a maximum of 15 years.*
   (a) *The request for the renewal shall be submitted until six months before the end of the term of protection, and shall be accompanied by proof of the payment of the respective fee and of the exploitation of the utility model in question, either by the patentee or by a third party.*
   (b) *In the event the third party is an infringer, the patentee shall submit proof that he/she has filed for an infringement suit against the third party.*
5. *All provisions concerning invention (or utility) patents shall apply to the prosecution and maintenance of utility model patents* mutatis mutandis.

9.2 Patents for Handicrafts

Here, the purpose is not to set a sui generis mechanism for the holistic protection of handicrafts, but rather using the Patent Act for covering a loophole left by the absence of that protection. As said, handicrafts are not inventions in the traditional sense of the term. They are closer to utility models, and thus the lawmaker may be satisfied by enacting provisions like those suggested above.

However, strictly speaking, handicrafts are not utility models either because their core features are not limited to a combination of shape and functionality. Handicrafts, as said, are elements of cultural identification of a community, and more than shapes, they display colors and symbols. Moreover, handicrafts last more than a simple industrial cycle or the mere lifetime of a product.

138. This language is borrowed from Brazil's Industrial Property Act of 1996.

As Octavio Paz wrote:

> Craftsmanship does not want to last for millennia nor is it possessed by the rush to die soon. It passes with the days, it flows with us, it is spent little by little, it does not seek death nor deny it: it accepts it. Between the timeless time of the museum and the accelerated time of technique, craftsmanship is the heartbeat of human time. It is a useful object but it is also beautiful; an object that lasts but that ends and is resigned to ending; an object that is not unique like the work of art and that can be replaced by another similar but not identical object. Craftsmanship teaches us to die and thus teaches us to live.[139]

Accordingly, the Patent Act of a country that hosts traditional communities that make of the creation and the commerce of new handicrafts their livelihood could include a rule providing for the grant of exclusive rights in those creations taking into account that: (i) they combine art and technique, esthetics and functionality, spiritual and economic values; (ii) their economic cycle goes beyond the common life cycle of industrial or consumption articles; and (iii) they operate as identifiers of the culture and the traditions of communities.

Moreover, the lawmaker should take the cultural value of those products into account, in the sense that their novelty should not be assessed in the same way as inventions for the purpose of obtaining utility patents. The suggestion is that traditional products or handicrafts abide by a concept of commercial novelty. This same idea has been in operation for decades as regards plant varieties are concerned, in the light of the various versions of the UPOV Convention, since 1961.[140]

Such provision could read as follows:

Article . . . Traditional products (handicrafts)

1. *Patents shall be granted to new products that are created within and with respect to the traditions of traditional communities recognized as such by the competent authority or, in the absence of such formal recognition, recognized as such by society.*
   (a) *A traditional craft is new where it has not been used commercially or industrially before the date of application.*
2. *Traditional products will be protected provided they present functionality and/or visual elements that are new or original, provided they are inserted into the traditional culture of the community.*
3. *The patent may be applied for by the creator or by the community, in accordance with the rules that traditionally govern the community. In the absence of those rules, the right to apply for the patent belongs to the creator.*
4. *The patent for a traditional product grants the right to the respective owner to—*
   (a) *object to its direct or indirect reproduction, imitation and/or use by unauthorized third parties for commercial purposes;*
   (b) *assign, transfer or license the rights, including transfer by succession;*

139. Octavio Paz, *Use and Contemplation*, available at <cordillerana.cl> [access on May 2025].
140. Article 6 of the UPOV Convention 1991 reads:

> *The variety shall be deemed to be new if, at the date of filing of the application for a breeder's right, propagating or harvested material of the variety has not been sold or otherwise disposed of to others, by or with the consent of the breeder, for purposes of exploitation of the variety . . . .*

(c) *oppose to and exclude from protection any traditional product under any other specific industrial property registration or unfair competition.*

5. *A patent for a traditional product shall be effective for a period of 50 years from the filing date, and may be renewed for an identical period.* [141]

As a general note to this provision, it should be understood that it does not eliminate the need for a sui generis regime for the protection of handicrafts. The main reason is that patents for handicrafts, as suggested, would cover individualized products, whereas a sui generis regime should take a holistic approach and protect the common denominators that identify an entire line of products and objects that are the handicrafts of one specific community. So, instead of having to apply for patents on a case-by-case basis, the community would be protected for all its products and articles that obeyed a number of common denominators, the Ariane thread that links all those products (raw materials, colors, types of figurative elements, methods of making, etc.).

141. In 2002, the Council of Ministers of Portugal approved Decree-Law No. 118/2002, of April 20, 2002, dealing with access to genetic resources and the protection of associated traditional knowledge, including "traditional crafts":

> *That includes, but is not limited to, knowledge of methods, processes, products and designations with applications in agriculture, food and industrial activities in general, including traditional crafts, commerce and services, informally associated with the use and preservation of local varieties and other spontaneously occurring autochthonous material covered by this Decree.*

Article 3 of the Decree-Law. The text in English is available at <faolex.fao.org/docs/pdf/por50973E.pdf>.

CHAPTER 4
On Formal and Substantive Requirements[142] of Patentability

We discussed above the necessity of carrying on the substantive examination of patent applications before their grant. The suggestion was that in countries with a very low number of filings that examination could be avoided until the moment the right is used, namely when the patent is licensed or enforced. In that case, before that moment arrives, the patent application is examined only as to compliance with formalities.

But this does not mean that the substantive examination—i.e., the examination as regards the patentability of the claimed invention—does not have to look at certain conditions of patentability that have a formal nature. Conditions of patentability are formal when they do not concern the invention itself (such as novelty, nonobviousness, and utility) but the form in which the invention is claimed. Examples of formal requirements are the mandatory enabling disclosure and the unity of invention.

1 FORMAL REQUIREMENTS

1.1 Unity of Invention

As far as the unity of invention requirement is concerned, the lawmaker is not expected to be too strict. As said, the requirement was introduced in the nineteenth century in the patent law of a number of countries that wished to ensure the collection of adequate

142. It should be noted that there is a difference between conditions of patentability and requirements of patentability. Requirements are all those obligations that the applicant must observe in order to successfully file a patent application. The observation of some of those obligations is crucial for obtaining the patent. In the case of failure to comply with them the patent shall be rejected (or, later, it may be revoked or invalidated). In other words, the observation of those requirements is a condition *sine qua non* for obtaining the patent. Therefore, conditions are species of requirements. For example, the invention that does not meet the *condition* of novelty is not patentable, whereas the patent whose application has failed to meet the *requirement* of unity of invention is not invalid.

fees. Therefore, the requirement was used as a mechanism to prevent applicants from filing a single application for several inventions, thereby circumventing the burden of increased fees.[143] However, there would be no major inconvenience in eliminating the unity requirement, provided that the different inventions were separately claimed and clearly distinguished in the application. Today, with the availability of electronic tools of search and retrieval, complex patents could very well serve as sources of technological information as well as those that are unity-compliant. The problem of the reduction in the revenue of patent offices could be solved by increasing the fees and basing those fees on the number of claims.

Anyway, the submission of inventions in a unitary manner is not essential for the quality of the patent. But patent examiners are invariably given by lawmakers the authority to submit patent applications to the scrutiny of unity and ask applicants to divide the applications in the case they claim different technical solutions that do not relate to the same inventive concept.

However, if the examiner does not take notice of such a formal failure and the patent is later found to be noncompliant with the unity requirement, the patent does not lose its validity.

At most, the law may determine that the maintenance fees will increase after the date the patent is determined not to have followed the unity requirement.

In a nutshell, the unity of invention is a requirement, not a condition of patentability.

Perhaps the best example of statutory language dealing with the unity requirement is found in Article 5 of the draft Treaty Supplementing the Paris Convention as far as Patents are Concerned, as follows:

> *"(1) [Requirement of Unity of Invention] The application shall relate to one invention only or to a group of inventions so linked as to form a single general inventive concept ('requirement of unity of invention')."*
>
> *"(2) [Validity of Patent not Affected by Lack of Unity of Invention] The fact that a patent has been granted on an application that did not comply with the requirement of unity of invention shall not be a ground for the invalidation or revocation of the patent."*

1.2 Enabling Disclosure

By contrast with the unity of invention requirement, the enabling disclosure requirement—which is another formal requirement, given that it concerns the form in

143. The best-known patent covering multiple inventions of different sorts is perhaps that granted by the Spanish Crown to Jeronimo de Ayanz y Beaumont, in 1606. The patent accorded the inventor the exclusive right to exploit for twenty years more than fifty inventions, including mills, hydraulic engineering devices, the steam engine and submarines. *See* Nicolás García Tapia, *Privilegios de Invención*, available at <ifc.dpz.es>. *See also Jerónimo de Ayanz: el Ingenioso Hidalgo de Navarra*, available at <www.defensa.gob.es/Galerias/gabinete/red/2024/07/p-62-65-red-418-ayanz.pdf> [access in May 2025].

which the patent application must be filed—is essential to the validity of the patent; i.e., it is a *formal condition of patentability*.

Article 29 of the TRIPS Agreement is explicit in this regard: its heading reads "Conditions on Patent Applicants." Paragraph 1 reads (in part):

> *Members shall require that an applicant for a patent shall disclose the invention in a manner sufficiently clear and complete for the invention to be carried out by a person skilled in the art . . . .*[144]

Article 29 of the TRIPS Agreement mentions two other formal requirements that are related to disclosure: the obligation to disclose the best mode of using the invention that is known to the inventor; and the obligation to inform the patent office concerning the applicant's corresponding foreign applications and grants. The lawmaker of a WTO Member is not obliged either to include these requirements in the statute or to impose them as conditions. After all, the first requirement calls for a subjective view, which may not necessarily correspond to technical reality. And the second requirement, although useful (in particular for those patent offices that take a long time for examining applications and therefore could benefit from the results of examinations carried out by foreign patent offices) is currently in a process of losing its practical value in view of the growing adhesion of countries to the Patent Prosecution Highway (PPH), which permits the sharing of examination results between patent offices.

The reason for the significance of the enabling disclosure condition lies in one of the social justifications of the patent system—to make patents to serve a function of technical teaching, in a manner that, when the patent expires, third parties do not need to engage in complex and costly activities of reverse engineering, in order to be able to reproduce the patented invention. Moreover, during the term of the patent, third parties should be able to invent around or to introduce improvements into the claimed invention, which, once patented, might enable them to obtain cross-licenses from the patentee.

When drafting a patent law, the lawmaker is, as a matter of course, concerned with ensuring the quality of patents that will be granted in his/her country. Frivolous patents, i.e., patents that do not correspond to genuine inventions, or inventions that do not result from an inventive activity of real significance, are more prejudicial than helpful.

---

144. The language employed in Art. 29.1 is far from being precise. To disclose means "to make known; reveal; lay open." *Webster's College Dictionary* (Random House, 1991). However, not all claimed inventions are disclosed. A number of them, in accordance with national law, will be kept secret, undisclosed, for the sake of national security interests. In other words, Art. 29.1—which also applies to patent applications that are to be kept secret—is about the *description* of the claimed invention, not of its *disclosure*. So, where Art. 29.1 reads that "an applicant for a patent shall disclose," it actually means that the applicant shall disclose the invention to the government authority in charge of granting patents. It does not mean that the applicant shall make the invention publicly known. This is a matter to be handled by patent offices, under Art. 12 of the Paris Convention. Actually, Art. 29.1 would be more precise if instead of using the verb "to disclose" it used the verb "to describe," which the same dictionary defines as "to tell or depict in words; give an account of."

It is true that several decades ago a number of national patent laws admitted the so-called patents of importation, that is, patents that were granted to inventions made in foreign countries and which might have lost novelty, with the purpose of luring foreign investors to bring their technology, machinery, and money to the granting country. This same idea was present in the industrial privileges that, during the Middle Ages and the Renaissance Era, were granted to foreign artisans by European States, with the intent of luring those artisans, so that they could bring their knowledge, their tools, and their apprentices and establish themselves (often with their families) in the granting country. It was by resorting to that sort of grants to Flemish artisans that England, in the fourteenth century, transformed its industry into a thriving center of manufacture of woolen cloth.[145]

But the Industrial Revolution, through the first modern patent laws, of the United States, in 1790, and of France, in 1791, has changed this perception of the patent system as a way of transferring technology through the migration of inventors (or of skilled artisans) into a system of circulation of ideas. Such a significant change was made possible by the progress brought by the Scientific Revolution, during which scientists and industrialists learned how to describe technological advances in a way that permitted their reproduction.[146] Suddenly, it was no longer necessary for an inventor to displace him/herself to make a demonstration of his/her knowledge: a full description of the invention on a piece of paper eliminated that necessity.[147]

As noted, sufficient disclosure is a crucial component of the patent system's function of technology dissemination. It is also an essential condition that permits patent examiners to assess the invention's novelty, inventiveness, and susceptibility of industrial application, or utility. The disclosure requirement is met, therefore, when the invention's description is made in a manner that permits its comprehension by others. A description that misses some essential components of the invention is insufficient and thus unacceptable. But so is a description that goes beyond the characteristics of the invention and contains too much unnecessary information, and, instead of clarifying how to carry out the invention, creates confusion.

---

145. *See* Nuno Pires de Carvalho, The Intellectual Property of Textiles and Fashion: From the Medieval Loom to the New York Fashion Week—A Sourcebook, at 185 et seq. (Wolters Kluwer, 2021).

146. Robert Friedel explains that, in his breakthrough technical book, *De Re Metallica*, published in 1556, Giorgio Agricola used plentiful woodcuts as illustrations. The reason was that the author "was acutely aware of the limitations of mere verbal description." Friedel adds that technical literature of that time was not aimed at disclosing and teaching new techniques, but rather to advertise what the authors were capable of, in the hope of attracting sponsors and clients. Robert Friedel, A Culture of Improvement—Technology and the Western Millennium, at 123, 136 (The MIT Press, 2007).

147. *See* Nuno Pires de Carvalho, A Estrutura dos Sistemas de Patentes e de Marcas: Passado, Presente e Futuro [The Structure of Patent and Trademark Systems: Past, Present, and Future], at 284-285 (Lumen Juris, 2009).

1.2.a Defining the Person Skilled in the Art for the Purposes of the Enabling Disclosure Condition

Once this is said, the developing country's lawmaker must pay a great deal of attention to the language he/she uses when drafting the provision establishing the enabling disclosure condition.

The disclosure requirement may be met by different means and may follow different standards, depending on the nature of the invention. Mechanical and chemical inventions, either products or processes, generally are sufficiently disclosed through their description. But there are inventions the description of which is extremely difficult. That is the case of microorganisms, for example. In order to address that problem, the Budapest Treaty on the International Recognition of the Deposit of Microorganisms for the Purposes of Patent Procedure has been established, so as to permit the deposit of microorganisms (as well as other assimilated biological materials, such as human cell lines) with one of the accredited International Depositary Authorities in order to meet the disclosure requirement.[148] Likewise, as mentioned above, the US Patent Act accepts that the disclosure of plants for the purposes of plant patent procedures be made through a description "as complete as is reasonably possible" (35 U.S.C. §162)—implicitly admitting that a full description of a plant may prove impossible.

Even though Article 29.1 does not say it clearly, the enabling disclosure requirement contains two elements that help define its scope: reasonableness and purpose.

The element of reasonableness is that patent applicants are not expected to give a full and detailed account of the technology involved in carrying out the invention, but rather the amount of information that is necessary for that purpose. The practice of patent disclosure follows the French saying "à un bon entendeur, un demi mot suffit." Under this practice, no applicant is required to describe the whole background of the claimed invention where such description is not practical and where the inventor can expect that a person skilled in the art is normally knowledgeable about it.

The reasonableness of disclosure may not be a matter of concern as regards products because in general those may be described by simply listing their components. But when it comes to processes, the task of disclosing them "in a manner sufficiently clear and complete" may prove very difficult, for it might require a long description of their technical background. Claimed processes, indeed, are frequently the tip of an iceberg, and for understanding that tip, it is necessary to have a complete grasp of what lies beneath the surface. For practical reasons, therefore, it is accepted that the inventor omits information to the extent that a person skilled in the art should be aware of it under normal circumstances (in other words, a person skilled in the art is deemed *un bon entendeur*, and therefore he/she only requires a *half word* rather than the complete word).[149]

148. *See* <www.wipo.int/treaties/en/registration/budapest/>.

149. The United States Supreme Court has acknowledged the limited value of patents as tools of technology dissemination in *Brenner v. Mansion*, 383 U.S. 519 (1966):

However, the concept of a person skilled in the art must reflect the average level of education of the granting country. Article 1.1 assumes that TRIPS implementation is carried out in accordance with practices and experiences that are specific to each individual WTO Member. The implementation of Article 29.1 at the national level, therefore, should be referred to the specific reality of each WTO Member. The average level of a person skilled in the art in one individual WTO Member may, and probably will, differ considerably from the average level in other WTO Members.[150] Consequently, patent applications that provide for a reasonably enabling disclosure in a developed country may not meet the same standard as established in a developing WTO Member. In spite of the language of Article 7 of the TRIPS Agreement ("The protection and enforcement of intellectual property rights should contribute . . . to the . . . dissemination of technology"), this fact greatly undermines the value of the international patent system as a source of technical dissemination among countries of different levels of technological development.

The TRIPS Agreement does not prevent patent examiners in poor countries from requesting applicants to supplement the specifications of applications (whether they claim a priority date or not) with additional information in order to make patent specifications more understandable to local researchers and inventors. If adopted, this should be a statutory matter, but the lawmaker should weigh the impact of this stricter enabling disclosure condition on the overall complexity of patent prosecution.

1.2.b Dos and Don'ts

This aspect has never been included in national patent laws, and yet its implementation would give the national patent system a true impact on the teaching function of patents. It is common in meetings with developing countries' researchers and inventors to hear from them the complaint that they are not able to apprehend the meaning and the reach of many patent applications that are originated in more developed countries, where patent attorneys draft the applications having the national technological landscape in mind. Therefore, those drafters, in good faith (but not always, as the U.S. Supreme Court acknowledged in *Brenner v. Mansion* (1966)), take shortcuts in describing the claimed inventions because they assume that national readers will be able to understand what is described and claimed—but they forget (or ignore) that in many developing countries that is not true.

> *It is true, of course, that one of the purposes of the patent system is to encourage dissemination of information concerning discoveries and inventions. . . However, in light of the highly developed art of drafting patent claims so that they disclose as little information useful as possible—while broadening the scope of the claim as widely as possible—the argument based upon the virtue of disclosure must be warily evaluated.*

Ibid., at 533-534.

150. The determination of such an average level is a matter of implementation of the TRIPS Agreement and is, therefore, subject to Art. 1.1. Therefore, WTO Members are free to determine it "within their own legal system and practice."

Therefore, it is recommended that the lawmaker in a developing country, in particular if it is a least-developing country, be stricter in requiring that the claimed invention be described in a way that national researchers and inventors be able to fully understand it and learn from it.

Because there are no national precedents, no national examples can be indicated in this regard. But, as a recommendation, it is suggested that the enabling disclosure condition be inserted in the National Patent Act with the language that follows:

Article . . . Enabling Disclosure

1. *The application shall disclose the claimed invention in a manner sufficiently clear and complete for the invention to be carried out by a person skilled in the art.*
   (a) *The disclosure of the claimed invention shall be considered sufficiently clear and complete if it provides information that is sufficient to allow that the invention be reproduced and used by a person skilled in the art, without undue experimentation.*
   (b) *For the purposes of assessing sufficiency of disclosure under paragraph (1), the disclosure on the filing date contained in the description, claims and drawings, eventually as amended and corrected under the law, shall be taken into account.*[151]
2. *For the purposes of determining the technical knowledge and experience of the person skilled in the art, the examiner shall consider the person with average technical skills and knowledge in the country.*
3. *When the examiner finds that the application either of a foreign or a national origin was filed taking into account a person with higher skills in the art than those that are the average in the country, he/she will request the applicant to complement the disclosure.*
4. *The failure to provide for disclosure that takes into account the average technical skills and knowledge in the country shall lead to the rejection of the application or the invalidation of the patent.*

As a *don't*, it should be noted that the notion of the "person skilled in the art" also applies to the assessment of the inventive step or nonobviousness, as it will be discussed below. By contrast with what was said above as regards the enabling disclosure condition, the suggestion is that the same approach be *not* adopted as regards the assessment of nonobviousness, by developing countries. The reasons are that, first, the enabling disclosure requirement plays a function that is different from that of nonobviousness; and, second, if that notion was related to the national level of average technical knowledge, developing countries would end up easing the patenting of minor inventions that in other countries would be deemed non-patentable for lack of sufficient inventiveness. Would such easing correspond to the national interests of developing countries? Most probably not. We will repeat this recommendation when looking at the condition of sufficient inventiveness.[152]

151. This language has been borrowed from the Draft Substantive Patent Law Treaty (Art. 10 (a) and (b)).
152. *See, infra*, subsection 2.2 in this chapter.

1.3 Best Mode

The requirement to indicate the best mode for carrying out the invention is optional because it is not strictly necessary for the complete understanding of the invention. But Article 29.1 of the TRIPS Agreement is silent about the possibility that WTO Members make the best mode indication mandatory at the national level, which implies that they may do so.[153] The best mode disclosure requirement refers to the date of filing or the priority date.

The enabling disclosure and the best mode disclosure are separate requirements because of their different subjects and standards. The enabling disclosure requirement aims at "placing the subject matter of the claims generally in possession of the public. If, however, the applicant develops specific instrumentalities or techniques [...], then the best mode requirement imposes an obligation to disclose that information to the public as well."[154] For this reason, where no "specific instrumentalities or techniques" have been developed for the invention (by the time of filing), the requirement cannot be complied with. This is one of the reasons why the TRIPS Agreement has made the best mode requirement an optional, nonmandatory matter for WTO Members. Article 24 of the Brazilian patent law, for example, makes it mandatory but only "when it applies"—which means that in those cases in which applicants have not developed a specific mode of using the invention, they are not expected to indicate the best mode in the specifications.

According to the TRIPS Agreement, the best mode is supposed to be known by the *inventor*, not by the *applicant*. This specific choice of words has not been accidental. TRIPS negotiators have simply recognized that inventors and patent applicants seldom are the same person or entity.[155]

There is the general belief that the main purpose of the best mode disclosure requirement is to help third parties use the invention after the patent expiry. This is not

153. The relevant part of para. 1 of Art. 29 of the TRIPS Agreement reads:

> *Members . . . may require the applicant to indicate the best mode for carrying out the invention known to the inventor at the filing date or, where priority is claimed, at the priority date of the application.*

154. *Spectra-Physics, Inc. v. Coherent, Inc.*, 827 F.2d 1524, 1532 (Fed. Cir. 1987), certiorari denied, 484 U.S. 954 (1987).

155. Interestingly, Art. 29.1 contains the only reference to the inventor throughout the entire TRIPS Agreement. That is not an accident. The TRIPS Agreement is not about *inventors*, but about *inventions*. Increasingly, it follows the trend of protecting *investors'* interests in technology. In this sense, *see* WIPO/GRTKF/IC/2/9, of December 3, 2001:

> [...] patent law is not necessarily about protection *inventors*, but about appropriating *inventions*. Likewise, copyright, especially in a TRIPS-context, is not about protecting *authors*, but rather about appropriating *works*.

Ibid., para. 24. The WIPO paper explains that the protection of inventors and authors is generally dealt with by contract and labor laws, not by intellectual property law.

correct. The best mode disclosure requirement may have that advantage, but that is not its main purpose. Its primary objective is to give evidence of possession of the invention at the time of the filing. In the course of prosecution proceedings (which may take several years), it is indeed possible that the applicant finds out new and better ways of putting the invention to practice, but even those laws that impose the best mode do not impose the obligation to update the patent specifications. The best mode corresponds to a precise time: the date on which the patent application was filed (nationally or abroad, when the priority right is claimed). If the idea were to assist third parties in benefiting from the claimed invention, patent offices should be entitled to require a regular updating of the best mode.

Other approach consists of requesting the applicant to disclose the several methods he/she knows of putting the invention in practice and, among those, define the best one. This solution is not a common one, however, given its redundancy. It can be found in the patent law of the Bahamas, as follows:

> *Article 19. Contents of specification.*
>
> . . .
>
> *(3) Every specification shall—*
>
> *(a) particularly describe the invention and the methods by which it is to be performed;*
>
> . . .
>
> *(c) disclose the best method of performing the invention which was known to the applicant (or his predecessor in title) at the relevant priority date and for which he is entitled to claim protection; . . .*

A more stringent approach can be found in the Industrial Property Law of Costa Rica, as follows:

> *Article 4.*
>
> *Descriptions shall describe the invention sufficiently clearly and comprehensively to evaluate it and to ensure that a person skilled in the art may carry it out. In particular, they shall specifically indicate the best way known to the applicant for carrying out the invention, giving one or more concrete examples where possible, and identifying, as the case may be, the one which would yield the most satisfactory results in terms of industrial exploitation.*

This text seems redundant. After all, the *best way* known to the applicant (or the inventor?) should be expected the one that yields "The most satisfactory results in terms of industrial exploitation."

Another possible approach is that of the law of Sierra Leone, which just asks the inventor to indicate one mode of carrying it out, as follows:

> *Article 11*
>
> . . .
>
> *(7) The description shall disclose the invention in a manner sufficiently clear and complete for the invention to be carried out by a person having ordinary skill in*

the art, and shall, in particular, indicate at least one mode known to the applicant for carrying out the invention.[156]

The approach of Sierra Leone's patent law should be preferred. The reason is that the requirement to disclose the best mode relies on a purely subjective approach. But nothing happens if another method of exploiting the invention proves subsequently to be more effective than the one indicated by the inventor. The latter is asked to indicate his/her preferred method (if he/she knows more than one, of course), not the method that objectively is shown to perform better. Sanctions could apply only if later it was shown that the inventor, on purpose, concealed the best mode, in order to make the invention's reproduction by third parties more difficult. But that would be a matter of fraud.

1.4 Information Concerning Foreign Applications and Patents

Paragraph 2 of Article 29 of the TRIPS Agreement authorizes WTO Members to request patent applicants (both national and foreigners) to submit information concerning the outcome of patent applications filed abroad (with or without a claim for priority).[157] In doing this, developing countries obtain help from other patent offices as regards searches and examinations of inventions.

That practice is entirely consistent with the principle of independence of patents, as established by Article 4*bis* of the Paris Convention, because independence does not concern the prosecution of patents and the assessment of the conditions of patentability, but the separation of the rights granted in different jurisdictions only.[158] But Article 29.2 does not impose a restrictive reading; i.e., the requirement does not concern exclusively the results of patent prosecution procedures. It also concerns the results of lawsuits or administrative procedures challenging the validity of patents granted in other countries. The purpose of Article 29.2 is to make information available as to whether in other jurisdictions a corresponding foreign patent has been deemed, by the patent office or by a court, not to meet all patentability conditions.

Moreover, access to information concerning grants in foreign countries helps patent offices to acquire knowledge of any changes made to the initial application after the priority date.

---

156. The Patents and Industrial Design Act, 2012. It should be noted that this provision makes reference to the "applicant," whereas Art. 29.1 of the TRIPS Agreement mentions the "inventor." The same choice of language by Sierra Leone's lawmaker can be found in other countries' patent laws.
157. Article 29.2 of the TRIPS Agreement reads:

    Members may require an applicant for a patent to provide information concerning the applicant's corresponding foreign applications and grants.

158. Consequently, the principle of independence of patents does not stand in the way of regional initiatives to integrate patent offices and patent grants, such as the EPO and the OAPI. Nor does it prevent national administrations from re-registering patents granted in foreign territories. On the principle of independence and its impact on the enforcement of patent rights, *see infra*, Chapter 8.

Article 29.2 allows Members to impose a strict inequitable conduct requirement as regards information on patent applications filed abroad. The patent statutes of many WTO Members have made this obligation dependent on an initiative by the patent office. This is, for example, the solution found in the WIPO Model Law for Developing Countries for Inventions, as we will *see* below. In other words, in those countries where the patent examiner does not solicit the patent applicant to submit information on patent applications filed for the same or essentially the same invention in other countries, the applicant is not obliged to do so. This means that, where the foreign patent application does not claim the benefit of priority corresponding to all other applications in other countries, or when the applicant is a national citizen (and therefore does not need to inform his own country's patent office about applications filed in other countries except under some very specific conditions, that will be mentioned in Chapter 11), Article 29.2 may be of little value. But the national law may require that the patentee at a later stage inform the patent office about the results of prosecution procedures as well as of post-grant challenges in other countries. Failure to inform could amount to inequitable conduct. In this case, the sanction against failure to comply with the requirement would be the invalidation of the patent, as the statute of Oman provides.[159]

Let us look now at a few examples.

First, a few examples concerning patent statutes that make the requirement to inform about foreign applications dependent on the examiner's request: the WIPO Model Law and the patent statutes of Brazil and Oman.

The WIPO Model Law for Developing Countries on Inventions contains a very detailed provision in this regard, as follows:

> *Section 128: Information Concerning Corresponding Foreign Applications and Patents or Other Titles of Protection*
>
> (1) *The applicant shall, at the request of the Patent Office, furnish it with the date and number of any application for a patent or another title of protection filed by him with a national industrial property office of another country or with a regional industrial property office ("foreign application") relating to the same or essentially the same invention as that claimed in the application filed with the Patent Office.*
>
> (2) *(a) The applicant shall, at the request of the Patent Office, furnish it with the following documents relating to one of the foreign applications referred to in subsection (1):*

159. The Delhi High Court, in *Chemtura Corporation v. Union of India & Ors*, held that the failure to comply with the requirement to disclose information about parallel patent applications in other countries, under sections 8(1)(b) and 8(2) of the Act, leads to the "prima facie attraction" of the ground for revocation as contained in section 64(1)(m). Consequently, the court vacated an interim injunction previously granted in favor of the plaintiff. Decision of August 28, 2009, available at < indiankanoon.org/doc/195444253/ > [access in May 2025]. The same court, in *F. Hoffmann-La Roche Ltd v. Cipla Ltd., Mumbai Central*, held that section 64(1)(m) gives it the discretionary authority to revoke or not the patent "on the peculiar facts and circumstances of the present case." The said discretion stems from the exact language of section 64(1), which says that the patent "may be revoked." The Act does not say that the patent *shall* be revoked. This means that, in the view of the court, the mere failure to comply with section 8 is not a sufficient ground for the revocation. Decision of August 28, 2009, available at <indiankanoon.org/doc/123231822/> (accessed in August 2025).

> (i) *a copy of any communication received by the applicant concerning the results of any search or examination carried out in respect of the foreign application;*
> (ii) *a copy of the patent or other title of protection granted on the basis of the foreign application;*
> (iii) *a copy of any final decision rejecting the foreign application or refusing the grant requested in the foreign application.*
>
> (b) *The applicant shall, at the request of the Patent Office, furnish it with a copy of any final decision invalidating the patent or other title of protection granted on the basis of the foreign application referred to in paragraph (a).*
>
> (3) *The applicant shall, at the request of the Patent Office, furnish it with the following documents relating to any foreign application other than the one referred to in subsection (2):*
> (i) *a copy of any communication received by the applicant concerning the results of any search or examination carried out in respect of the foreign application and in which publications or other documents establishing the prior art are mentioned;*
> (ii) *a copy of any final decision rejecting the foreign application or refusing the grant requested in the• foreign application.*
>
> (4) *The documents furnished under this Section shall merely serve the purpose of facilitating the evaluation of the novelty and inventive step of the invention claimed in the application filed with the Patent Office or in the patent granted on the basis of that application.*
>
> (5) *The applicant shall have the right to submit comments on the documents furnished under this Section.*

This language includes not only applications that claim priority but also independent applications (provided, of course, they concern the same or essentially the same invention). The final text of patents obtained abroad must also be submitted. But the provision does not cover the opinions of foreign courts in proceedings concerning the invalidation of the patent.

As a second example, the Industrial Property Act of Brazil, of 1996, reads:

> *Article 34.*
>
> *Once the examination is applied for, the following must be submitted within 60 (sixty) days, whenever requested, under penalty of the application being archived:*
>
> *I— objections, searches for prior art and examination results for granting a corresponding application in other countries, when there is a claim for priority;*
>
> . . .

The problem with this approach is that the applicant is not obliged to inform about the results of invalidation lawsuits in other countries, if they have terminated before the patent application was examined in Brazil—which is not out of question, in view of the long delays taken by the Brazilian patent office in carrying out the prosecution. Moreover, the requirement is confined to the cases where priority has been claimed, which may leave independent patent applications out of the requirement.

The law of Oman also makes the submission of information as regards patent applications filed abroad dependent on a request by the examiner (or, more specifically, by the Registrar). But it goes further than the WIPO Model Law:

Article (8):

If the Applicant filed, by himself or by his predecessor, a patent application outside the Sultanate, for the same or essentially the same invention as that claimed in the application filed in Oman, the Registrar may request the applicant to furnish him with the following documents:

1— Date and number of any application filed abroad;

2— A copy of any communication concerning the date of any search or examination carried out in respect of the foreign application;

3— A copy of the patent granted on the basis of the foreign application;

4— A copy of any final decision rejecting the foreign application or refusing the grant requested in the foreign application; and

5— A copy of any final decision invalidating the patent granted on the basis of the foreign application.

By providing the Registrar with this information, the applicant of a patent in Oman is informing not only about the existence of applications filed abroad concerning the same (or essentially the same) invention but also the results of examinations, the content of patents obtained (because, as said before, these may have been amended during the prosecution or as a result of invalidation proceedings), and the results of eventual decisions by foreign courts concerning patents for the same invention.

Some countries, however, impose the duty of informing about patent applications (for the same invention) filed abroad as a general requirement, without the need for the patent office to take the initiative in such regard. This is the case of Bahrain, for example:

Section 4. An applicant shall submit all the details and information related to any application previously submitted abroad for the same patent subject to the claim and decisions issued for these applications.

The law of Bahrain confines the requirement to applications filed abroad before the application was filed in the country. The law is silent about applications filed subsequently.

Following an approach very similar to (probably inspired in) that of the WIPO Model Law, the Patent Act of Costa Rica regulates the submission of information concerning patent applications filed abroad with great detail. This is the text:

Article 14.—Information relating to patent applications

1. *Applicants for or owners of patents in Costa Rica shall indicate the date and number of any patent application or other title of protection they have submitted to or any rights they have obtained from an Industrial Property Office in any other country or from a regional Industrial Property Office, which refers in full or in part to the same invention claimed in the application filed in Costa Rica.*
2. *Where foreign inventors are unable to produce the patent certificate issued in the country of origin but can provide documentary proof that the country in question has no patent register for the class of inventions involved, a certificate of patent registration from any other country in which the patent has been registered shall be valid. In any case, documentary proof shall be provided as to the expiry date of the patent abroad.*
3. *Applicants or patent owners shall provide the following documents in respect of foreign applications or titles:*

(a) *copies of all communications received by the applicant which refer to the results of a search for prior art or examinations conducted in respect of the foreign application;*
(b) *copies of patents or other protection titles granted on the basis of foreign applications;*
(c) *a copy of any final decision rejecting a foreign application or refusing to grant the concession sought;*
(d) *information on disputes or complaints regarding the invention which are known or related to it.*

4. *Patent applicants shall also provide the Industrial Property Registry at its request with a copy of any final decision invalidating the patent, or another protection title granted on the basis of the foreign applications referred to in paragraph 1.*
5. *Documents provided under this Article shall be used to facilitate the examination of novelty and the inventive step of the invention claimed with the Industrial Property Registry.*
6. *If patent applicants fail to provide the information or documentation sought within the prescribed period, the patents shall be refused. In duly justified cases, applicants may request an extension of the period for submitting the corresponding information or documentation.*
7. *Patent applicants may submit observations and comments on the information and documents they provide.*

Above we said that the lawmaker should not be too laconic, so that the law does not become obscure. But the reverse is also true: the lawmaker should avoid being too verbose, in order not to fall into contradiction or give rise to ambiguity. This is the case of the provisions above. Indeed, on the one hand, paragraph 5 says that the information on patent applications filed abroad serves as elements of assistance to the examination of the application filed in Costa Rica. But, on the other hand, paragraph 1 mentions "applicants for or owners of patents in Costa Rica." Does the requirement apply after the patent has already been granted (in an invalidation proceeding, for example)? Another aspect of difficult understanding is that the first three paragraphs indicate that the applicants are supposed to submit the required documents without the need for a specific request by the patent examiner (or the patent office). But paragraph 4 explicitly mentions the request by the patent office as regards "any final decision invalidating the patent, or another protection title granted on the basis of the foreign applications referred to in paragraph 1." Is the request necessary for one particular type of document and unnecessary for another sort of documents? Costa Rican courts will have to clarify these (apparent) contradictions.

But, importantly, the law of Costa Rica provides, in paragraph 6, that "If patent applicants fail to provide the information or documentation sought within the prescribed period, the patents shall be refused." It follows that, subsequently, such failure may lead to the invalidation of the patents, if they were not refused. In this manner, Costa Rica makes of this requirement a condition of patentability, even in the absence of any fraudulent intent.

By a striking contrast, the statute of Oman provides:

Article (14)

. . .

3— *The lack of compliance with any formal requirements shall not be ground for the invalidation of the patent unless the non-compliance in question occurred as a result of a fraudulent intention.*

This seems to be the correct approach, if we understand that the reference to formal requirements in Article 14(3) does not include enabling disclosure, which, as explained, is more than a mere requirement—it is a condition of patentability. Information about patent applications filed abroad may be relevant, but not to the point of prejudicing the value of the patent, even more so if we take into consideration the growing number of countries engaging in PPH deals.

In regard to the need for submitting information concerning foreign patent applications, the lawmaker of Botswana has found a different solution: the applicant is requested to provide that information at the moment he/she files the application; eventually, the Registrar may later request that the applicant submit the corresponding documents:

Section 19.

(1) *An applicant shall indicate in the application for a patent the date and the number of other applications filed by him or her or his or her predecessor in title outside Botswana relating to the same or essentially the same invention as that claimed in the application filed in Botswana.*

(2) *The applicant shall, when requested by the Registrar, furnish the following documents relating to any of the applications referred to in subsection (1)—*

. . .[160]

This seems a good solution. It would only need to be improved by requesting the applicant to submit information about the results of examinations and invalidation proceedings abroad until the date the Registrar publishes the decision concerning the grant or the refusal. For countries that have not adhered to any PPH schemes with larger and more resourceful patent offices, that simple mechanism would ensure that the patent office would be informed of the results of patent applications for essentially the same invention in other countries.

1.5 The Requirement to Disclose the Origin of Genetic Resources and/or Traditional Knowledge Used in the Making of the Claimed Invention

On May 24, 2024, WIPO Member States adopted a Treaty on Intellectual Property, Genetic Resources and Associated Traditional Knowledge, the main clause of which is to impose on Contracting Parties the requirement to inform the patent office (hence, the public) of the origin of genetic resources and/or traditional knowledge used in the making of the claimed invention. The relevant clause reads:

160. Industrial Property Act, Act No. 8 of 2010.

Article 3. Disclosure requirement

3.1. Where the claimed invention in a patent application is based on genetic resources, each Contracting Party shall require applicants to disclose:

(a) the country of origin of the genetic resources, or,
(b) in cases where the information in Article 3.1(a) is not known to the applicant, or where Article 3.1(a) does not apply, the source of the genetic resources.

3.2 Where the claimed invention in a patent application is based on traditional knowledge associated with genetic resources, each Contracting Party shall require applicants to disclose:

(a) the Indigenous Peoples or local community, as applicable, who provided the traditional knowledge associated with genetic resources, or,
(b) in cases where the information in Article 3.2(a) is not known to the applicant, or where Article 3.2(a) does not apply, the source of the traditional knowledge associated with genetic resources.

The disclosure requirement has a single objective: to help biodiversity-rich countries to monitor and assess compliance with the legal or contractual obligation of sharing benefits derived from the commercial use of genetic resources (GRs) and/or associated traditional knowledge (TK), in the light of the recommendation contained in Articles 8(j) and 15.7 of the Convention on Biological Diversity (CBD).[161] Furthermore, under Article 16 of the CBD, countries should give access to the technology derived from the use of GRs and covered by patents to those countries where those resources have been obtained. Article 16.2 adds that:

In the case of technology subject to patents and other intellectual property rights, such access and transfer shall be provided on terms which recognize and are consistent with the adequate and effective protection of intellectual property rights.

Even before the WIPO Treaty was adopted, a number of WIPO Member States had already sought ways of adopting the Requirement. Some have introduced the

---

161. Article 8(j) of the Convention on Biological Diversity (in part) provides:

Each Contracting Party shall, as far as possible and as appropriate:

[...]
(j) Subject to its national legislation, respect, preserve and maintain knowledge, innovations and practice of indigenous and local communities embodying traditional lifestyles relevant for the conservation and sustainable use of biological diversity and promote their wider application with the approval and involvement of the holders of such knowledge, innovations and practices and encourage the equitable sharing of the benefits arising from the utilization of such knowledge, innovations and practices.

Article 15.7 of the CBD provides:

Each Contracting Party shall take legislative, administrative or policy measures, as appropriate, . . . and, where necessary, through the financial mechanism . . . with the aim of sharing in a fair and equitable way the results of research and development and the benefits arising from the commercial and other utilization of genetic resources with the Contracting Party providing such resources. Such sharing shall be upon mutually agreed terms.

Requirement in their national laws as an additional formal condition of patentability. Other countries have preferred to sanction the failure to comply with the Requirement by measures outside the patent system, such as fines.

For example, Article 26(4) of the patent law of China (as amended in 2020) provides that:

> *Where an invention-creation is accomplished by relying on genetic resources, the applicant shall indicate, in the patent application documents, the direct and original source of the genetic resources. Where the applicant fails to indicate the original source, he or it shall state the reasons thereof.*

The sanction for failure to comply with that disclosure requirement is the rejection of the patent application, as provided in Article 5, paragraph two:

> *No patent right shall be granted for any invention-creation where the acquisition or utilization of the genetic resources, on which the development of the invention-creation relies, violates the provisions of laws or administrative regulations.*

China's law does not say what happens to the patent that has been granted in violation of Articles 5 and 26, concerning the disclosure of the source of genetic resources, but, in view of the language of Article 5, one can only conclude that such patent can be invalidated.

The same solution is expressly provided by the patent law of Vietnam, as follows:

> *Article 96. Cancellation of effectiveness of protection titles*
>
> 1. *A protection title shall be entirely invalidated in the following cases:*
>
>   . . .
>
>   c) *Patent applications for inventions which are directly created based on genetic resources or traditional knowledge associated with genetic resources but fail to disclose or incorrectly disclose the origin of genetic resources or traditional knowledge associated with genetic resources in the application.*[162]

The same orientation is followed by the Andean Community countries, whose Directive 486, on Industrial Property, provides:

> *Article 3. Member countries shall ensure that the protection conferred on the various forms of industrial property shall be granted in such a way as to safeguard and respect their biological and genetic heritage and also the traditional knowledge of their indigenous Afro-American or local communities. By virtue of the foregoing, the grant of patents relating to inventions developed on the basis of material derived from that heritage or knowledge shall be subject to that material having been acquired in accordance with international, community and national legal provisions.*
>
> . . .
>
> *Article 26. The application for a patent shall be filed with the competent national office and shall contain the following:*

162. Law No. 07/2022/QH15, of June 16, 2022, amending and supplementing a number of articles of the Law on Intellectual Property.

. . .

(h) *where applicable, a copy of the access contract where the products or processes for which a patent is sought have been obtained or developed from genetic resources or products derived therefrom of which any of the member countries is the country of origin;*

(i) *where applicable, a copy of the document accrediting the licensing or the authorization of the use of the traditional knowledge of the indigenous Afro-American or local communities of member countries where the products or processes for which protection is sought have been obtained or developed from such knowledge of which any of the member countries is the country of origin, in accordance with the provisions of Decision 391 and such of its amendments and implementing regulations as are in force;*

. . .

Article 75. The competent national authority shall decree the absolute invalidity of a patent at any time, either ex officio or at the request of any person, where:

. . .

(g) *where applicable, a copy of the access contract has not been filed where the products or processes to which the patent application relates have been produced or developed with genetic resources or derived products of which any of the member countries is the country of origin;*

(h) *where applicable, a copy of the document evidencing the licensing or authorization of the use of traditional knowledge of the indigenous Afro-American or local communities of the member countries has not been filed where the products or processes for which protection is sought have been produced or developed on the basis of such knowledge of which one of the member countries is the country of origin; . . .*

The Industrial Property Act of Samoa also requires that the patent applicant disclose the use of TK that is of relevance for the making of the claimed invention. This is the language of Samoa's statute:

7. Application for a patent—

(3) *An application must contain the following:*

. . .

(g) *a statement stating whether or not the invention for which protection is claimed is based on knowledge available within any local or indigenous community whether from Samoa or elsewhere;*

(h) *a statement disclosing the source and geographical origin of any biological material used for the invention;*

. . .

(10) *Subject to subsection (11), if the application is based on or derived from biological material or knowledge available within any local or indigenous community the Registrar may direct the applicant to furnish evidence as to the applicant's title or authority to make use of such material or knowledge.*

(11) *The Registrar is only to direct an applicant for evidence under subsection (10) when the applicant makes a written statement that the invention for which protection is claimed is based on or derived from biological material or knowledge available within any local or indigenous community.*

(12) *If an applicant fails to provide evidence as directed by the Registrar under subsection (10), the Registrar may, cease to deal further with the application.*

The expression "knowledge available within any local or indigenous community" is obviously incorrect. After all, there is a great deal of knowledge that is available within local communities that is not private to those communities. The statute should have made reference to knowledge that has been created/invented/found by the indigenous community and is specific to it.

The law of Samoa instructs the Registrar to deny the patent if the applicant omits information concerning the use of TK and GRs. But the law also provides for the invalidation of the patent by the Supreme Court that fails to comply with the disclosure requirement (section 17(2)(a)).

Those countries that have accepted and wish to implement the WIPO Treaty of 2024 will have to review these provisions, so as to adopt post-grant sanctions that do not include the invalidation of the patent.

As explained elsewhere, the problem with imposing the disclosure requirement as a formal condition of patentability is in its incompatibility with the TRIPS Agreement.[163,164] The reason is that under Article 62.1 of the TRIPS Agreement, formal requirements additional to those that are accepted by the TRIPS Agreement (such as the disclosure of the invention, the designation of an address for service and the appointment of an agent) and the Paris Convention (such as the declaration of priority, the mention of the inventor and the payment of maintenance fees) must be reasonable. "Reasonableness" means a certain sense of appropriateness with the objectives sought. Whereas formal requirements concerning the payment of prosecution fees, for example, seem reasonable, the obligation of fulfilling a cumbersome requirement of disclosing the origin of GRs and TK, in the absence of a formal contract of access, in order to comply with a provision of a treaty—the CBD—that is outside the jurisdiction of the WTO, and to which certain WTO Members cannot even adhere because they are not States, does not seem to be reasonable.

163. *See* Nuno Pires de Carvalho, *Requiring Disclosure of the Origin of Genetic Resources and Prior Informed Consent in Patent Applications Without Infringing the TRIPS Agreement: The Problem and The Solution*, 2 J.L. & Policy 371, 399-400 (2000).

164. The Requirement also contradicts Art. 29(1) of the Patent Cooperation Treaty (PCT), which reads:

> *No national law shall require compliance with requirements relating to the form or contents of the international application different from or additional to those which are provided for in this Treaty and the Regulations. . . .*

Significantly, the WIPO Treaty on Intellectual Property, Genetic Resources and Associated Traditional Knowledge, in note 4, expresses the request by Contracting Parties to the Assembly of the International Patent Cooperation Union that it "consider the need for amendments to the Regulations under the PCT and/or the Administrative Instructions thereunder." The Note means that WIPO Member States acknowledge the conflict between the new Treaty and the PCT (i.e., with the Treaty itself, and not only with its Regulations). However, an observer might ask why WIPO Member States did not first seek to make an amendment to the PCT before embarking on diplomatic negotiations for another treaty containing a clause that contradicts it. Actually, an amendment to the PCT Regulations in order to admit the disclosure requirement has already been proposed (by Switzerland), but without success. *See* Nuno Pires de Carvalho, The TRIPS Regime, *supra* note 3, at 317.

This is the probable reason for the wording of paragraphs 3 and 4 of the WIPO Treaty on Intellectual Property, Genetic Resources and Associated Traditional Knowledge, which read:

> *5.3 Subject to Article 5.4, no Contracting Party shall revoke, invalidate, or render unenforceable the conferred patent rights solely on the basis of an applicant's failure to disclose the information specified in Article 3 of this Treaty.*
>
> *5.4 Each Contracting Party may provide for post grant sanctions or remedies where there has been fraudulent intent in regard to the disclosure requirement in Article 3 of this Treaty, in accordance with its national law.*

Moreover, Article 16 of the CBD says that compliance with the Convention is subject to the observation of international treaties on intellectual property. In other words, it must be access to the genetic resources and traditional knowledge that must comply with intellectual property protection requirements, and not the opposite.

The shortcoming with the solution of imposing administrative sanctions, such as the levying of fines, is that it may not be effective. Indeed, the difficulty in assessing the damages (to the country and/or to traditional communities) arising from the violation of laws on access to genetic resources may be an obstacle to the establishment of proportionate fines. Additionally, infringers of the disclosure requirement may understand that paying the fines will be less stringent than complying with the requirement.

But the more serious, fundamental mistake in the WIPO Treaty of 2024 is that it does not link the disclosure requirement to any formal claims of ownership or other entitlements to the GRs and TK involved in the claimed inventions. The existence of a national inventory of GRs that are specific to a country or a region, and which cannot be found in any other place in their natural state, and a national system of registration and protection of TK, should be designated as mandatory conditions for a country to impose the Requirement.[165]

165. An identical flaw is found in the new requirement established by the Riyadh Design Law Treaty, adopted by WIPO Member States on November 22, 2024. Paragraph 2 of Art. 4 (on Application) reads (in part):

> *(2) [Indication of Information] A Contracting Party may require, where permitted under the applicable law, that an application contain an indication of any prior application or registration, or of other information, including information on traditional cultural expressions and traditional knowledge, of which the applicant is aware, that is relevant to the eligibility for registration of the industrial design.*

The ambiguity in the language of this provision seems to be even worse than that of the WIPO Treaty on Intellectual Property, Genetic Resources and Associated Traditional Knowledge, in the sense that it does not provide for any clarification on what can be deemed "relevant to the eligibility for registration." The reference to an indication of "any prior application or registration" suggests that the drafters of the Riyadh Treaty understood that the eventual preexistence of traditional cultural expressions (TCEs) and TK could be seen as an impediment to acquiring rights in the claimed design. But here a problem of legal security emerges: which TCEs and TK could constitute impediments? Prior applications and registrations are recorded in public documents. But most TCEs and TK are undocumented and unregistered, and therefore they are not accompanied by any sort of legal certainty. A second major flaw in this provision of the Riyadh Treaty is that, by contrast with TCEs—and with industrial designs—TK consists of technical knowledge, i.e., of ideas, and not of their expressions. For example, how can the knowledge of the process of making the textiles of a

1.5.a Dos and Don'ts

In reality, the disclosure requirement is of very doubtful value and may even be counterproductive. An undue burden imposed on patent applications may create serious difficulties for the management of national and international patent systems and deflect the focus of the whole patent system from contributing to the progress of useful arts to the acknowledgment of third parties' stakes in claimed inventions. The transaction costs arising from uncertainties as to ownership of TK, in the absence of a national or international system for its registration and protection, may be disproportionate.

Moreover, the disclosure requirement undermines the value of patents as effective means of securing property rights in inventions. The possibility of attacking the validity of those rights because of factors concerning conditions that are intrinsic to or associated with raw materials used in the making of the invention, although remotely, and extrinsic to the invention itself or to inventorship, will create unpredictability. Patents will lose much of their value, given that acquiring and maintaining them may depend on elements that have nothing to do with the invention. Patents are certificates of *inventive* behavior, and that is in that capacity that they perform their social function. If transformed into certificates of *good* behavior, patents cease being patents as such and become certificates of origin of genetic materials.

Incidentally, once such an approach is deemed acceptable by the international community, the validity of patents could also be scrutinized vis-à-vis the legitimacy of the acquisition of raw materials and research tools, such as microscopes and other laboratory equipment, and their purpose of securing intangible assets would necessarily become meaningless.

The WIPO Treaty on Intellectual Property, Genetic Resources and Associated Traditional Knowledge attempts to circumvent this shortcoming by allowing noncompliant patents to be revoked on grounds of fraud only. However, the problem of unpredictability remains as far as patent applications are concerned. The inventor of a new pharmaceutical or biochemical compound will never be sure if his/her patent application will be opposed based on the alleged failure to disclose the origin of the raw materials used in his/her experiments. Indeed, the WIPO Treaty does not provide any clue on the evidence that must be presented by eventual challengers to the patent application on grounds of failure to disclose the origin of GRs or to submit proof of consent by the holders of associated TK.

The national lawmaker should take into serious consideration that the disclosure requirement, when designated as a condition of patentability, does not promote benefit sharing: it simply generates information about the use of GRs and associated TK in the making of claimed inventions. Most patents fail to generate any economic revenue, particularly in the pharmaceutical industry, where patent applications are filed very

specific community, including the techniques of weaving and dying them, interfere with the registration of a design? Only designs (or, at most, their verbal description) can be of relevance "to the eligibility for registration" of other designs—not the knowledge of how to make the respective material supports.

early in the research process, and patent applicants are still far away from obtaining a positive commercial outcome. Thus, as a monitoring tool, the disclosure requirement does not go beyond informing the TK holder about the existence of a patented invention that has been made upon some hint or clue given by that holder concerning the practical utility of the GR involved. The patent does not inform them about the commercial exploitation of that invention, let alone the financial gains of the patent owner.

Things can get even more complicated if the TK holder is aware of a practical use of a specific GR—for example, in the preparation of a potion used to relieve patients from a headache—but the pharmaceutical company that has collected that GR and, several years later, upon examining it finds that it has potentially positive effects in treating a completely different health condition. That will be a very difficult task for the patent office or an opponent of such a patent application to show that "the claimed invention in a patent application is *based*" on that specific piece of TK.

Moreover, one should not underestimate the difficulties of patent applicants in identifying the origin of GRs, the properties of which might have found their way into a claimed invention. The Requirement may prove impossible to meet in many instances, and therefore it only adds to the already existing complexities of obtaining a patent.

Let us admit, however, that the national lawmaker is aware of all of these constraints and yet he/she wishes to set in the Patent Act some language that, on the one hand, intends to show sensitivity with the legitimate interests of TK holders, and, on the other, aims at securing the legality of access to the national trove of biodiversity. For that to take place in a manner that has a really significant impact without serving merely as a trap against inventors in the pharmaceutical and biotechnological fields, the lawmaker, first, must be certain that any references to GRs and TK are founded on well-defined legal concepts, i.e., that the country has laws or regulations that clarify rights and obligations in those areas.

Second, the lawmaker should not fall into the trap of attempting to treat TK in the same manner as patentable inventions. The (obvious) reason was explained elsewhere: TK holders are not generally engaged in commercial competition with other TK holders. The same rationale of commercial rivalry that presides over patent laws does not apply to the vast majority of TK holders—except in the special field of handicrafts, which, as noted above, are a combination of commercial and cultural objects.[166]

Therefore, in reflecting the legitimate interests of documented TK holders, the lawmaker should look at solutions preventing *misappropriation*, rather than *counterfeiting*.

Following this reasoning, here is an example of what a provision in the Patent Act dealing with inventions based on the use of GRs and/or the help (or inspiration) of associated TK could look like:

166. Nuno Pires de Carvalho, *Sisyphus Redivivus? The Work of WIPO on Genetic Resources and Traditional Work of WIPO on Genetic Resources and Traditional Knowledge*, in Charles McManis and Burton Ong (eds.), ROUTLEDGE HANDBOOK OF BIODIVERSITY AND THE LAW, at 337-349 (Routledge, 2017).

Article . . . Disclosure requirement

1. *Without prejudice to the provisions of Article . . .* [the Article listing the documents that must accompany the request for the patent], *in the case the invention is based on the use of genetic resources and/or of associated traditional knowledge, the applicant shall submit, with the request, proof that access to the genetic resources and/or the acquisition of the associated traditional knowledge on which the invention is based was obtained in a manner that is compliant with the applicable laws and regulations.*[1]
   a. *For the purposes of this paragraph, an invention shall be deemed to be based on a genetic resource when the resource or any of its components has been employed in the making of the invention, in a manner that without such employment the invention could not have been made;*
   b. *For the purposes of this paragraph, an invention shall be deemed to be based on traditional knowledge when the inventor has resorted to the teachings of traditional knowledge, by using it as guidance or by reproducing it, in order to find the technical solution that the invention represents, in a manner that, in the absence of such teachings, the inventor would not have been able to find the solution or, if he/she had been able, he/she would have taken a significantly longer time to find the solution.*[2]
2. *The genetic resources that this Article concerns are those that are identified and classified in the central registry of biodiversity, in the Ministry of . . ., or are otherwise autochthone to this country and not available in the territory of any other country.*
   a. *Genetic resources from other territories or countries shall also be taken into consideration, on a reciprocity basis.*[3]
3. *The traditional knowledge that this Article concerns is the knowledge of products and processes that is held by traditional and indigenous communities that are based totally or in significant part on the territory of this country.* [4]
   a. *Traditional knowledge held by traditional and indigenous communities that are based totally or significantly in the territories of other countries shall also be taken into consideration, on a reciprocity basis.*
4. *The patent office shall not verify ex officio the authenticity of the proof submitted by the applicant, as mentioned in paragraph 1.* [5]
   a. *The holders of traditional knowledge or their representatives and, in the case of genetic resources, the governmental body in charge of administering access to and the management of national biodiversity, may file an opposition against the decision to grant the patent and/or, as appropriate, file an appeal against the decision granting the patent.*[6]
   b. *The applicant may apply for the rectification of his/her application concerning the disclosure requirement in the same manner of amendments and corrections as provided in Article . . .*[7]
5. *After the patent is granted, when a court finds that the patent owner has failed to comply with the disclosure requirement, as established in the present Article, the following sanctions may be imposed on the patent owner:*
   (a) in the case of misappropriation of TK:
      - *compensation for any losses caused to the TK holder;*
      - *punitive damages, when the TK holder is unable to give evidence of losses caused by the misappropriation, as well as when the patent owner's failure to give the proof mentioned in paragraph 1 of the present Article is shown to represent a gross misconduct; in this last hypothesis, the damages shall be cumulatively accorded;*

(b) *if it is impossible to verify the losses incurred by the TK holder, the court may take into account the profits obtained by the patent holder from the exploiting and/or licensing and/or licensing the patented invention;*

(c) *in the case of unauthorized access to GRs:*
- *a fine to be set as established on the applicable laws and regulations mentioned in paragraph 1;*
- *upon request by the Ministry of . . ., in the case the patented invention consists of the GR itself, either in its natural form or in a synthesized formulation, the court may transfer the ownership of the patent to the Ministry;*
- *when the patented invention consists of the GR itself, either in its natural form or in a synthesized formulation, upon request by the Ministry of . . ., the court may prohibit the patent owner from commercially exploiting it, either directly or through its assignment or licensing in the territory of the country or abroad, until the patent owner is able to secure from the Ministry the permission to use the GR in question.*[8]

Notes:

1. As discussed above, for the sake of legal security and predictability, it is recommended that only those GRs and TK components that have been the subject matter of some sort of formal registration or documentation should serve as elements for the conditioning of the grant of a patent.
2. For the purposes of the disclosure requirement, it is of the essence that the elements of TK in question have had a preponderant role in the inventive activity that led to the solution claimed in the patent. Sometimes, that role consists in a simple hint. For example, a shaman informs a bioprospector of the use he makes of the seeds of a certain plant from his garden for preparing a potion, which he administers to those members of his tribe who come to his hut complaining of some illness. That information serves as guidance to the researchers of a biotechnological company that those seeds contain some powerful active ingredient. Sometimes, that hint serves as a crucial clue for finding some powerful cure. Some other times, the merit of the TK is in simply helping the inventor save time in selecting active components that show positive effects. In both cases, the TK has been used by the inventor and, in the absence of the informed consent by the rights holder, an act of misappropriation has taken place.
3. As noted above, the Requirement undoubtedly makes the prosecution of patents more burdensome. Therefore, the patent office should not waste resources in protecting the biodiversity of other countries, unless the country has to gain from that. Reciprocity is, as a rule, banned from international protection of IP. However, here, first, we are not dealing with IP, but with access to GRs and, eventually, with benefit-sharing. And, second, GRs are not mentioned either in the Paris Convention or the TRIPS Agreement, so they are excluded from the constraints of national treatment and most-favored-nation treatment principles.
4. This language addresses the situation of many traditional communities that are found in more than one national territory, particularly of neighboring countries. This situation is common in the Amazon and the Congo rainforests, for example.
5. The same considerations of note 3 apply here, *mutatis mutandis*. The reason for not applying those considerations *ipsis verbis* is that in several countries, TK is understood as a modality of IP. That same understanding led to the establishment, in 2001, of the WIPO Intergovernmental Committee on Genetic Resources, Traditional Knowledge and Folklore (the IGC), and has presided the work of the Organization for the last twenty-five years. But that is a wrong concept—which has eventually led to the failure of WIPO, after such a long period, to achieve a relevant result on the protection of TK, other than the misguided and poorly negotiated 2024 Treaty. IP primarily serves a function of differentiating products and services (as well as their makers and providers) and is

conceived to be used in a setting of commercial rivalry. However, traditional and indigenous communities do not engage in commercial rivalry with one another (except, as already said, in the case of handicrafts, which are of a combined commercial-cultural nature). One does not envisage the situation of a shaman who invents a new potion in order to new lure clients and divert those of other tribes' shamans to himself, as a pharmaceutical company does. Nor does one imagine a shaman suing the shaman of the neighboring tribe who somehow has acquired knowledge of that potion, on grounds of infringement. Eventually, such an acquisition by the latter shaman may have meant a cultural offense, but indigenous communities have other ways of solving those conflicts.
5. This proviso corresponds to Article 3.5 of the WIPO Treaty. The patent office will not take the initiative to verify whether the applicant has used protected GRs and/or TK to make the invention, but if an opposition or an appeal is submitted, then the patent office has to respond to the third party's intervention, through an *inter partes* proceeding.
6. The idea is to avoid that nongovernmental organizations and third parties, moved by purely political interests and other hidden agendas, on the false claim of protecting the rights of traditional communities, create unjustified obstacles and difficulties to the grant of patents for pharmaceutical and biotechnological inventions.
7. The suggestion here diverges from the solution for rectifications as provided by the WIPO Treaty on Intellectual Property, Genetic Resources and Associated Traditional Knowledge, in Article 5.2:

> *Subject to Article 5.2(bis), each Contracting Party shall provide an opportunity to rectify a failure to disclose the information required in Article 3 before implementing sanctions or directing remedies.*
>
> *A Contracting Party may exclude from the opportunity to rectify under Article 5.2 cases where there has been fraudulent conduct or intent as prescribed by national law.*

This paragraph assumes that the applicant is ready to make the rectification after some proceedings that may reveal that the absence of the relevant proof of authorized access is the result of fraud. However, the Treaty does not mention any pre-grant proceeding that may lead to such finding. Article 5.2 implies that the patent has been granted and that a court has identified the fraud. Then, as the Treaty goes, the patent holder would have his/her patent cancelled. But the point in the suggested language is that the applicant *sua sponte* wishes to amend or rectify the application. Where the applicant, spontaneously, offers to rectify the application, the concept of fraudulent intent should be automatically put aside.
8. Paragraph 5 addresses the topic of sanctions to be imposed on the patent owner who, in the prosecution of the patent, has failed to comply with the disclosure requirement. The WIPO Treaty on Intellectual Property, Genetic Resources and Associated Traditional Knowledge, in this regard, provides that:

> *5.3 Subject to Article 5.4, no Contracting Party shall revoke, invalidate, or render unenforceable the conferred patent rights solely on the basis of an applicant's failure to disclose the information specified in Article 3 of this Treaty.*
>
> *5.4 Each Contracting Party may provide for post grant sanctions or remedies where there has been fraudulent intent in regard to the disclosure requirement in Article 3 of this Treaty, in accordance with its national law.*

It is intriguing that the drafters of the WIPO Treaty have been bold enough to impose the disclosure requirement as a mandatory obligation for the Contracting Parties ("Where the claimed invention in a patent application is based on genetic resources, each Contracting Party *shall require* applicants to disclose . . . .") but, by contrast, have been so laconic in setting the sanctions for noncompliance. Apparently, paragraphs 3 and 4 of Article 5 seem to indicate that sanctions may only lead to the invalidation/cancelling/revocation of the patent when the patent owner has committed some fraudulent act:

- concerning either the acquisition of the GR in itself or in failing to disclose the origin of the GR of which he/she was aware during the prosecution of the patent; and/or
- concerning the manner in which he/she acquired the associated TK (e.g., by failing to inform the traditional community in question of the commercial objectives of the bio-prospection) or in failing to inform the origin of the associated TK.

It is obvious that the Treaty has been drafted in a careless manner, but one wonders: what happens when the patent owner has acquired some piece of TK and has used it to reach some technical solution that is inventive enough (and new) to justify the grant of a patent? If the patent owner has not requested express permission from the TK holder and has not informed the patent office about the source where he/she has obtained the piece of TK, he may have practiced an act of misappropriation, but not necessarily one of fraud. Fraud would take place if the patent owner had lied to the patent office (or to the TK holder). But simply omitting the information does not seem to consist in a fraud. Misappropriation is not synonymous with fraud. Thus, in that event, there would be no sanction against the patent owner, according to the WIPO Treaty. For a Treaty that is entitled (albeit in a misleading fashion) *WIPO Treaty on Intellectual Property, Genetic Resources and Associated Traditional Knowledge*, one should expect some provisions to be more effective in granting protection for TK holders.

In view of this, the suggested language goes beyond the WIPO Treaty and, without conflicting with it, proposes an array of sanctions that might give some effectiveness to the disclosure requirement.

2 SUBSTANTIVE REQUIREMENTS

2.1 Novelty; The Grace Period

The condition of novelty for inventions has been a feature of the patent system since its early origins, in the time of industrial privileges. As a matter of course, there has never been a justification in according to someone a legal favor to exclude others from using some technique that was in the public domain.[167] What might change was the scope of novelty; that is, the granting authority could well accord the favor to someone who introduced some technique that was new in the granting territory, regardless of whether that same piece of knowledge was known in other territories.

Historically, novelty as a condition of patentability was explained by the plaintiff's attorney in *Darcy v. Allen* (the King's Bench, 1603)—and the court agreed with that explanation. Criticizing the grant of a monopoly that would give to the defendant the exclusivity in the trade of making, importing and selling playing cards, which was already being exploited by several crafters and merchants, he said:

> This same (monopoly) leadeth to the empoverishing of divers Artificers and others, who before by labor of their hands in their Art or Trade had kept themselves and their families, who now of necessity shall be constrained to live in idleness and beggary; [...]. And the Common Law in this point agreeth with the

167. It was the grant of this sort of abusive industrial and commercial privileges by the British crown that led to the Parliament's reaction and the enacting of the Statute of Monopolies, in 1623.

> equity of the Law of God, as appeareth in Deut. cap. xxiv. ver. 6, *Non accipies loco pignorisinferiorem et superioremmolam, quiaanimamsuamapposuittibi*; You shall not take in pledg the neathet and upper millstone, for the same is his life; by which it appeareth, That every mans Trade doth maintains his life, and therefore he ought not to be deprived or dispossessed of it, no more than of his life.[168]

It follows that the grant of patents should not interfere with the freedom of work of those that were established in the market before the application. This was true in 1603, and still is today.

Novelty can take a number of forms. It may be absolute as to territory or it may be local. It may be absolute as to time or it may be relative (i.e., only disclosure made from a certain date forward destroys novelty). Novelty may also be of a technical or a commercial nature, as noted above. Today, although the TRIPS Agreement, in Article 27.1, does not qualify novelty, the common practice is to require that inventions be absolutely new, as regards both the territory and the time of disclosure. Utility models and patents for inventions follow the rule of technical novelty, whereas plant variety certificates obey commercial novelty.

But the condition of novelty, as absolute as it may be, admits three exceptions: priority (Article 4(B) of the Paris Convention), disclosure at official or officially recognized exhibitions (Paris Convention, Article 11), and the grace period.

As far as the right of priority is concerned, the lawmaker has no options or flexibilities to seek: priority is firmly grounded on the Paris Convention since its first version of 1883, as a mechanism that facilitates the access of inventors to protection in other countries without losing the benefit of novelty. The Paris Convention, in subsequent versions, has dealt with subsidiary aspects of priority, namely those that concern the formalities necessary to prove the right to priority and the consequences of the abandonment of an application that has not been published.

On the consequences of disclosure of the invention at official or officially recognized exhibitions, the national lawmaker does not have much leeway either. Such an exception to novelty is a well-settled matter—and served, actually, as the core reason for the triggering of the negotiations that led to the Paris Convention, in view of the fear of U.S. inventors that, if they disclosed their inventions at the international exhibitions that were organized in Europe in the second half of the nineteenth century, without any sort of protection, they would lose the possibility of seeking patent protection outside the United States.

By contrast, when it comes to the grace period, the national lawmaker cannot rely on international guidance for clarity. Indeed, national laws diverge as regards two elements: the duration of the grace period and the causes that may trigger it.

The grace period is the time span that precedes the filing of a patent application during which the disclosure of the invention under certain circumstances does not prejudice its novelty and nonobviousness, such as disclosure by the inventor or his/her successor or by a third person without the permission of the inventor. The grace period is of special interest to individual inventors and small companies, which do not need to

168. Steve Sheppard (ed.), THE SELECTED WRITINGS AND SPEECHES OF SIR EDWARD COKE, vol. 3, at 400 (Liberty Fund, 2003), available at <oll.libertyfund.org> [access August 2025].

fear the imprudent or uninformed disclosure of inventions by collaborators that are in the making or being tested. The grace period is also of relevance to universities and other academic institutions, whose inventors frequently have an urgency in publishing their findings. The grace period is, however, an exception to the fundamental condition of novelty and therefore should be treated carefully.

In reality, the grace period can be seen as an expansion of the exception to novelty provided by Article 11 of the Paris Convention. That exception was of enormous importance in the nineteenth century—an era when businesses in general participated in national and international exhibitions, some of them of large dimensions, to publicize and advertise their articles.

By admitting that inventions be disclosed by the inventor, or his/her successors, without losing novelty for a certain period, the grace period encompasses the exhibition-related exception to novelty. The difference is that the latter is not precisely defined in the law: it applies while the exhibition takes place, provided that, in the case of international applications, it does not go beyond one year (given that the exhibition-related exception cannot extend the periods of priority). In order that the impossibility of cumulation of priority with the exhibition-related exception be indisputable, Article 11 of the Paris Convention adds that "if, later, the right of priority is invoked, the authorities of any country may provide that the period shall start from the date of the introduction of the goods into the exhibition." The employment of the term "may" suggests that national lawmakers may be more tolerant and add the regular period of priority to the previously acknowledged temporary protection, but the phrase "Such temporary protection shall not extend the periods provided by Article 4" strongly indicates otherwise.

One might find here a sort of contradiction. But there is not. What cannot be extended is the right of priority, i.e., the period in which the applicant may file in other countries without losing novelty. But there is nothing against extending the protection of inventors against certain sorts of disclosure. Such an extension, however, shall not expand the period in which he/she can file abroad and still claim priority.

An example:

- an inventor introduces his/her invention at an officially recognized exhibition;
- the exhibition keeps its doors open for nine months;
- as soon as the exhibition ends, the inventor files a patent application;
- the inventor has twelve months from the date of his/her application to file in other Members of the Paris Union (and of the WTO); i.e., he/she may claim priority in other countries until twenty-one months after he/she disclosed the invention.

It is here that the inventor's problems start. If the exhibition is of a purely national dimension, in other countries, patent examiners may find that the disclosure of the invention has occurred outside the period of priority, and therefore it has lost novelty. But if the exhibition is of an international dimension, which means that it has been officially recognized by a multitude of countries, in those countries, depending on national law, the exhibition-related exception may add to the priority. But a caveat is of crucial importance here: *depending on national law*. Indeed, some national laws make the grace period (which, in practice, has replaced the exhibition-related exception) count for six months only. Some national laws also make the duration of the grace period depend on the filing date, not the priority date. In both cases, the invention that the inventor had disclosed at that exhibition would have lost its novelty.

The grace period has been part of the patent law in many countries for several decades. Section 114 of the already mentioned WIPO Model Law for Developing Countries on Inventions, for example, provides for that exception to novelty. The period is limited to one year before the filing date, and the causes that trigger the exception are the same two that were mentioned above:

> *(3) A disclosure to the public of the invention shall not be taken into consideration with regard to the patent application referred to in subsection (2)(a) if it occurred within one year preceding the date at which the applicant filed that application and if it was by reason or in consequence of acts committed by the applicant or his predecessor in title;*
>
> *(4) A disclosure to the public of the invention shall not be taken into consideration with regard to the patent application referred to in subsection (2)(a) if it occurred within one year preceding the date at which the applicant filed that application and if it was by reason or in consequence of an abuse committed with regard to the applicant or his predecessor in title.*

In the commentary to the text above, the WIPO Secretariat has emphasized the particular relevance of the grace period for developing countries:

> Such a period of grace is of particular interest for a developing country since it is not always to be expected that the nationals of such countries will be fully aware at the time of making an invention of the importance of keeping it secret until a patent application is filed. The period of grace therefore enables them to avoid the loss of their rights through sheer inexperience.[169]

A few years later, in 1986, the WIPO Secretariat proposed to insert the grace period in international law by launching discussions on a draft Treaty Supplementing the Paris Convention as far as Patents are Concerned.[170] The language of the draft Treaty concerning the grace period was as follows:

169. *Ibid.*, at 60.
170. The main aim of the Secretariat's proposal of the draft Treaty was to introduce a provision concerning the grace period. That specific and limited proposal was later broadened, and the proposed Treaty encompassed several other substantive aspects of patent law, such as disclosure and description of inventions, the right to a patent, fields of technology, conditions of patentability, the rights conferred by the patent, and the reversal of the burden of proof, among other provisions. In fact, the draft Treaty anticipated several topics that the TRIPS Agreement would later cover. It was the opposition that developing countries raised against both the revision of the Paris Convention and the adoption of higher standards of patent protection within WIPO that led to the suspension of negotiations on the draft Treaty, in 1991, at The Hague. In parallel, developed countries, led by the United States, the European Communities, Canada, and Japan (known collectively as the "Quad"), by offering commercial favors in the areas of tariffs and phytosanitary measures to developing countries, were able to include the same proposed substantive standards of IP protection in the Uruguay Round, thus leading to the subsequent approval of the TRIPS Agreement.

Article 12

Disclosures Not Affecting Patentability (Grace Period)
(1) [Circumstances of Disclosure Not Affecting Patentability]

Disclosure of information which otherwise would affect the patentability of an invention claimed in the application shall not affect the patentability of that invention where the information was disclosed, during the 12 months preceding the filing date or, where priority is claimed, the priority date of the application,

(i) by the inventor,
(ii) by an Office and the information was contained
(a) in another application filed by the inventor and should not have been disclosed by the Office, or
(b) in an application filed without the knowledge or consent of the inventor by a third party which obtained the information direct or indirectly from the inventor,
(iii) by a third party which obtained the information direct or indirectly from the inventor. . .

This language, almost *ipsis verbis*, was inserted into the draft SPLT, with an important change: where the provision of the draft Treaty Supplementing the Paris Convention reads "during the 12 months," the draft SPLT reads "during the [12][six] months." The options between square brackets express a major split among those WIPO Member States that have introduced the grace period into their patent laws. Actually, the way the period of grace is reflected in national patent laws follows more than one line of divergence. Laws diverge not only as regards the period's length but also as regards how it is counted (whether until the priority date, or until the filing date, or until both) and in relation to the motives that trigger the period.

Table 1 gives us a good illustration of these divergences.

Table 1 Provisions Dealing with the Grace Period

					Early Disclosure Caused By		
Country	*6 Months*	*12 Months*	*Priority Date*	*Filing Date*	*The Inventor*	*A Third Party, Abusively*	*A Patent Office, Unduly*
Algeria[171]		x	x	x	x	x	
Andean Community		x	x	x	x	x	x
Barbados[172]		x	x	x	x	x	

171. Ordinance No. 03-07 of 19 Joumada El Oula 1424 corresponding to July 19, 2003, on Patents.
172. Patents Act, Chapter 314 (Act 2001-18, as amended by Act 2006-2).

					Early Disclosure Caused By		
Country	*6 Months*	*12 Months*	*Priority Date*	*Filing Date*	*The Inventor*	*A Third Party, Abusively*	*A Patent Office, Unduly*
Brazil		x	x	x	x	x	[the national patent office, only]
China	x			x	- in case of public interest; - int'l exhibition; - academic or technological conference	x	
Indonesia	x	x		x	- nat'l or int'l exhibition; - use for research and experimentation; - academic publication	x	
Kenya[173]		x	x	x	x	x	
Nigeria[174]	x			x	int'l exhibition		
Oman		x	x	x	x	x	

173. Industrial Property Act, 2001 (Act No. 3 of 2001, as amended up to Act No. 11 of 2017).
174. Patents and Designs Act (Chapter 344).

					Early Disclosure Caused By		
Country	*6 Months*	*12 Months*	*Priority Date*	*Filing Date*	*The Inventor*	*A Third Party, Abusively*	*A Patent Office, Unduly*
Panama[175]		x	x	x	x	x	
Philippines		x	x	x	x	X [but no reference to abuse]	x

The patent law of Indonesia makes a clear distinction between the disclosure of the invention by the inventor(s) and by third parties, abusively. In the first case, the grace period has a six-month duration. In the second case, a twelve-month duration. The law of Indonesia, very wisely, aims at ensuring special protection for inventors against abuses.

Another interesting aspect concerning the grace period is found in the law of Mozambique, as follows:

> *Article 37*
>
> *Invention not devoid of novelty*
>
> 1. *An invention shall not be considered as forming part of art if it was disclosed during the twelve months preceding the filing date or the priority date of the patent application, in the following circumstances:*
>   (a) *Where the disclosure of the invention was promoted by the inventor or his successors in title, to professional or scientific institutions or publications, in competitions at exhibitions or trade fairs which are official or officially recognized by the government;*
>   (b) *Where the disclosure was a result from an obvious[ly] abusive act by third parties against the inventor or his successors in title.*
> 2. *In the case of paragraph (a) above, the inventor shall, at the time of filing the application, declare in writing that the invention was actually disclosed or published and shall provide evidence of this fact within three months from the filing date.*

This is indeed a simple measure that may avoid complex debates in the course of the examination: preventively, the applicant claims his/her entitlement to the grace period exception in view of his/her early disclosure of the invention. Actually, the law of Mozambique could have gone further and include as one of the exception's triggering factors the use of the invention by the inventor with a view to experimenting with it. It is true that it may be difficult to distinguish commercial use from experimental use, but the lawmaker should have taken the risk of mentioning the latter, for the sake of permitting the invention to reach the market earlier.

175. Law No. 35 of May 10, 1996, on Industrial Property.

2.1.a Dos and Don'ts

As proposed by the WIPO Model Law and reflected in many national statutes, linking the duration of the grace period to the date of filing of the patent application does not make much sense as far as international applications are concerned. In fact, the priority exception would absorb the grace period. Thus, in order to make the grace period of some value, it should be linked to the date of priority—in the case of international applications that claim it—or to the filing date—in the case of national applications. But the duration of the grace period should be one year. It is unfortunate that, due to the lack of international harmonization, national patent laws adopt different periods for the grace period, which introduces inconsistency in the international system, to which the mechanism of priority is intended to facilitate an easier access. By adopting the grace period of one year, the national lawmaker will make the national patent system consistent with those foreign systems that adopt similar periods and still make it compatible with those that admit periods of six months only.

Moreover, the causes for adopting the period of grace should be confined to the two that were mentioned in the initial proposal by the WIPO Model Law: disclosure (inadvertently or deliberately) by the inventor or his/her successors; and abusive (or unauthorized) disclosure by a third party. In the first case, as mentioned by the WIPO Secretariat, the lawmaker will be respecting the particular circumstances that surround individual inventors and small firms in developing countries (and some developed countries too), who are usually unaware of the need for keeping the inventions secret before bringing them to the patent office. In the second case, the lawmaker is protecting the legitimate interests of inventors, both small and large ones, who should not be prejudiced in their plans to file for patent applications.

It does not make much sense to include the undue disclosure of some invention by the patent office (either national or of a foreign country or region) as a trigger of the grace period. The reason is that such an exception diverges entirely from the fundamental purpose of the grace period, which is protecting small, inadvertent inventors. A mistaken publication by a patent office does not relate to the particular nature of a given inventor. Neither does the publication of a patent application abusively filed by a third party have any correlation with the idea of protecting small inventors. Moreover, it is not usual for patent offices to publish patent applications in such a short period as the grace period implies.

2.2 Nonobviousness (Sufficient Inventive Step)

On the condition of the inventive step, given that the matter is reasonably harmonized in the laws of developed and developing countries alike, there is not much to recommend as regards the implementation of public policies.

However, two points should be made.

First, if the lawmaker cares about precision in language, he/should not limit the law to requiring that the invention be new, nonobvious (or inventive) and useful. The reason is that in such (common) formulation lies a redundancy: an invention may not be new because a reinvented technical solution continues being an invention for all purposes; an invention may also lack utility if it is purely abstract and/or if, in practice, it proves to be of low efficiency, but there is no invention that is not the result of a certain level of inventiveness. This is an idea that the WIPO Secretariat stated in one of its most thought-provoking papers, which was submitted in 2003 to the IGC. The particular excerpt in that regard reads as follows:

> To some extent, it could be argued that these criteria [novelty, non-obviousness and utility] are overlapping with the inherent notion of "invention." However, it is possible for an invention, so defined, to fail to meet the criteria, for instance for want of novelty or utility. The reverse engineering of a technique that the emulator ignored had been previously disclosed is an invention, in spite of not being new. The only criterion that is actually overlapping with the notion of "invention" is non-obviousness. There are no obvious inventions. But there are inventions that are more inventive than others. In other words, in contrast with the two other criteria, non-obviousness is a relative one. Patentability depends on the amount of level of inventiveness. If correctly worded, a statutory provision on patentability should actually read: "patents shall be available for any invention provided that it is new, *involves a sufficient inventive step* and is useful."[176]

The second recommendation was stated above: in designating a (relatively) objective threshold for the condition of nonobviousness, the lawmaker should not use the same notion of a person skilled in the art that was suggested above in the context of the enabling disclosure. Otherwise, developing countries, and, in particular, those countries less developed technologically could be flooded with international patent applications that, in their countries of origin, would not meet the patentability conditions, for reasons of insufficiency in inventiveness. In this regard, it is more prudent for national lawmakers to be strict, and not permit technical ideas that are freely available in countries of higher economic level to be of exclusive use in the territory of their countries:

> *Article ... Patentability*
>
> 1. *An invention is patentable if it is new, involves a sufficiently inventive step and is industrially applicable.*
>
> ...
>
> 2. *An invention shall be considered as involving a sufficiently inventive step if it would not have been obvious to a person skilled in the art at the filing date or at priority date of the claimed invention.*
>   (a) *The provisions of paragraph 2 of Article . . . [on Enabling Disclosure]*[177] *shall not apply for the purposes of assessing compliance with the condition of the sufficiently inventive activity.*

The effect of proviso (a) is to restore, for the purposes of assessing nonobviousness, the notion of the person skilled in the art that is applied generally by patent examiners (and court experts) around the world—that of an ideal technical person with

176. *See Composite Study on the Protection of Traditional Knowledge,* Intergovernmental Committee on Intellectual Property and Genetic Resources, Traditional Knowledge and Folklore, Fifth Session, Geneva, July 7 to 15, 2003, WIPO/GRTKF/IC/5/8, April 28, 2003, at 19 (note 48).
177. *See supra* note 150 and accompanying text.

a level of technical knowledge that corresponds to a global or regional standard, as opposed to a strictly national level. The assessment of nonobviousness is always of a subjective nature, and patent examiners will tend to use their own knowledge and experience as a standard. Given the professional experience that is required from examiners and the intense technical training they are usually submitted (often through international programs), patent examiners will finish by having technical skills that are higher than those of the average technical person in their country. For the purposes of assessing nonobviousness, patent examiners should not be expected to lower the standard of normal skills below their own.

CHAPTER 5
Amending the Application

1 AMENDMENTS BY THE APPLICANT'S INITIATIVE

In the prosecution of patents, inventors and society seek to secure the protection of two major values: legal security and predictability.

As far as the inventor's perspective of those two values is concerned, he/she is (or should be) the first to be interested in obtaining a title of property that is able to resist to challenges by third parties and is enforceable in a relatively straightforward manner—this meaning that the claims are of easy reading and understanding (and interpretation) by judges and court experts.

But as far as society's expectation of security and predictability is concerned, two dimensions must be considered: one is the same that concerns the inventor himself/herself—the patent should be of *good quality*, with claims well defined; the other dimension is related to the interests of third parties by and large, such as other inventors and researchers, as well as potential users of the claimed invention. The rights granted by the patent, like those that result from a property deed, are confined to the matter that appears in the claims. So, once the application is published, third parties acquire knowledge of what they can and cannot do as regards the use of the invention, either for commercial purposes or for the other purposes accepted by the patent statute as exceptions to rights granted, such as use for experimental purposes or use for anticipating the obtaining of marketing approval in the cases of regulated products and processes.

It is here that one particular element that is usually found in patent laws, of both developing and developed countries, can generate difficulties. That element can be associated with amending, correcting or complementing the various components of the application, in particular the claims, either directly or through continuation patent applications, or as a result of the division of the patent application. Third parties who have noticed the filing of a certain patent application may be later taken by surprise with an expansion of the scope of the claims. One who sees advantage in that the lawmaker is permissive with the amendment of claims could say that third parties should wait for the patent to be granted before embarking on the use of the invention. But an opponent would have a good argument that third parties should not wait that long, and that the date on which the application is published should operate as a watershed. Unclaimed matter should be deemed, from a specific date on (i.e., the date of publication) as public domain matter.

This discussion covers four sorts of amendments that the applicant may wish to introduce in the application:

(i) corrections of factual errors;
(ii) amendments to the claims in order to clarify their meaning and scope;
(iii) changes in the scope of the claims with the intention of reducing the claimed matter; and
(iv) changes in the scope of the claims with the intention of expanding the claimed matter; this last variety of amendments has two sub-types:
  (1) the changes expand the claims by including matter that *has been* disclosed in the specifications but has not been claimed;
  (2) the changes expand the claims by including new matter that *has not been* disclosed in the specifications, either because of an omission by the applicant or because he/she made some additional findings/ improvements after the patent was filed (and before it was granted).

An additional aspect of the amendments is that they may, eventually, be submitted to the patent office *after* the patent is granted. In general, those amendments are acceptable only when they cover obvious mistakes or clerical errors—hence, without any substantive effect on the scope of exclusivity—or when they aim at reducing the scope of protection. This is the solution proposed by the WIPO Model Law, as follows:

Article 17

Changes in Patents

(1) [Limitation of Extent of Protection] The owner of a patent shall have the right to request the competent Office to make changes in the patent in order to limit the extent of the protection conferred by it.

(2) [Obvious Mistakes and Clerical Errors] The owner of a patent shall have the right to request the competent Office to make changes in the patent in order to correct obvious mistakes or to correct clerical errors.

(3) [Additional Changes That May Be Allowed] Each Contracting Party may provide that the owner of a patent shall have the right to request the competent Office to make changes in the patent in order to correct mistakes or errors, other than those referred to in paragraph (2), made in good faith, provided that, where the change would result in a broadening of the extent of protection conferred by the patent, no request may be made after the expiration of two years from the grant of the patent and the change shall not affect the rights of any third party which has relied on the patent as published.

(4) [Changes Affecting the Disclosure] No change in the patent shall be permitted under paragraphs (1) or (3) where the change would result in the disclosure contained in the patent going beyond the disclosure contained in the application as filed.

Today, the idea of making post-grant amendments to patents (except for those that are mentioned in the WIPO Model Law) has been put aside in most countries. The legal insecurity that might result from introducing changes to claims of already granted patents, albeit of a minor nature, would be unacceptable. At most, one could admit the patent to be revised as far as clerical errors or typos are concerned, given that they help make the patent more exact, and thus serve better its purpose of serving as a tool of technological teaching. Where the WIPO Model Law refers to "mistakes or errors, other than [obvious mistakes and clerical errors]," it is pointing to substantive components of the patent. The solution, where that occurs, should be the invalidation of the claims concerned, not their amendment. After all, we are dealing here with patents granted that are already producing exclusionary effects.

In addition to the correction of clerical mistakes and typos—which does not produce results of material relevance—amendments to patents should not go beyond those aiming at reducing the claims. By releasing claimed matter to the public domain, by sharp contrast with expanding that matter, the patent owner is not creating legal insecurity to third parties.

Anyway, as said, most national laws do not accept the amendments to patents unless as a consequence of lawsuits challenging their validity that result in cancelling one or more claims, or parts thereof.

So, what about amendments to patent *applications*? How far should the inventor be allowed to go? Obviously, the modalities mentioned in provisos (i) to (iii) should be accepted by the lawmaker. They contribute to clarifying the meaning of the claims and of the disclosed matter as a whole. But when it comes to the two sub-types of amendments mentioned in proviso (iv), the solution should be different.

The idea of allowing the inventor to amend the patent application by including in the claims inventive matter that he/she had disclosed either in the description or in the drawings but had failed to claim is not of mandatory obeyance under the fundamental rationale of the patent system. Such failure could be seen by the lawmaker as a punishment to the naïf or negligent inventor who has failed to hire a competent attorney.

But the truth is that, for the sake of the *in dubio pro inventore* principle, lawmakers tend to be tolerant with those failures, provided that the matter to be added to the application (hence, to the claims) does not go beyond what has been disclosed in the application as a whole (this meaning, the description, the claims, the drawings, if any, and the abstract). This is the general practice, actually.

Another question that amendments may raise concerns the opportunity for their submission during the course of the prosecution. When should patent applicants be allowed to submit requests for amending the specifications, or elements thereof?

The answers to these various questions have to do with those basic values mentioned above, which consist of ensuring security and predictability, both for the inventor and for society as a whole. The inventor naturally wishes that the patent, once granted, be free of mistakes and ambiguities—patents are made of human language, lest we forget—that later might create difficulties and barriers against their licensing, assignment or enforcement. And society does not want the leeway attributed to amendments in patent applications (and patents) to become a problem of competition and an obstacle against technical improvements.

Let us now have a brief, schematic look at a number of different avenues that a few national laws and international agreements have followed as regards amendments filed by the applicant's initiative. As a matter of course, amendments introduced in response to actions by the patent examiner or in the course of infringement or of invalidation proceedings are not discussed here. The reason is that when the applicant responds to the patent examiner or to the court, he/she is limited in making the amendments in pursuance of the requests he/she has received. The applicant has no choice.

Table 2 Amendments to the Patent Application Introduced by the Applicant's (or Patentee's) Own Initiative

Country	*Purpose*	*Opportunity*	*Limitations*
Brazil	Better clarification or definition of the application	Until the examination request	The amendments shall not go beyond the matter disclosed in the initial application.
China	Not defined[178]	Not defined	The amendments may not go beyond the scope of disclosure contained in the original description and claims.
Cook Islands[179]	The applicant or patentee shall state the nature of the proposed amendment and shall give full particulars of the reasons for which the application is made.	*After the acceptance of the complete specification*, only disclaimers, corrections, or explanations shall be accepted; no new claims about matter not in substance disclosed or that does not fall wholly within the specification or the scope of a claim, before the amendment.	No amendments during infringement procedures

178. Where Table 2 mentions "Not defined," the reference is exclusively to the statute. Where the statute is silent, these matters may also be covered by regulations and/or administrative orders, which have not been examined for the purposes of this book.
179. Act No. 64 of 1953.

Country	*Purpose*	*Opportunity*	*Limitations*
Fiji Islands[180]	The applicant shall state the nature of the proposed amendment; give full particulars of the reasons for the request; and observe the prescribed manner (if any).	*Before the acceptance* of the complete specifications *After the acceptance* of the complete specifications	*After the acceptance of complete specifications*: amendments shall not claim or describe matter that was not in substance disclosed in the specification before the amendment; or claim matter that would not fall wholly within the scope of a claim of the specification before the amendment. This does not apply to amendments for the purpose of correcting an obvious mistake made in, or in relation to, a complete specification. *After the date of the publication of the accepted complete specification*: the right of the patentee or applicant to make the amendment must not be called into question except on the ground of fraud; the amendment must be treated as forming part of the specification.
Saudi Arabia	Not defined	Not defined	The amendments shall not change what was disclosed in the original application.

180. Patents Act 2021 (Act No. 37 of 2021).

Country	*Purpose*	*Opportunity*	*Limitations*
South Africa	It is up to the applicant to set out the nature of the proposed amendment and furnish his full reasons therefor.	Before or after the grant.	If the amendment of a provisional specification aims at correcting the application, it shall be authorized. The amendment to a provisional specification[181] (and, *mutatis mutandis*, to a complete specification) shall not introduce new matter or matter not in substance disclosed in the specification. Third parties may oppose the amendment if the specification is open to inspection.
WIPO Model Law	Not defined	Not defined	The amendments shall not go beyond the disclosure in the initial application.
Draft Treaty Supple-menting the Paris Conven-tion	*Before the grant*: not defined. *After the grant*: limitation of the extension of protection; correction of obvious mistakes and clerical errors; correction of	*Before the grant*: up to the time when the application is in order for grant; in those countries that provide for substantive examination, the law may permit amendments only up to the time allowed for the reply to the first substantive communication from the Office.	*Before the grant*: no amendment or correction of the application may go beyond what has been disclosed in the application as filed. *After the grant*: changes made in patents shall not affect the rights of any third party which has relied

181. Provisional specifications correspond to inventions that are still being finalized or tested. They must be replaced by complete specifications within twelve months. The system of provisional specifications, that is common to a number of common law countries, corresponds to the mechanism that in other countries is designated as provisional applications or provisional protection. *See supra*, Chapter 2, section 2.

Country	Purpose	Opportunity	Limitations
	other mistakes and errors made in good faith.	*After the grant*: the request for corrections of other mistakes and errors in patents made in good faith can be made within two years from the grant.	on the patent as published; changes shall not cause the disclosure contained in the patent, going beyond the disclosure contained in the application as filed.
SPLT[182]	As regards the application, the purpose is not defined. Amendments or corrections to the patent have the purpose of limiting the extent of the protection conferred by it.	At any time (before or after the grant)	*Before the grant*: no amendment or correction of the description, the claims [the abstract] and any drawings, other than the correction of a clear mistake, may be permitted, where the amendment or correction would result in the disclosure contained in the amended or corrected application going beyond the disclosure. *After the grant*: no amendment or correction in a patent may be permitted where the amendment or correction would result in the disclosure contained in the amended or corrected patent going beyond the disclosure (including the description, the claims and any drawings).

182. The records of the latest version of the draft SPLT, with a large number of strikethroughs and square brackets, reveal that the topic of amendments submitted by the applicant's initiative was the subject of strong dissent among WIPO Member States.

Country	*Purpose*	*Opportunity*	*Limitations*
TRIPS Agreement, Article 70.4	To claim enhanced protection provided in the TRIPS Agreement for pending patent applications	At any time before the grant of the pending patent applications	Amendments shall not include new matter (i.e., amendments can include matter that existed at the time of the filing (or of priority) but which had not been included in the application).[183]

In addition to the examples included in Table 2, it is worth mentioning the provisions of the PCT concerning amendments introduced by the applicant. The PCT refers to amendments that can be submitted by the applicant in four different phases:

(i) amendments (to the claims only) submitted before the International Bureau; these amendments can be submitted within two months from the date of transmittal of the international search report to the International Bureau and to the applicant by the International Searching Authority or sixteen months from the priority date, whichever time limit expires later (Rule 46.1);
(ii) amendments to the application submitted to the International Preliminary Examination Authority; these amendments may be submitted at the time of filing the demand or until the international preliminary examination report is established;
(iii) amendments to the application (i.e., to the description, the claims, and the drawings) submitted to the designated office (i.e., the national or regional office designated by the applicant in the international phase, under Chapter I of the PCT); and
(iv) amendments to the application submitted to each elected office, i.e., the national or regional office elected by the application under Chapter II of the PCT.

Amendments under the PCT shall not go beyond the disclosure in the international application as filed, unless the national law of the designated or elected States permits them to go beyond the disclosure. In cases (iii) and (iv), time limits and formalities are those established by national laws. However, the elected or designated office shall grant a patent, or refuse the grant of a patent, before such time limits have expired, except with the express consent of the applicant.

183. The amendments admitted by Art. 70.4 of the TRIPS Agreement were of a different nature: they were of a transitional nature and were aimed at compensating the inventors in those sectors that were excluded from patentability before the Agreement applied to Members. For example, in a WTO Member that, before the TRIPS Agreement applied to it, excluded pharmaceutical products from patentability, but admitted the patentability of the processes for making them, the inventor who had previously applied for a patent for the process could amend the application and include the product obtained through that process, provided that product had already been invented and publicly disclosed at the time of the filing of the application.

2 CONTINUATION AND CONTINUATION-IN-PART APPLICATIONS

Continuation and continuation-in-part applications are part of U.S. patent law and practice. The former consists of a second application repeating a previous one, which is still pending, with amendments. Continuation applications are the equivalent of amendments to the original applications.[184] Continuation-in-part applications are those that, besides repeating, at least in a significant portion, the original patent application, still pending, add new elements not previously disclosed and/or claimed in the parent application. In other countries, continuation-in-part applications are known as patents of addition, when they add new inventive matter to a previous patent, but which is not sufficiently inventive to deserve an independent new application.

The matter of relevance in continuation-in-part applications as well as in patents of addition is to secure the original filing date (and, consequently, the priority date). The explanation is that newly added subject matter, if it were sufficiently inventive, would be the subject matter of a new patent application, with its specific filing and priority date. But because the invention remains, ultimately, the same, the filing date does not change.

3 AMENDMENTS SUBMITTED IN RESPONSE TO THE PATENT EXAMINER'S ACTION, OR AS A CONSEQUENCE OF THE DIVISION OF APPLICATIONS, OR IN THE COURSE OF INVALIDATION PROCEEDINGS

Until now, we have dealt with amendments submitted by the applicant's initiative. But amendments may also occur: (i) during the course of examination proceedings, when the patent examiner calls the applicant's attention to eventual errors, or ambiguities; (ii) as a result of the division of the application, as a consequence of the failure to comply with the rule of unity of invention (when new claims need to be drafted for each of the new applications, which may entail changes to the manner in which the original invention is claimed); or (iii) in the context of invalidation proceedings, when the court may allow the patentee to amend the patent (by rephrasing the specifications or by reducing the claims).

In no event may those amendments lead to the expansion of the claimed matter, even when made under the supervision of the court. The reason for that is the same that was provided before: third parties have created certain expectations in taking knowledge of the application at the time of its publication and may have started using unclaimed matter based on those legitimate expectations; they should not be taken by surprise, therefore, with the subsequent expansion of the claims.

184. *See* J. Thomas McCarthy et alii, McCarthy's Desk Encyclopedia of Intellectual Property, at 106 (3rd ed., BNA, 2004).

4 *DOS AND DON'TS*

Coming back to this chapter's starting point, the lawmaker, in addressing amendments submitted by the initiative of the applicant, should be careful in not destroying the delicate balance between the private interests of the inventor and society's collective interest. Amendments are useful for the purpose of clarifying the future patent document and, eventually, of reducing the scope of the claimed invention when the inventor finds out, upon practicing the invention, that some elements are not relevant (or even inconvenient) upon experimenting and/or exploiting it for commercial purposes. This sort of amendments has no consequences upon the market, other than those that result from a better-drafted title. But amendments may lead—and, in practice, tend to lead—to an expansion of the disclosed (and, more specifically, of the claimed) matter, which may have serious consequences upon third parties, such as researchers interested in using the claimed invention for scientific purposes and entrepreneurs who, as it happens frequently, follow the patenting activities of their competitors in search of opportunities given by disclosed but unclaimed technologies.

In this second case, those third parties should be entitled to believe that, in claiming only part of the described invention, the applicant was indirectly or impliedly waiving the right to claim ownership in the unclaimed elements of that invention.

It is therefore recommended that the applicant should only expand the claims to matter not claimed but described before the publication or before the disclosure of the invention by any means. After either of those moments, any amendments should be restricted to the claimed matter:

Article … Amendments to the application

1. *The application may be amended in order to correct errors and mistakes or clarify the manner in which the invention is described and claimed.* [1]
2. *Up to the publication of the application by the patent office, or by the applicant, or by a third party, with or without his/her consent, the applicant may amend the application, provided the amendments do not go beyond the matter that is disclosed in the description, the claims or the drawings.* [2]
3. *After the publication of the application, as per paragraph 2, and up to the moment the decision to grant the patent is notified through the official gazette, the applicant may still introduce amendments, provided they shall not go beyond the matter claimed in the initial application.* [3]
4. *Any amendments introduced in the course of the examination or any applications resulting of the division of the application into two or more applications, shall not go beyond the matter disclosed in the original application as of the date of its publication. Each divisional application shall be entitled to the filing date and the priority date of the initial application.*[4]
5. *Amendments to the patent shall be limited to the purpose of correcting obvious mistakes and clerical errors, and in no way should they expand the subject matter as claimed at the date of the publication of the corresponding application.*[5]
6. Amendments with the purpose of reducing the scope of the disclosed or claimed invention may be submitted at any time between the filing date of the original application and the date of expiry of the corresponding patent or patents.

Notes:

1. The spirit of the language provided is to limit amendments. They should be accepted only with the purpose of contributing to making the patent clearer and free of mistakes.
2. In the case, the contents of the patent application have not yet become publicly known, the applicant is allowed to expand the claims but not beyond the matter that has been disclosed in the description, the claims and the drawings of the initial application. If the applicant described an invention that is broader in scope than the invention that appears in the claims, he/she will have the opportunity to expand the claims so as to cover that unclaimed matter. But that it will be his/her last window of opportunity to expand the claims. For the purposes of the publication, it does not matter who has caused it. What matters is that the application has been published and third parties have acquired knowledge of the scope of the claimed invention.
3. Once the application has been published, and up to the moment the decision to grant the patent is published in the official gazette, the applicant may still amend the application, but he may no longer expand the claims. The suggested language refers to the "moment the decision to grant the patent is notified through the official gazette," instead of the more common term "up to the time when the application is in order for grant," which is found in several national patent laws. The reason of the choice of language is that the applicant does not know the exact date when the application is in order for grant. That date is known to the patent examiner only when he/she closes the file and gives his/her approval to the application. The applicant becomes aware of the favorable decision only when he/she is notified of the decision to grant.
4. Paragraphs 2 and 3 concern amendments made by the applicant's initiative. Paragraph 4 concerns amendments made either at the request of the examiner or by the applicant in response to the examiner's action.
5. Paragraph 5 deals with amendments to the patent, as granted. No expansion of the claimed invention is allowed, taking the application at the date of the application's publication as reference.

CHAPTER 6

Pre-grant and Post-grant Challenges, Third-Party Observations, Invalidation, Revocation

The possibility of third parties having something to say as regards the prosecution of patent applications (either before or after the grant) has been a topic of debate for many years. Two opposite arguments are at stake here. On the one hand, there is the voice of those who maintain that the patent office (this meaning the patent examiner, in a first phase, and the board of appeals, in a second moment) should be assisted in their complex task of examining the patentability of the claimed invention. Interested third parties can be in possession of elements that are not easily accessible to the examiner, in particular when those third parties are competitors of the applicant and are well acquainted with the practice in the industry. Moreover, patents subject to the scrutiny of third parties (even when such scrutiny does not lead to any action) tend to be more secure, i.e., less prone to being challenged in invalidation proceedings—which shall be available anyway, both in direct lawsuits or as a defense against infringement allegations.

On the other hand, there is the position of those who defend that the prosecution of a patent application is already complex enough, and that the examiner, particularly that one who works in the framework of one or more PPH arrangements, has already enough tools that allow him/her to issue a correct, well-based final decision. That reduces the risks of patents being wrongly granted. Nevertheless, if the patent is wrongly granted, third parties will always have the possibility of seeking its invalidation in court.

Statutes provide for a relatively vast array of possibilities for third parties to contribute with subsidies and comments so as to assist patent offices. Some of those possibilities entail ex parte proceedings, such as pre-grant oppositions (which can be filed immediately after the application is published, or after the examination is requested, but, in any event, before the decision to grant the patent is notified through the official gazette) and appeals against the decision to grant. They are ex parte because both the opponent/appellant and the applicant are heard by the patent office, under the due process of law. Also, ex parte are invalidation requests that third parties can file with the patent office as well as with courts after the patent has been finally granted and the patent letter has been delivered to the inventor. We will see later in this chapter that the first possibility, although admitted under several national laws, is not recommended. Invalidation of patents after their grant should be left to courts exclusively.

Other possible avenues for the intervention by third parties are of an *inter partes* nature, when only the third party is heard by the patent office, without any intervention—at least at that stage—by the inventor.

The lawmaker in a developing country must take two major considerations into account in regard to third-party challenges to the application (or the grant), which may sound conflicting: first, the lawmaker needs to ensure that patents be well granted, in the sense that they correspond to genuinely new and sufficiently inventive technical solutions; second, the lawmaker needs to ensure that the exercise of granting patents does not become too burdensome, generating heavy administrative costs or, worse, causing the patent office to appear as unresponsive to the demands of inventors, thereby contributing to the loss of significance of the whole patent system.

The *dos* as far as this topic is concerned are in providing third parties with the opportunity to assist the patent office in an effective manner but without giving rise to burdensome proceedings, in particular, because, once the patent is granted, those interested third parties may seek the invalidation of wrongly granted patents through invalidation procedures or in defense against infringement lawsuits.

The solution that seems to address the concerns above is the one that permits third parties, in an initially ex parte procedure, to file subsidies and observations with the patent office at any time until the decision to grant is made public through the official gazette. If the patent examiner sees some merit in those subsidies and observations, he/she may still set an action, through which the patent applicant will have an opportunity to rebut the third party's allegations and/or amend the application—hence, the procedure becomes *inter partes*.

Once the decision to grant the patent is publicly notified, third parties should have another opportunity to manifest their objections through an appeal. And, once again, the appeal should be set by the statute, initially, as an ex parte procedure. The patent office would notify the patent applicant of the filing of such an appeal, thereby informing the latter that there may be some delay in the issuance of the patent, but it would be up to the civil servant (or board) in charge of reexamining the application to decide whether the appeal has some merit. If yes, then the applicant would be given an opportunity to be heard—thus converting the procedure into an *inter partes* one. The decision either of accepting the appeal (after hearing the applicant) or of rejecting it (after hearing the applicant or not) should be final. Subsequent complaints should be addressed to the courts.

This is how the statute could look like:

Article . . .

1. *Any interested parties, after the application has been published and until the date the decision to grant the patent is published, may submit subsidies and observations aimed at showing that the claimed invention fails to attend, in total or in part, the conditions* [1] *as set in Article(s) . . . of the present law.*
2. *When the examiner understands that the subsidies have merit and contain elements that may lead to the rejection, in part or entirely, or the modification of the application, he/she will give notice to the applicant, who will have 60 (sixty) days for submitting his/her comments.*

Article . . .

1. *Within 60 (sixty) days counted from the publication of the decision to grant the patent, any interested parties may file a request for the reexamination of the claimed invention aimed at showing that the claimed invention fails to attend, in total or in part, the conditions of patentability as set in Article(s) . . . of the present law.*
2. *Where the reexaminer [the board] is satisfied that the request has merits, in total or in part, the patent applicant shall be notified of the request, and of the reasons of the reexaminer. Within 60 (sixty) days from receiving the notice of the reexamination request, the applicant may submit a response in defense of the application or submit amendments.*
3. *The reexaminer [the board] shall issue a final decision within 90 (ninety) days from the date the applicant has filed the response.*

Article . . .

Any interested party may ask the court[2] *to invalidate the patent on grounds of failure to observe the conditions of patentability set in Articles ... [novelty, non-obviousness, utility, insufficient disclosure, exclusion from patentability]*[3] *at any time during the patent term and until the end of the period of five (5) years beyond the expiry.*[4]

Notes:

1. The opportunity given for third parties to intervene in the application procedures so as to express their discontent with the claimed invention should concern *conditions of patentability* only. As explained above, those conditions may be of a formal or substantive nature, but they are set in the statute as requirements the compliance with which is mandatory. Failure to observe those conditions leads the patent to be rejected or to be invalid (in whole or in part).
2. Invalidation of the patent can be handled through proceedings between private parties in courts only. The patent office should not be involved in debates concerning this matter. First, there is an obvious conflict of interest in a patent office's reviewing a final decision on granting a patent. Second, if the patent office accepts a challenge to the patent, it would be contradicting its previous work and, eventually, creating a problem for the patent examiner who had agreed to grant the patent and received a bonus for that decision. The lawmaker could, however, draft language in a different sense, admitting the patent office's direct intervention (as a plaintiff, for example) in the event the patent has been fraudulently obtained (through the so-called inequitable conduct).
3. As it will be discussed below, invalidation should only occur when the conditions of patentability are not met.

4. On some occasions, to invalidate a patent already expired may be of interest—for example, when there are still royalties whose payment is pending after the expiry of the patent.

On invalidation, it was already mentioned above that it should not be taken as a synonym of revocation on grounds of public interest. A patent is invalidated when it was granted in spite of not observing all the mandatory requirements (or conditions) for it to be granted in the first place. The sake of convenience (e.g., vis-à-vis the public interest) should not justify a patent to be invalidated, thereby frustrating the efforts and the expectations of inventors.

It is worth noticing that, as far as substantive conditions of patentability are concerned, Article 27.1 of the TRIPS Agreement mentions three only: novelty, nonobviousness, and utility. There is no reference to the public interest in Article 27.1. Public interest is mentioned in Article 27.2, through the designation of two of its modalities: *ordre public* and morality. Social concerns as regards the protection of "human, animal or plant life or health" and the avoidance of "serious prejudice to the environment" are also mentioned in the same paragraph. The exclusion of certain inventions from patentability, however, as noted, is conditioned to the passing of a two-step test: (i) the fact that the exclusion of an invention from commercial exploitation contributes indeed to the protection of morality or *ordre public* must be verified; and, once the patent examiner is satisfied that the first step was successfully overcome, (ii) then he/she must determine whether there is necessity in denying the patent so as to prevent its commercial exploitation. Otherwise, if for some reason a patent is contrary to some public interest that was not foreseen at the time of its prosecution, when there are no grounds for its invalidation, then what public authorities should do is to expropriate the patent (against adequate remuneration) and either give it some use or simply release it into the public domain.

An example of this solution can be found in the (real) case of a patented invention that proved to be of crucial utility for a large class of poor citizens—small farmers—who could not afford to pay the royalties and/or acquire the patented product—a device to dig cheaply and effectively wells and irrigation canals. In this case, the patent was of great inconvenience to the public, but it was not prone to invalidation. The solution was for the government to expropriate the patent (against the payment of fair compensation) and abandon it for public use (citizens still paid for the patent in the form of taxes, but the cost was spread throughout the entire population).

And yet, we can find a few examples of patent laws that run against this basic notion of protection of private property (and of respect for the rationale of the patent system, under which the patent is a tool for the inventor to reap the rewards from his/her inventive efforts from the market), such as the statute of Namibia:

Section 68. Revocation of patent in public interest

(1) *Where the Board is of opinion that a patent or the mode in which it is exercised is inimical to the interests of the State or generally prejudicial to the public, and the Board is satisfied that the prejudice cannot be remedied by way of a compulsory licence, the Board may, after giving the patentee an opportunity to*

be heard, make a declaration to that effect in the Gazette and thereupon the patent is deemed to be revoked. . . .[185]

A similar provision is found in the Patent Act of India:

Section 66. Revocation of patent in public interest.—

Where the Central Government is of opinion that a patent or the mode in which it is exercised is mischievous to the State or generally prejudicial to the public, it may, after giving the patentee an opportunity to be heard, make a declaration to that effect in the Official Gazette and thereupon the patent shall be deemed to be revoked.

This particular topic was once the subject matter of a debate in the TRIPS Council, when India defended its legal provision. But a vast majority of WTO Members, led by the United States, which opened the debate, expressed an opposite view.[186]

An additional point concerning invalidation of a patent poorly granted is the provision that a few patent statutes provide for the exemption of the patent office (and the government as a whole) from any liability in the event the patent is cancelled (by a court or by the patent office, in those countries that admit that patent offices conduct invalidation procedures) on grounds of failure to comply with conditions of patentability.

One example is the law of Antigua and Barbuda, which reads:

Section 62. Immunity regarding official acts

Neither the Minister nor any person employed by the State or the Intellectual Property Office shall—

. . .

(b) incur any liability by reason of or in connection with any examination or investigation required or authorised by this Act or any report or other proceeding consequent upon any such examination or investigation.

Identical language is found in the patent statute of Belize (section 64) and a very similar provision is included in the Patent Act of the Cook Islands (section 18).

In this same regard, the previous industrial property code of Brazil (Law No. 5,772, of 1971), abrogated by the Act of 1996, contained a very curious provision:

Article 21.

. . .

§ 2 The patent must contain the respective number, name, nationality, profession and domicile of the inventor, . . the title and nature of the privilege and its duration, . . . reserving the rights of third parties and exonerating the Government's responsibility regarding novelty and utility, . . .

185. Industrial Property Act, 2012 (Act No. 1 of 2012) (Amended by Act No. 8 of 2016).

186. One of the earliest drafts of the TRIPS Agreement contained a provision that permitted that patents be "revoked on grounds of public interest and where the conditions for the grant of compulsory licenses are not fulfilled." However, such proposal has been rejected. For a more extensive discussion of this topic, *see* Nuno Pires de Carvalho, THE TRIPS REGIME, *supra* note 3, at 446.

The original sentence, in Portuguese, is somewhat ambiguous because it employs the same verbal form *ressalvando-se* in connection with the rights of third parties and with the government's responsibility, but with a different meaning, as the translation above shows. On the one hand, the provision reserves the rights of third parties, in the case the patent has been mistakenly granted and impacts the rights of those third parties (e.g., an inventor applied earlier for a patent for the same invention, and the patent office has ignored the prior rights of that inventor). On the other hand, the provision says the government is not liable for errors in granting the patent.

It is here that the interesting element of the Brazilian old provision comes: the government's liability is exempted only as far as novelty and utility are concerned. There is no exemption in relation to the examination of inventiveness and the scrutiny of the other conditions of patentability, such as exclusions from patentability and enabling disclosure.

As noted, this version of the Brazilian industrial property statute was abrogated in 1996, and there is no notice that a particular provision has ever been invoked by a patentee who may have felt harmed by the patent office's error in granting a patent. However, if the lawmaker understood that forgiving the patent office for mistakes made in the fields of novelty and utility was acceptable because of the virtual impossibility for scrutinizing those two matters in a total error-proof manner, one may wonder why the exemption has not been extended to nonobviousness. Nonobviousness, although based on an objective concept—the state of the art—depends on an analysis that is entirely subjective. In the same patent office, two patent examiners may have different approaches to the assessment of the inventive step, one being stricter than the other.[187]

If the lawmaker wishes to exempt the patent office from any liability concerning the quality of the patents granted, then the exemption should be total, not partial, as under the old Brazilian statute.

But is that a good measure? Probably not, and that is why today that orientation has been abandoned in the vast majority of patent statutes. Patent offices should have the responsibility for granting patents whose validity is presumed. Gross negligence or, worse, eventual biases against (or in favor of) certain technologies that lead to patents being wrongly denied or granted should not be exempted from liability.

187. In the beginning of his career, between 1902 and 1909, Albert Einstein served the Swiss Federal Institute for Intellectual Property as a patent examiner. The legend goes that, when examining patent applications, he would often write comments on the applications such as "dumb!," "ridiculous!", and other similar expressions of disdain for what he saw as lack of creativity by inventors.

Chapter 7

On the Rights Conferred by the Patent: Setting and Calibration

1 COMPULSORY LICENSES: EFFECTIVE TOOLS OR MIRAGES?

1.1 Definition and Essential Points

The term "compulsory license" means the authorization given by an administrative authority (such as the head of the patent office or a minister) or a court, in the sense that a third party performs acts that, but for that authorization, are exclusive of the patent owner, namely making and selling the patented product.

The word "license" in the term "compulsory license," therefore, is somewhat misleading because, under a compulsory license, the rights of the beneficiary do not arise from a private contract. In a compulsory license, there is no *licensor* or *licensee*, but a *granting authority* and a *beneficiary*. Indeed, the conditions of the compulsory license are, within the limits set in the law, established by the administration or the court, not by private parties. In this case, a compulsory license is much closer to a public easement than to a private contract. However, under the laws of certain countries, a court or a governmental agency (such as a competition authority) may order the patent owner to accept negotiating on reasonable commercial terms a license to a third party. In this case, the deal, although celebrated under pressure, will be closer to a real license.

Compulsory licenses are seen in many developing countries as a sort of general panacea against the inconveniences that result from the TRIPS principle of national treatment: given that developing countries can no longer refuse patent protection to certain inventions, national entrepreneurs are not allowed for an average twenty-year period to reproduce a vast number of inventions that are made abroad. Developing countries are, therefore, under the burden of granting titles that may amount to an exclusive right to import foreign goods. Those countries believe that they can, at least, resort to the compulsory license mechanism in order to give national undertakings access to coveted technologies of foreign origin.

There is a sophism, however, in such a reasoning: if national entrepreneurs cannot invent in some technological fields because of lack of knowledge and of tools, the same applies to the exploitation of the inventions covered by patents granted to foreigners in those same fields. The grant of a compulsory license supposes a situation of rivalry between the patent owner and the candidate to obtain the authorization from the government. It follows that the patent owner will not transmit to the beneficiary of a compulsory license the know-how and other information complementing the invention as disclosed in the patent, which is necessary for its successful exploitation.[188]

This explains why the number of compulsory licenses granted all over the world is so small, except in the cases of the application of the *unclean hands* doctrine and in some antitrust-related events. In the first case, the beneficiary of the compulsory license is an infringer who, in the course of infringement procedures, has been able to persuade the court that the patent owner has engaged in abusive practices (e.g., when the patent owner has wrongly terminated a licensing agreement that he/she had previously celebrated with the defendant).[189] The second case occurs, for example, when a competition authority orders the patent owner involved in some merger or acquisition to license the patented invention (and to teach about its exploitation) as a condition for that operation to be approved. These two cases occur with relative frequency. But, other than those very specific circumstances, compulsory licenses have very rarely been granted, and, when granted, have not had significant success. The reason is worth being repeated: the patent owner will not be enthusiastic about voluntarily transfer know-how and other information of a technical and commercial nature to an undesired partner.

Before we look at the circumstances in which compulsory licenses can be admitted by the lawmaker, we should emphasize a few basic points of essential

188. There have been isolated attempts by developing country lawmakers to overcome this obstacle by requiring that the patent owner transfer to the beneficiary complementary knowledge, know-how and other data necessary to put the invention into practice, on the penalty of the invalidation of the patent on grounds of the failure to comply with the enabling disclosure condition. Examples of those attempts can be found in the law of Uruguay (Art. 67) and in a regulation approved in Brazil (Decree No. 3, 201, of 2001, as amended by Decree No. 4,830, of 2003, Art. 5§1). Of course, such a measure is not only disrespectful to the proprietary nature of the patent but also contrary to the true dimension of the enabling disclosure, which should be strictly confined to the contents of the claims. For example, information that relates to the unclaimed ingredients used in exploiting a patented process, for example, is not supposed to be described in detail in the specifications. However, this does not mean that the refusal by the patentee in helping the beneficiary exploit the invention should go without any consequences. After all, we should not forget that we are here dealing with the public interest, and not only with the profit-oriented interests of the beneficiary. The consequence here is that the authority granting the license, in calculating the remuneration, should take into consideration, among the other factors that will be mentioned below, the costs the beneficiary will have to face in order to fully understand and reproduce the invention.
189. As it will be explained in *infra* note 200, in spite of being well settled and profoundly rooted in the U.S. judicial application of patent law, the judicial construction that led to the unclean hands doctrine is not necessarily correct if applied without a careful consideration of the circumstances surrounding the abuse.

importance that the patent statute should reflect. These points are mentioned in the TRIPS Agreement, Article 31.

1.1.a Compulsory Licenses Must Take the Individual Circumstances of Each Case into Account

First, the grant of a compulsory license "shall be considered on its individual merits" (Article 31(a) of the TRIPS Agreement). This means that authorities and courts in WTO Members (regardless of their being developing or developed countries/territories) may not grant compulsory licenses that operate as blankets as regards their conditions and terms as well as the beneficiaries. Each case has to be a case.

This rule is of particular importance in the field of public health, in view of ex officio systems of compulsory licensing established by several national laws aimed at dealing with situations of crisis. In the last years, the rule became even more relevant in the context of telecommunications and the so-called standard-essential patents (SEPs)—patents that cover inventions that are components of technical standards, without which the standards cannot be implemented. There have been some initiatives in the sense of compelling SEP owners to grant blanket, worldwide licenses to implementers of those standards in conformity with some general conditions and terms, known as FRAND (fair, reasonable, and nondiscriminatory). The problem does not lie in finding limits to the conditions and terms themselves, which are frequently voluntarily proposed by SEP owners to the Standard-Setting Organizations in question, but in their horizontal, nonindividualized application to implementers that may be based in different jurisdictions and present different entrepreneurial profiles.

Where a competition authority or a court imposes compliance with certain licensing terms and conditions against the will of the SEP owner, we are in the face of a compulsory license for all purposes. And, in accordance with Article 31(a) of the TRIPS Agreement, that license should take into account the particular characteristics of the beneficiaries as well as of the territory where the patented invention will be exploited. We will come back to this topic when we cover the territorial independence of patents and the rights they confer.

As far as this matter is concerned, the patent law of Chile is adequately drafted, as follows:

> *Article 51 bis C.*
>
> *The competent authority shall decide on the request for non-voluntary license based on its particular circumstances.*[190]

By contrast with Chile, the Industrial Property Act of Guatemala not only fails to mention the necessity for a compulsory license to take the particular circumstances of

190. Law No. 19,039 of March 6, 2006, on Industrial Property (Consolidated Law approved by Decree-Law No. 4 of June 30, 2022, incorporating amendments up to Law No. 21,355 of July 5, 2021).

the deal into account but also suggests that its terms and conditions may be predetermined. Guatemala's law reads:

> *Compulsory Licenses*
>
> *134. For reasons of public interest, and in particular for reasons of national emergency, public health, national security, or non-commercial public use, or to remedy any anti-competitive practice, after hearing the interested party, the Registry may, at the request of the authority or an interested party, order at any time:*
>
> . . .
>
> *(b) That the invention which is the subject of a patent or a pending patent application be open to the granting of one or more compulsory licenses, in which case the competent national authority may grant such a license to any applicant, subject to the conditions established.*

It is true that Guatemala's provision does not read "subject to the conditions previously established," but neither does it read "subject to the conditions to be established, taking into account the particular circumstances of the case," as it should.

Another problem of Guatemala's law is that the reasons of national emergency, national security, and noncommercial public use are not designated by the TRIPS Agreement as causes for the granting of compulsory licenses. After all, they all are naturally included in the concept of "public interest"—the first and fundamental justification for the intervention in the domain of private property by the State. Those circumstances are mentioned by Article 31(b) of the TRIPS Agreement as causes for eliminating the beneficiary's obligation to seek a voluntary license, before he/she starts exploiting the invention, but not for any other purpose.

1.1.b Infringers Should Not Be Allowed to Benefit from Compulsory Licenses

Second, compulsory licenses may not be granted for the benefit of infringers (except when the *unclean hands* doctrine applies, as noted above, or in cases of national emergency or other circumstances of extreme urgency or in cases of public noncommercial use). Article 31(b) is unequivocal in this regard:

> . . . *such use may only be permitted if, prior to such use, the proposed user has made efforts to obtain authorization from the right holder.* . . .

The term "*such*" refers to the wording employed in the *caput* of Article 31, which mentions the "use of the subject matter of a patent." Here, the Agreement refers to the *use of the invention* (i.e., its exploitation through making the product and/or using the process), not to the *use of the patent right* (which has three modalities: licensing, assigning, and enforcing).

Therefore, Article 31(b) means that, in the absence of the few exceptional circumstances that it mentions, the potential beneficiary of the authorization may not start using the invention before he/she attempts to obtain a voluntary license. The only exception to this, as already observed, applies when the patent owner has practiced some abusive act and additional conditions apply, as discussed below. Infringers, as a matter of principle, should not be rewarded with compulsory licenses.

This provision has also gained great significance in the enforcement of SEPs against infringing implementers. Although SEP owners may have offered to license the patents under FRAND conditions, such offers cannot benefit infringers, including those that engage in *holding out* the patentees, by engaging in licensing negotiations in bad faith, with the only intent of gaining time or of forcing the patentee to license the patent under conditions that are not fair or not sufficiently remunerating. In this context, an SEP is enforced like all other patents, and infringers are not entitled to any special treatment.

1.1.c The Scope and Duration of a Compulsory License Should Be Adapted to Its Purpose

This element is redundant to some extent: given that the grant of compulsory licenses shall be considered on their individual merits, it follows that the terms and conditions fixed by the granting authority shall also vary in accordance with those same merits, and thus the licenses (and the duration) must be adapted to their purpose.

This rule impacts on the duration and the scope (both geographical and technical) of the grant. Where the compulsory license aims at solving supply problems in some relevant sector caused by the suppression (or lack or insufficiency of exploitation) of a patented invention, and where the patent owner is able to prove that within a certain time limit he/she will be able to supply the market, the duration of the license shall be limited to that period, plus an extra time necessary for the beneficiary to be compensated by the loss of access to the invention.

As regards its scope, where the problem the compulsory license is supposed to solve is confined to one region within the country, then the compulsory license shall confine the use of the invention to supply that particular territory, not the whole country. Moreover, where the patented invention can be exploited in more than one manner and is claimed in a way that leads to obtaining different industrial outputs, the license shall be limited to the one use that is necessary to achieve the purpose of the grant. The most obvious example is the patent for a product and the process of making it. When the compulsory license is granted for the purpose of using that process for the making of a different product (eventually unpatented or covered by a different patent), then the product that is covered by the licensed patent is out of bounds. If the beneficiary of the license uses that process for making both products, he/she will be breaching the license (and infringing the patent, in part).

An example of a correct drafting approach to this point can be found in the Industrial Property Law of Chile, which reads:

> *Article 51 bis C.—*
>
> *[The authority granting the authorization] shall, on the one hand, set the duration and the scope of the authorization, limiting it to the purposes for which it has been granted . . .*

1.1.d Compulsory Licenses Shall Be Nonexclusive and Nonassignable (with One Exception)

The mandatory nonexclusive nature of compulsory licenses has three dimensions: (i) the patent owner does not lose his/her right to use the invention, where economic regulations do not determine otherwise (e.g., in the case of an invention that applies in the field of transmission of energy, where the patent owner has not received a permission to engage in the business of providing public utilities, he/she will not be allowed to exploit the patented invention);[191] (ii) the patent owner reserves the right to contract voluntary licenses with other parties (most probably, competitors of the beneficiary); and (iii) the granting entity keeps the authority for granting additional compulsory licenses to other beneficiaries, where circumstances justify such grants.

These three dimensions, actually, operate as obstacles to the dissemination of compulsory licenses, adding to the already mentioned impossibility of eventual beneficiaries having access to the know-how and other complementary information and data necessary for the successful exploitation of the invention, unless the patentee voluntarily supplies those elements.

The compulsory license shall be nonassignable, except, as Article 31(e) of the TRIPS Agreement goes, "with that part of the enterprise or goodwill which enjoys the use." However, the assignment is not automatic. Where the beneficiary is sold, in total or in part, the granting authority needs to verify whether the beneficiary's successor is qualified to continue exploiting the invention. Where it is decided that the beneficiary's successor does not meet the required conditions, the compulsory license should be cancelled.

1.1.e The Rights Conferred by the Compulsory License to the Beneficiaries Shall Not Include Exporting the Patented Product or the Product Made with the Patented Process (Except Where the Law Provides Otherwise)

The grant of a compulsory license is supposed to attend to the conditions of the national economy, not of other countries. If other reasons were not available, the fact that the same invention can be (and frequently is) covered by patents in various countries, where they confer rights independently, makes compulsory licenses for exporting a legal impossibility and a logical contradiction.

The opposite, however, is possible: to grant a compulsory license with the purpose of importing the patented invention. Such licenses are not frequently granted, and the reason is that national authorities tend to envisage that certain compulsory

191. In this regard, it is always useful to remind that patents do not confer the right to use the claimed inventions. Such right results, in general, from economic freedom, as secured by constitutional provisions. Limits to that right are acceptable under special regulations, which must be in conformity with those constitutional provisions. The rights conferred by the patent are, essentially, the right of prohibiting others from exploiting the invention (through enforcement), as well as the consequential rights of authorizing others to exploit the invention (through licensing and assigning).

licenses may operate as means of luring foreign technology and productive investments into the country—hence the provisions (albeit contrary to the principle of national treatment of goods, as it will be explained below) present in a large number of countries dealing with compulsory licenses on the grounds of the lack of local manufacturing.

The exception to the rule was introduced through the 2003 Decision of the WTO General Council, aiming at permitting the grant of compulsory licenses in developed countries (or in developing countries hosting a pharmaceutical industry) with the purpose of making anti-HIV drugs and exporting them to other developing countries under health crises. In 2017, that Decision was incorporated into the TRIPS Agreement and became Article 31*bis*.

When the 2003 Decision was approved, a few countries that host an industry of production of pharmaceutical generics saw it as a business opportunity for increasing exports without the risk of facing the barriers caused by market segmentation and the eventuality of prohibitions against parallel imports. But they were wrong. The exception to Article 31(f) has never been put into practice. One attempt, described elsewhere,[192] aimed at exporting anti-HIV medicines made in Canada under a compulsory license to Rwanda, took place in 2008, and served to test the practicality (or lack thereof) of the solution. The Canadian generic manufacturer that benefited from the compulsory license has complained bitterly of the complications in obtaining all the necessary approvals for making and exporting the drugs. It is worth noticing that in this regard there were two elements that could have greatly facilitated the deal: not only the generic manufacturer (APOTEX) had the knowledge for making the patented ingredients but Rwanda had also claimed its right to delay the application of the provisions of the TRIPS Agreement dealing with pharmaceutical patents and trade secrets, this meaning that there was no need to grant a parallel compulsory license for the importation of the drugs. And yet, in spite of the patent owner (GSK) having waived its right to claim the payment of royalties—thus making this entire exercise an operation of charity—no country has tried to repeat the experience.

Countries interested in adopting the solution of Article 31*bis* have two avenues at their disposal for transposing it into the national patent statute. One avenue is transposing its provisions to national legislation. That is a complex solution, given the many small details that the 2003 Decision has incorporated. For evidence of that complexity, a quick reading of the statutes enacted by Canada and the European Union will serve as a good illustration.[193] However, exactly because the 2003 Decision (and

192. *See* Nuno Pires de Carvalho, THE TRIPS REGIME, *supra* note 3, at 424 and 443.

193. Bill C-9 (entitled An Act to amend the Patent Act and the Food and Drugs Act [*The Jean Chrétien Pledge to Africa*]) was passed by the House of Commons on May 4, 2004. Its text is available at <www.parl.gc.ca>. It was later converted into law by means of amendments to Canada's Patent Act (sections 21.02 to 21.2) and the Food and Drugs Act. Bill C-9 (as well as the final statutory language) reflects well the complexity of transposing the General Council's Decision (and Art. 31*bis*) into national legislation: it is indeed a long, complex and obscure piece of legislation, which aims more at making a political statement (hence its curious name) than at establishing a practical and effective waiver from Art. 31(f). Another example of a statute that implemented the Decision is Regulation (EC) No. 816/2006 of the European Parliament and of the Council, of May 17, 2006, on compulsory licensing of patents relating to the manufacture

Article 31*bis* and its Annex) has been drafted with great detail, there is no need for the national lawmaker to repeat its provisions.

An example of a simple manner of transposing the Decision into national law can be found in the amendment of 2005 to the Indian Patents Act of 1970, which added a single provision (section 92A) permitting the granting of compulsory licenses for the purposes of exporting pharmaceutical products to countries without manufacturing capacity. That provision does not enter into details, which suggests the automatic application of the operational conditions contained in the Decision. However, the Indian Patents Act would not accept the granting of compulsory licenses where the country stands as an importer because it contains a provision that establishes that compulsory license grantees will not be allowed to import the licensed product. The Indian Patent Act's provision reads:

> *92A. Compulsory licence for export of patented pharmaceutical products in certain exceptional circumstances.—*[194]
> *(1) Compulsory licence shall be available for manufacture and export of patented pharmaceutical products to any country having insufficient or no manufacturing capacity in the pharmaceutical sector for the concerned product to address public health problems, provided compulsory licence has been granted by such country or such country has, by notification or otherwise, allowed importation of the patented pharmaceutical products from India.*
> *(2) The Controller shall, on receipt of an application in the prescribed manner, grant a compulsory licence solely for manufacture and export of the concerned pharmaceutical product to such country under such terms and conditions as may be specified and published by him.*
> *(3) The provisions of sub-sections (1) and (2) shall be without prejudice to the extent to which pharmaceutical products produced under a compulsory licence can be exported under any other provision of this Act.*
> *Explanation.—For the purposes of this section, "pharmaceutical products" means any patented product, or product manufactured through a patented process, of the pharmaceutical sector needed to address public health problems and shall be inclusive of ingredients necessary for their manufacture and diagnostic kits required for their use.*

Another approach possible, and even simpler, was adopted by Oman's Industrial Property Act of 2008, which contains two references to the Decision (one, on the possibility of granting a compulsory license for exporting pharmaceutical products and another, on avoiding double remuneration in this event), both conditioned to the

---

of pharmaceutical products for export to countries with public health problems. O.J. L157/1 of June 9, 2006. Like the Canadian statute, the European one is a complicated text (even if not as much as the Canadian legislation).

194. Section 92A takes the standing of exporting pharmaceuticals only. India has seen the Decision of 2003 as an opportunity to foster its generic industry. Moreover, section 90(2) of the Indian Patents Act does not admit the granting of compulsory licenses for the purposes of importing. The relevant part of the provision reads:

> *No licence granted by the Controller shall authorise the licensee to import the patented article or an article or substance made by a patented process from abroad where such importation would, but for such authorisation, constitute an infringement of the rights of the patentee.*

observation of the 2003 Decision. Indirectly, therefore, but more explicitly than the Indian statute, the Omani law has incorporated the Decision into national law.

Given that the Decision has language that is vastly operational and detailed, there is indeed no need to follow the example of Canada or the European Union. The relevant provisions of the Omani Industrial Property Act are as follows:

> *Article 13:*
>
> 1\. . . .
>
> (B) . . . *The exploitation of the invention shall be limited to the purpose for which it was licensed, provided that an adequate remuneration be paid to the patent owner in the circumstances of each case, taking into account the economic value of the Minister's decision, and the provisions of the WTO General Council, when applicable [,] with regard to the determined remuneration on granting a compulsory license of a patent claiming a pharmaceutical product or a process of making such a pharmaceutical product.*
>
> . . .
>
> 8— *The exploitation of the invention for which a compulsory license has been issued shall be predominantly for the export of a pharmaceutical product or a process to make such a protected pharmaceutical product for supply of the market in Oman or for a foreign territory or country with no or with insufficient manufacturing capacity of this pharmaceutical product or the process to make it, in accordance with the terms and conditions of the Decision of the General Council of the WTO.*

Today, a developing country would just need to replace the reference to the 2003 WTO General Council Decision with a reference to Article 31*bis* of the TRIPS Agreement.

In 2022, the WTO Ministerial Conference debated again eventual amendments to the Agreement in order to facilitate access to COVID-related vaccines and treatments. The final decision[195] deals with vaccines only (but a possible expansion to diagnostics and treatments is mentioned, pending an agreement). The 2022 decision goes even further than the 2003 Decision to the extent it calls for the eventuality of Members' ignoring the need to protect test data under Article 39.3, for the sake of speeding the approval for use of a COVID-19 vaccine. Anyway, the 2022 Ministerial Decision is temporary; thus, the lawmaker should not feel under the same pressure so as to transpose it into national law.

1.1.f *Remuneration*

As the fourth paragraph of the Preamble of the TRIPS Agreement puts it unequivocally, IP rights are private rights. It follows that they cannot be taken by governmental initiative, regardless of the purpose, without due compensation (except in some cases of anticompetitive practices).

Of course, the lawmaker, in requiring the payment of remuneration to the owner of a patent that has been the subject matter of a compulsory license, does not need to

195. WT/MIN(22)/30, WT/L/1141, of June 22, 2022.

enter into the details on the way of calculating it. That will be a topic to be discussed with the authority in charge of granting the remuneration. The role of the lawmaker is to ensure that, when setting the amount to be paid to the patent owner, that authority will not fail to take into account the conditions set by the TRIPS Agreement—which should correspond to the normal value of a compulsory license; remuneration is mandatory (unless the patent owner waives from his/her right to be paid); it shall take the circumstances of each case into consideration; and it shall be adequate, in the sense that the economic impact of the compulsory license must be taken into account. It will be up to the national authority to assess that economic impact: the profits the beneficiary is expected to obtain; the loss in the patentee's revenue; and eventual costs in technical assistance that the patent owner may be willing to provide to the beneficiary. In the event the patentee refuses to provide for technical assistance, as noted above, then the costs the beneficiary will have to face in order to fully understand and reproduce the invention should be taken into account in the final decision on remuneration.

The exception is the grant of a compulsory license as a remedy against an act of antitrust violation, when the remuneration may be reduced and, in some extreme cases, even be eliminated.

1.2 Circumstances That May Trigger the Grant of a Compulsory License

Compulsory licenses can be granted whenever the public interest so requires. That is a general principle of constitutional law: sometimes the interests of the society, as a whole, overcome the constraints that society imposes on itself concerning the interference with private property rights. In those opportunities, society admits that the rights of patent owners can be reduced through compulsory licenses. The TRIPS Agreement does not mention it (but implies it), and yet under many countries' constitutional law, patent rights may also be compulsorily assigned to the government, against adequate remuneration, as a form of expropriation for reasons of public interest.

Within the concept of public interest, the lawmaker can find some special variations of grounds for the grant of compulsory licenses within the TRIPS Agreement, namely:

- to remedy a practice determined after judicial or administrative process to be anticompetitive (Article 31(k));
- to permit the exploitation of a patent which cannot be exploited without infringing another patent (Article 31(l));
- to prevent abuses which might result from the exercise of the exclusive rights conferred by the patent, for example, failure to work (Article 5(A)(2)(3) of the Paris Convention).

1.2.a Compulsory Licenses to Remedy Anticompetitive Acts

The first modality, as said, should be dealt with in a special norm or regulation concerning the interface between the use of patent rights and antitrust. Eventually, depending on the country's constitutional regime, this topic should be covered by a directive of an administrative nature or a statute passed by parliament. Anyway, the respective text should be prepared in coordination between the patent office and the competition authority. It should cover the (as few as possible) *don'ts* as regards the licensing and the assignment of patents. It should also provide for guidance on how the anticompetitive abuse of patent rights (with some examples) will be sanctioned by the authority. Of particular interest is the identification of the situations that the competent authority will treat as per se anticompetitive as well as those that the authority will approach under the rule of reason. This type of guidance—eventually not with the same level of detail—is available in a number of the most developed countries in the world, such as the United States, Canada, the European Union, Japan, and the Republic of Korea. However, it would be of great advantage for developing countries to follow that example, in order to increase legal security and provide the basis for a culture of free competition in the field of patents.

The patent statute of Eswatini (formerly Swaziland) contains a provision that, if well drafted, could be of interest for other developing countries. It is subsection 5 of section 5, which reads as follows:

> (5) *The Minister may prescribe regulations allowing the use of a patent without the authorization of a right holder to remedy an anti-competitive practice.*[196]

Actually, instead of making the issuance of regulations on the anticompetitive use of patent rights depend on the will of the Minister, the provision should have given instructions in that sense.

Of great interest to developing countries would also be the establishment of a system of registration of patent licensing agreements, but in this regard three words of caution are necessary: (1) the Contracting Parties should not be requested to submit confidential clauses involving technical, commercial, and financial matters; (2) the authority in charge (either the patent office or, preferably, the competition authority) should not be expected to engage in a substantive examination of contractual clauses; it may, however, issue some recommendations or suggestions to the parties, which shall not be published, and may be or not accepted by them; and (3) in the event the parties do not submit the licensing agreement for registration, the license will still produce effects between the parties, but not against third parties.

At this point, it is important to note that Article 31(k) of the TRIPS Agreement deals with compulsory licenses that are granted *to remedy* anticompetitive acts, i.e., *after* the acts were practiced. By contrast, Article 5(2) of the Paris Convention concerns compulsory licenses granted *to prevent* the abusive use of patent rights, i.e., *before* the acts were practiced.

The notion of abusive use of patent rights encompasses both anticompetitive acts and unfair acts, meaning those acts that infringe the laws for the repression of unfair competition. Compulsory licenses motivated by unfair trade practices are not impacted by the provisions of Article 31(k) and, therefore, the corresponding remuneration

196. Patents Act, Act No. 19 of 2018.

should follow the general rules on adequacy to the economic value of the license (Article 31(h)).

1.2.b Compulsory Licenses of Dependent Patents

The case of compulsory licenses for dependent patents is very much straightforward, given that it is regulated in detail and with clarity by Article 31(l) of the TRIPS Agreement. The transposal of those rules to the national law should be therefore an easy task.

1.2.c Compulsory Licenses on Grounds of Lack of (Sufficient) Exploitation (or Suppression)

The same goes for the obligation to exploit the patented invention. The language of Article 5(A)(2)(3)(4) and (B) of the Paris Convention and of the last sentence of Article 27.1 of the TRIPS Agreement is sufficiently detailed and may serve as guidance for the lawmaker who wants to draft a provision on compulsory license of patents.

This said, the lawmaker has to make a decision, first, on whether it is worthy to impose the exploitation requirement. It is true that the vast majority of WTO Members and Paris Contracting Parties have adopted it, but one may seriously challenge the validity of such a constraint on inventors. The deal behind patents is that they are granted to inventors in exchange for their inventive contribution to the advancement of arts, regardless of their putting them into practice or not. In principle, the exploitation of the patent is a matter of commercial opportunity. Reasonable inventors will do their best to extract as much profit as they can from their inventions. The exploitation requirement, therefore, is built on an assumption of inventors' economic irrationality.

Like the wrong but generalized association of patents with monopolies, which was originated with the passing of the Statute of Monopolies, of 1623, the working requirement is grounded on very old patent law practices that presided over the granting of industrial privileges in the Middle Ages, when foreign artisans were lured to bring the techniques they mastered, with their apprentices and tools, to the cities that were engaged in competition with other cities. The working of the inventions was necessary not only to increase the industrial base of the granting cities but also as a way of teaching and disseminating the technique among local artisans. As said above, this last function of industrial privileges has been replaced after the Industrial Revolution with the enabling disclosure requirement.

This explains the requirement adopted in some national laws that patents be not only exploited but also *locally* exploited. If today the justification of enabling the person-to-person teaching of foreign inventions to local artisans is abandoned, the purpose of using patents as tools for promoting industrialization and importation of technology remains. In this regard, the Patent Act of India, of 1970, could not be more expressive:

> *Section 83. General principles applicable to working of patented inventions.—*
>
> *Without prejudice to the other provisions contained in this Act, in exercising the powers conferred by this Chapter, regard shall be had to the following general considerations, namely:—*
>
> *(a) that patents are granted to encourage inventions and to secure that the inventions are worked in India on a commercial scale and to the fullest extent that is reasonably practicable without undue delay;*
> *(b) that they are not granted merely to enable patentees to enjoy a monopoly for the importation of the patented article;*
> *(c) that the protection and enforcement of patent rights contribute to the promotion of technological innovation and to the transfer and dissemination of technology, to the mutual advantage of producers and users of technological knowledge and in a manner conducive to social and economic welfare, and to a balance of rights and obligations.*

Paragraph (c) of section 83 of the Indian Act results from a misquotation of Article 7 of the TRIPS Agreement, which reads (in part):

> *The protection and enforcement of intellectual property rights* should contribute *to the promotion . . .* (emphasis added).

Article 7 of the TRIPS Agreement reads *should contribute*, whereas section 83 of the Indian Patents Act reads *contribute*. There is a huge difference in the meaning of the two terms. The Indian lawmaker understands that the granting of patents to foreign inventors in itself ensures the transfer of the corresponding technology, whereas the drafters of the TRIPS Agreement have seen that result as a trend, an ambition, a wish. The understanding of the Indian lawmaker has necessarily led to the imposition that patent owners work the inventions "in India on a commercial scale and to the fullest extent that is reasonably practicable without undue delay." This obligation is addressed to both foreign and national inventors, but it is undoubtful that the lawmakers had the former in mind when they stated that "*[patents] are not granted merely to enable patentees to enjoy a monopoly for the importation of the patented article.*"

It happens that the local exploitation requirement has been banned by the TRIPS Agreement, in the last sentence of Article 27.1, as follows:

> *. . . patents shall be available and patent rights enjoyable without discrimination as to . . . whether products are imported or locally produced.*

This provision, with its unambiguous language, reflects the globalist nature of the WTO, which has been made mandatory through the principle of national treatment of goods (Article III.4 of the General Agreement on Tariffs and Trade 1947 [GATT 1947]). Under this principle:

> *The products of the territory of any contracting party imported into the territory of any other contracting party shall be accorded treatment no less favourable than that accorded to like products of national origin in respect of all laws, regulations and requirements affecting their internal sale, offering for sale, purchase, transportation, distribution or use. . . .*

As a result of this principle, the WTO Member that imposes the mandatory exploitation of patents granted must admit, as evidence of such exploitation, proof of the commercialization of patented goods (or goods made with the patented process) regardless of their having been manufactured in the country's territory or their having been imported.

Unfortunately, this TRIPS (and WTO) requirement is not well understood by many IP academics and commentators, who defend the local working requirement, thereby showing their lack of familiarity with the WTO rationale. Indeed, if all countries on Earth imposed the local exploitation requirement, the international commercial flow of goods incorporating patented inventions would immediately cease, and the usefulness of the WTO and its rules for the international trade of technology-based goods would disappear. The WTO would be left supervising the trade of commodities—but not all of them because some commodities incorporate patented technologies.

And yet, there is a large number of WTO Members that refuse to comply with that requirement, such as India (as already observed), Croatia, OAPI Member States, and Brazil.

The relevant provision in the patent law of Croatia reads:

Article 104

(1) *The court referred to in Article 103 paragraph (1) of this Act may allow any person to exploit the subject matter of a patent without consent of the holder of a patent by granting a compulsory license in cases where the holder of a patent does not at all or insufficiently exploit the subject matter of a patent in the territory of the Republic of Croatia or has not made effective and serious preparations for its exploitation.*

(2) *A compulsory license cannot be granted if the holder of a patent provides legitimate reasons to justify non-exploitation or insufficient exploitation of the protected invention.*[197]

The Brazilian statute reads:

Article 68

. . .

§ 1° The following shall also allow for compulsory licensing:

I— *the non-exploitation of the subject matter of the patent in Brazilian territory due to lack of manufacture or incomplete manufacture of the product, in addition, the lack of full use of the patented process, except in cases of economic unfeasibility, in which case import will be permitted; or*

II— *the commercialization that does not satisfy the needs of the market.*

The Bangui Agreement, of OAPI, in this same regard, reads:

Article 37

Non-voluntary license for non-working

197. Patent Act, NN 16/2020, in force from February 20, 2020.

> (1) *At the request of any person made after four years with effect from the filing date of the application for the utility model certificate, or three years with effect from the date of the issuance of a certificate, whichever period expires later, a non-voluntary license may be granted where one or more of the following conditions are met:*
> (a) *the utility model is not being worked on the territory of a Member State at the time the request is made;*
> (b) *the working of the utility model on such territory does not meet the demand for the protected product on reasonable terms; . . .*

Significantly, although the topic of local exploitation is very dear to developing countries, which would like to use the patent system as a tool for luring foreign technology and direct investment, some developed countries have also fallen into the temptation of inserting it in their laws. We saw above that is the case of Croatia, formerly part of the socialist group of backward countries that formed Yugoslavia, but presently a relatively developed country, with a GDP per capita of USD 21,865, in 2023 (World Bank data), and Member of the European Union since 2013.

Even the United States requires the local exploitation of inventions made with financial and technical federal assistance as well as of federally owned inventions when they are licensed. Indeed, sections 204 and 209 of the US Patents Act read (in part):

> *§204. Preference for United States industry*
>
> *Notwithstanding any other provision of this chapter, no small business firm or nonprofit organization which receives title to any subject invention and no assignee of any such small business firm or nonprofit organization shall grant to any person the exclusive right to use or sell any subject invention in the United States unless such person agrees that any products embodying the subject invention or produced through the use of the subject invention will be manufactured substantially in the United States. However, in individual cases, the requirement for such an agreement may be waived by the Federal agency under whose funding agreement the invention was made upon a showing by the small business firm, nonprofit organization, or assignee that reasonable but unsuccessful efforts have been made to grant licenses on similar terms to potential licensees that would be likely to manufacture substantially in the United States or that under the circumstances domestic manufacture is not commercially feasible.*
>
> . . .
>
> *§209. Licensing federally owned inventions*
>
> . . .
>
> (b) *Manufacture in United States.—A Federal agency shall normally grant a license under section 207(a)(2) to use or sell any federally owned invention in the United States only to a licensee who agrees that any products embodying the invention or produced through the use of the invention will be manufactured substantially in the United States.*

Ironically, in 2000, the United States requested consultations with Brazil, alleging a conflict between Article 68 of Brazil's Industrial Property Law, on the one hand, and the GATT 1947 and the TRIPS Agreement, on the other hand. In 2001, after the WTO

Dispute Settlement Body established a panel to address the United States' complaint, Brazil, instead of submitting a defense of its Article 68—which obviously violates the country's commitments under the WTO—requested consultations with the United States, alleging that its Patent Act, in sections 204 and 209, also infringed those same commitments.

The outcome is known: the United States has dropped its request for the Panel, and Brazil has not pursued its request for consultations.[198]

1.2.c.1 Dos and Don'ts of Requiring the Working of the Patent

Even though the exploitation requirement may be in conflict with the modern rationale of the patent system, and in its local modality, it is a blatant violation of one of the most fundamental principles of the WTO—the national treatment of goods—one has to admit that the lawmaker of a developing country may have good motives to impose the requirement (even in its local modality), for the sake of pursuing national objectives of industrial and technological development. The trick is how to do it without infringing trade-related international commitments and keeping the patent system consistent with its values.

The best approach in order to secure those two goals is to link the granting of compulsory licenses for lack of exploitation to the need for sanctioning abusive uses of patent rights, as Article 5(A)(2) of the Paris Convention admits.

But, before explaining the solution possible, it is convenient to clarify the true meaning of Article 5(A)(2) of the Paris Convention. It is usually accepted that the paragraph can be read as providing that failure to work, without any other qualification, may be taken as an abuse of the rights conferred by the patent. This reading can be found actually in a few patent statutes, such as that of Israel:

> *Section 119.*
>
> *The exercise of a monopoly conferred by a patent shall be deemed abusive, if one of the following circumstances exists in respect of the invention, the product or the process which is the subject of the patent, and if the patent holder did not provide a reasonable justification for its existence:*
>
> *(1) all the demand for the product is not satisfied in Israel on reasonable terms;*
> *. . .*[199]

But this is a wrong reading of the Paris Convention. To work the invention is not and may never be an abuse in itself because, as said above, working the invention is a prerogative that results from the laws ensuring economic freedom, not from the patent. A patent abuse may lie in enforcing or licensing it only because it is in those two acts that the rights conferred reside. As said above, when the patent is granted for an

198. A detailed account of these cross-disputes can be seen in Nuno Pires de Carvalho, *Um Episódio da Diplomacia Comercial Brasileira: A Controvérsia iniciada pelos EUA sobre o art. 68 da Lei de Propriedade Industrial e a Resposta do Brasil*, [*An Episode of Brazilian Commercial Diplomacy: The Dispute initiated by the USA concerning Art. 68 of the Law on Industrial Property and Brazil's Response*], Revista dos Tribunais, vol. 106, No. 975, at 243-290 (January 2017).

199. Patent Law, 5727-1967, amended up to 5774-2014.

invention that falls within a technological field that corresponds to a sector monopolized by the state, the patentee needs permission from the public authority to exploit the invention. The patent in itself does not confer that right. The right the patent owner has is to exclude others from using the invention for commercial purposes.

Moreover, the idea of granting a compulsory license as a preventive measure, as Article 5(A)(2) of the Paris Convention says, in order to sanction the patentee who does not exploit the invention, is a complete nonsense. That is why the Paris Convention sets minimum periods for that nonuse to occur in order to justify the compulsory license for lack of exploitation. A compulsory license on grounds of lack of exploitation has to be granted *ex post*, never *ex ante*.

This means that the correct reading of Article 5(A)(2) of the Paris Convention is that Members of the Paris Union (and of the WTO as well) shall have the right to take legislative measures providing for the grant of compulsory licenses to prevent (and to remedy) the abuses which might result from the exercise of the exclusive rights conferred by the patent, in the case of the patent owner who does not exploit an invention of economic and technical significance to society but nevertheless enforces or threatens to enforce his/her exclusive rights against a potential infringer. In that case, courts may refuse injunctive relief and order the defendant to pay damages to the patent owner. This solution is equivalent to a compulsory license.[200] However, this

200. In the United States, in lawsuits aimed at enforcing nonpracticed patents, courts have consistently ordered the accounting for damages but denied to issue injunctive relief against infringers (*see, e.g.*, *Hoe v. Knap*, 27 F. 204 (N.D. Ill. 1886); *Landis Tool Co. v. Ingle*, 286 F. 5 (3rd Cir. 1923), *cert denied*, 257 U.S. 644 (1921); *Foster v. American Mach. & Foundry Co.*, 492 F.2d 1317 (2nd Cir. 1974), *cert. denied*, 419 U.S. 833 (1974)). In *Foster*, the court ordered a compulsory license and refused the accounting of damages. Instead, it ordered the payment of royalties. But *see King Instruments Corp. v. Luciano Perego*, 65 F.3d 941 (Fed. Cir. 1995). In *King*, the court held that the Patent Act provided for the payment of adequate damages even in the absence of the exploitation of the patent by its owner. The court said:

> Requiring exploitation of the claimed invention for a recovery of lost profits would cause a systematic failure to award "damages adequate to compensate for the infringement" in cases where the patent holder could otherwise prove causation. Requiring exploitation would force patent owners to accept a reasonable royalty in cases where a reasonable royalty is inadequate compensation. Infringers would in effect receive the windfall of a retroactive compulsory license from the patent owner.

Ibid., at 951 (emphasis added). U.S. courts have also consistently denied to accord injunctive relief where it might cause serious harm to the public (*see, e.g.*, *City of Milwaukee v. Activated Sludge, Inc.*, 69 F.2d 577 (7th Cir. 1934); *Activated Sludge Inc. v. Sanitary Dist. of Chicago*, 64 F. Supp. 25 (N.D. Ill. 1946), *aff'd per curiam*, 157 F.2d 517 (7th Cir.), *cert. denied*, 330 U.S. 834, *reh'g denied*, 330 U.S. 856 (1947), *2nd petition for reh'g denied*, 331 U.S. 866 (1947); *Guthard v. Sanitary Dist. of Chicago*, 8 F. Supp. 329 (N.D. Ill. 1934); *Bliss v. Brooklyn*, 3 Fed. Cas. 706, Case No. 1.544 (E.D.N.Y. 1871); *McCreery Eng'g Co. v. Massachusetts Fan Co.*, 180 F. 115 (D. Mass. 1910)). The problem in this judicial construction that is designated by the term "*unclean hands*" is that an infringer is not or should not be entitled to be always treated with favor by the court. An infringer is an infringer. The hands of the patentee may be unclean because he is enforcing a noncommercially exploited patent, but the infringer's hands are likewise unclean. The *unclean hands* doctrine should be applied in those very rare cases where the defendant has unwillingly engaged in infringing (as in the case when the patentee without good cause terminates a licensing agreement) or when the patent covers an invention of particular economic and social significance.

applies vis-à-vis a potential infringer, not an actual infringer. The reason, as said, is that infringers are not (or should not be) benefited with compulsory licenses. A request for a voluntary license in reasonable commercial terms and conditions must be submitted to the patent owner preceding any request for or any grant of a compulsory license.

We can find examples of the second case in various statutes, such as that of Qatar and the Bangui Agreement.

Article 15, proviso (c) of the patent law of Qatar reads:

> *Whoever it may concern shall be allowed, after the expiration of three years of patent granting date, to apply for a mandatory license for exploiting the invention under any of the following causes:*
>
> . . .
>
> *c) Refusal by the patent owner to give contractual licensing for exploiting the invention thus impeding the establishment or development of industrial and commercial activities in the State. In all cases, mandatory license shall not be issued if the patent owner provides legitimate reasons. However, importing the product shall not serve as legitimate reason.*[201]

In the same token, Article 37 of the Bangui Agreement reads (in part):

> *Article 37*
>
> *Non-voluntary license for non-working*
>
> *(1) At the request of any person made after four years with effect from the filing date of the application for the utility model certificate, or three years with effect from the date of the issuance of a certificate, whichever period expires later, a non-voluntary license may be granted where one or more of the following conditions are met:*
>
> . . .
>
> *(c) on account of the refusal of the holder of the certificate of registration to grant licenses on reasonable commercial terms and procedures, the establishment or development of industrial or commercial activities on such territory is unfairly and substantially prejudiced. . . .*

Both enforcing and refusing to license a nonworked patent without good cause constitute effective abuses of the patent right in the proper sense of the term because, as said above, enforcing and licensing are the expressions of the use of the right.

1.3 Drafting the Provisions Dealing with Compulsory Licenses

Before presenting suggested language that addresses compulsory licenses in a way that avoids the most common mistakes, some of which were indicated above, a few observations are necessary.

201. This last sentence is in conflict with the TRIPS Agreement. Importing the patented product should be considered as working the patent.

The first observation is that the lawmaker of a developing country should not expect much from compulsory licenses. He/she should give them the same consideration as a person who lives in a desertic area and keeps an umbrella in a corner of his/her house. The umbrella may eventually be of use one day, but very rarely.

The second observation is that, in spite of being built on an assumption of the patentee's economic irrationality (i.e., that he/she neglects to extract money from his/her patent by working the invention), it is undeniable that the exploitation requirement has the advantage of avoiding or eliminating the problem of the so-called patent trolls or, in a more neutral jargon, "non-practicing entities" (NPEs). NPEs usually are firms specialized in buying patents with market value and enforcing them. In that way, NPEs make money out of enforcing the patents, or rather out of the working of the inventions by infringers (or alleged, threatened, infringers), not by them.

Third, the lawmaker, in the matter of compulsory licenses, should not feel compelled to avoid the drafting of a long and detailed provision. The reason is that, in spite of their scarcity, compulsory licenses constitute an intervention in the private proprietary rights of inventors. Therefore, the law should set rigorous (and detailed) guarantees so that inventors do not fall prey to opportunistic interests. This said, the lawmaker should insert in the law an article setting:

(a) the grounds for the granting of compulsory licenses (this should not be neglected, given that, as said, compulsory licenses are an interference in citizens' private property, which is usually protected by constitutional orders);
(b) the mandatory observation of the conditions listed in the Agreement as well as the number of additional requirements imposed by the lawmaker for the sake of legal security of both the patentee and the beneficiary;
(c) in specific cases, such as compulsory licenses granted for the purposes of addressing problems of public health, a cross-reference to Article 31*bis* of the TRIPS Agreement; and
(d) the authority of courts to determine additional requirements, terms, and conditions, in accordance with international treaties (this meaning the Paris Convention and the TRIPS Agreement).

Moreover, the topic of granting compulsory licenses in order to prevent or repress abusive behavior, with or without anticompetitive effects, should be the subject matter of a special regulation—or law—discussed and adopted—or submitted to the competent legislative body—jointly by the patent office and the competition authority.

Here goes the suggested language:

Article . . .

Compulsory licenses

1. (a) *The Patent Office [the Minister] [the Court]* [1] *shall give the authorization to a natural or legal person, or a private or public entity, to exploit a patented*

invention or a registered utility model in [name of the country], without the approval of the right holder. Compulsory licenses are granted where:

- *(i) the public interest justifies the grant;*[2]
- *(ii) the invented product or process has significant economic or technical relevance and is not available in sufficient quantities or quality or at predetermined reasonable prices in [name of the country], either through manufacture in [name of the country] or through importation;*[3]
- *(iii) another patent (the "second patent") claims an invention that involves an important technical advance of considerable economic significance in relation to an invention claimed in the first patent and which cannot be exploited without infringing the first patent.*

2. *No compulsory license shall be granted if the request for its grant has not been preceded by a written request from the proposed beneficiary addressed to the patentee for a voluntary license, on reasonable commercial terms and conditions, and that request has been either not responded or rejected by the patentee within a period of six months.*
   - *(a) This requirement shall be waived in the case of a national emergency or other circumstances of extreme urgency or in cases of public non-commercial use.*
   - *(b) In situations of national emergency or other circumstances of extreme urgency, the patentee shall, nevertheless, be notified as soon as reasonably practicable.*
   - *(c) In the case of public non-commercial use, where the government or contractor, without making a patent search, knows or has demonstrable grounds to know that a valid patent is or will be used by or for the government, the right holder shall be informed promptly;*
3. *The exploitation of the invention under the compulsory license shall be limited to the purpose for which it was granted, as regards both the duration of the scope;*
4. *The patent owner shall be paid an adequate remuneration taking into account the circumstances of each case and the economic value of the authorization, except where the provisions of Article 31bis of the TRIPS Agreement apply.* [4]
5. *A compulsory license may not be applied for on the ground of insufficient availability of the patented product or of the product manufactured with the patented process, as established in paragraph 1(a)(ii), of this article before the expiration of a period of four years from the date of filing of the patent application or three years from the date of the grant of the patent, whichever periods expires last; it shall be refused if the patentee justifies his/her inaction or insufficient action by legitimate reasons.*
6. *Upon request of the owner of the patent, or of the Government agency or of the third person authorized to exploit the patented invention, the Patent Office [the Minister] [the Court] may, after hearing both parties, if either or both wish to be heard, modify the terms of the decision authorizing the exploitation of the patented invention to the extent necessary to attend the circumstances that may have changed after the authorization was given.*
7. *(a) Upon the request of the patentee, the Patent Office [the Minister] [the Court] shall terminate the compulsory license upon verification, after hearing both parties, if either or both wish to be heard, that the circumstances which led to the grant of the compulsory license have ceased to exist and are unlikely to recur or that the beneficiary of the compulsory license has failed to comply with the terms of the decision.*

(b) *The Patent Office [the Minister] [the Court] may decide not to terminate the compulsory license upon verification that the need for adequate protection of the legitimate interests of the beneficiary of the compulsory license justifies the maintenance of the authorization. The extension of the authorization shall never be extended beyond the time strictly necessary for the protection of the beneficiary's legitimate interests.*[5]

8. *The compulsory license may only be transferred with the enterprise or business of the beneficiary or with the part of the enterprise or business within which the patented invention is being exploited. The transfer will not be authorized if the Patent Office [the Minister] [the Court] is not satisfied that the transferee has technical and financial capacity to exploit the invention commercially in the same terms and conditions as those set initially. In such an event, the compulsory license shall be cancelled.*
9. *The compulsory license shall always be non-exclusive. Therefore, it shall not exclude:*
   (a) *the exploitation of the invention by the patent owner him/herself, either through manufacture in [name of the country] or through importation or both; and*
   (b) *the conclusion of license contracts by the patent owner; and*
   (c) *the exercise, by the patent owner, of his/her rights under the provisions of this law.*
10. *The request for the compulsory license shall be addressed to the Patent Office [the Minister] [the Court]. It shall be accompanied by evidence that the requirement established by paragraph (2) of this Article has been complied with.*
11. *The exploitation of the invention for which a compulsory license has been issued shall be predominantly for the supply of the domestic market of [name of the country] except when the circumstances and terms of Article 31bis apply.*
12. *Compulsory licenses of patented inventions in the field of semi-conductor technology shall only be granted for public non-commercial use or to remedy a practice determined after the court or the competition authority has determined to be anti-competitive.*
13. *Where a compulsory license is granted under paragraph (1)(a)(iii):*
   (a) *the owner of the first patent shall be entitled to a cross-license on reasonable terms to use the invention claimed in the second patent; and*
   (b) *the license of the first patent shall be non-assignable except with the assignment of the second patent.*
14. *The provisions of this article shall apply, where appropriate and mutatis mutandis, to pending patent applications, except in the case of insufficient availability of the patented product or of the product manufactured with the patented process.* [6]
15. *Compulsory licenses granted on grounds of abusive and/or anti-competitive conduct by the patent owner shall be governed by the Directive jointly issued by the Patent Office and the Competition Authority [by the special law]. These compulsory licenses shall be granted by the authority in charge of hearing the respective cases.*[7]
   (a) *The refusal to accept a voluntary license, even if offered in reasonable commercial terms and conditions, by a patentee who does not exploit the patent commercially shall not be a sufficient reason for the grant of a compulsory license.*
   (b) *For the compulsory license to be granted, in addition to the submission of evidence that a request for a voluntary license has been refused, the following conditions must be met:*

(i) *the invention is deemed of great social interest and the lack or insufficiency of its exploitation harms the economy of the country or a particular sector of the industry of high social interest, such as health and the environment; this includes inventions whose use is essential for the implementation of technical standards that is required by law or regulations; or*

(ii) *the periods set in Subsection (5) of the Section have expired without the patentee's taking serious preparations or starting the effective commercial exploitation of the invention; and*

(iii) *the patentee has no reasonable justification for refusing the voluntary license and/or for his/her omission in exploiting the invention.*[8]

16. *Any decision on the grant or denial of a compulsory license, including on the determination of the remuneration, shall be subject to a review by the court [the court of appeals in the case the authority to grant compulsory licenses has been attributed to the court], upon the initiative of the aggrieved party.*

Notes:

1. The designation of the authority in charge of hearing requests of compulsory licenses and of granting (or denying) them depends on the legal structure of each country. In small countries, where the patent office tends to be small, it is preferable to attribute this task to a Ministry (of Justice, for example) or to a public agency with experience and human resources, such as the Office of the General Attorney. Some developing countries leave the matter of granting compulsory licenses to courts. This may be a good solution, given that courts are constitutionally authorized to decide on limitations to private rights, but it should depend on whether the country has a good court system, with judges not too overwhelmed with legal disputes on other topics, and reasonably educated in patent law.

2. As said, the public interest is the main reason for the granting of compulsory licenses. In fact, the public interest encompasses all other reasons. The reference to the public interest that is made in this article dealing with compulsory licenses will be reinforced with the provision dealing with injunctions, which, as it will be explained below, should be refused when they harm the public interest.

3. It is suggested that simply not working the patent should not lead to a compulsory license. The invention must have some technical or economic relevance—for example, when it concerns a medicine or is important for a sector of the country's industry—in order to justify the interference in the private property of the patentee. A rational patentee who does not see value in working the invention will end up ceasing to pay maintenance fees, and the patent will lapse. However, where the patent owner enforces a nonworked patent, the abuse becomes clear. But this notion evokes two ideas: there may be some very rare occasions when the patent owner has legitimate reasons for suppressing the invention—for example, a patent covering an invention that greatly facilitates the process of abortion, when the patentee sustains a pro-life position; the second idea, already mentioned above, is that, even in the face of an abusive patentee, the infringer is no less an infringer. So, the court must weigh prudently the interests at stake and refuse the injunction (i.e., grant a compulsory license) in cases of serious abuses only. On another point, the expression "through importation" makes compulsory licenses granted on grounds of failure to work compatible with Article 27.1 of the TRIPS Agreement and Article III.4 of the GATT 1947.

4. Where the country grants a compulsory license for importing products made abroad under a compulsory licensing for exporting pharmaceutical products, in accordance with Article 31*bis* of the

TRIPS Agreement, there is no need to pay remuneration. By contrast with the WTO Ministerial Council Decision of 2022, concerning COVID vaccines, Article 31*bis* does not refer to the possibility of reducing the remuneration having in view charitable considerations. As said, this latest Decision is of temporary nature, and therefore there is no immediate utility in incorporating or transposing it into national law.
5. This second part of the sentence may seem redundant, but it is necessary as a clarification that the protection of the legitimate interests of the beneficiary of the compulsory license will not, in principle, justify its duration until the patent expires.
6. This is a topic usually overlooked by patent statutes, but the lawmaker should not forget that patent applications may give rise to some rights. For example, depending on the country's law, the patent owner, once the patent is issued, may enforce it retroactively and recover damages since the date of the filing, or of the publication, of the application. The exception is a nonworked patent, in view of the clear language of paragraph (A)(4) of Article 5 of the Paris Convention.[202]
7. This provision makes it clear that the abuses that may justify a compulsory license are not necessarily anticompetitive. Certain cases involving unfair trade or unfair competition practices, depending on their seriousness, may very well justify the granting of compulsory licenses—as Article 5(A)(2) of the Paris Convention makes it clear.
8. In view of the discussion on the requirement that the pretendent requests a voluntary license from the patentee before he/she applies for the grant of a compulsory license, and taking into consideration what was said above about the unclean hands doctrine, a brief note on refusals to license is necessary. The requirement that a voluntary license be requested (in normal commercial terms and conditions) and that the patentee refuses it does not mean that the simple refusal serves as ground for the grant of the compulsory license. This has already been said, but it is worthy being repeated. The right to say "no" to commercial rivals is a corollary of the right to say "yes." This obvious but important rule is found clearly stated in the patent statute of the United States, as follows:

> *§271. Infringement of patent*
>
> . . .
>
> *(d) No patent owner otherwise entitled to relief for infringement or contributory infringement of a patent shall be denied relief or deemed guilty of misuse or illegal extension of the patent right by reason of his having done one or more of the following: . . .*
> *(4) refused to license or use any rights to the patent; . . .*

However, some lawmakers (and courts) have taken a different stance when the patent owner suppresses the invention, i.e., when he/she does not exploit the invention and nevertheless enforces it or refuses to license it. This is acceptable only when some conditions are met, namely: (i) when the invention is of particularly social interest and its suppression is socially inconvenient; (ii) when the period(s) determined in the law for the mandatory exploitation of the patent has ended; and (iii) the patentee has no acceptable justification for the suppression.

202. Article 5.(A)(4) of the Paris Convention reads (in part):

> *(4) A compulsory license may not be applied for on the ground of failure to work or insufficient working before the expiration of a period of four years from the date of filing of the patent application or three years from the date of the grant of the patent, whichever period expires last; . . . .*

2 ON EXHAUSTION: NEITHER NATIONAL NOR INTERNATIONAL—ALTERNATIVES ARE AVAILABLE

Exhaustion is the mechanism under which the rights that the patent confers to the owner are terminated upon the legitimate transfer of the title to the product covered by the patent or made with the concourse of the process covered by the patent. Exhaustion, therefore, does not occur only after the first sale of the product. It also occurs when the product is donated or seized. What matters is that the transfer of the title be legitimate. It must be practiced by the patentee, his/her successor, or by someone under the control of the patentee, or by operation of the law (seizure by a court or the transfer of the good by the beneficiary of a compulsory license). Therefore, the designation that is usually given to exhaustion—the "first sale doctrine"—in spite of being common, is misleading.

Exhaustion, naturally, occurs at the national level. In view of the principle of independence of patents, which we will briefly discuss below, sales or other facts leading to the transfer of the patented good that occur in other countries should not affect the rights that result from the patent in one given country. But the patent statutes of most countries adopt the modality of international exhaustion, this meaning that the legitimate transfer of the good in another country where the same patent owner has been granted a patent for the same invention leads to exhaustion in the country in question. International exhaustion permits the so-called *parallel imports*, this meaning that independent importers, without the authorization of the patent holder, may import the patented goods from other countries, provided they have been put on those countries' markets legitimately and under a patent for the same invention. International exhaustion, although authorized by Article 6 of the TRIPS Agreement, is in conflict with the principle of independence of patents, and thus it contradicts the provisions of Article 4*bis* of the Paris Convention.

Which mechanism should a developing country adopt?

The two modalities of exhaustion have both advantages and disadvantages.

2.1 Advantages and Disadvantages of National and International Exhaustion

International exhaustion seems to be the preferred avenue for developing countries. And yet, it harms those inventors who obtained a patent for an invention obtained in more than one country. The reason is that those inventors lose their ability to grant exclusive licenses limited to the territory of each country—since parallel imports can lead to the invasion of licensees' exclusive territories by products manufactured (legitimately) by other licensees in other territories.[203] In this sense, international exhaustion is contrary to international technology transfer, as both the licensor and the

203. An exception to this rule is found in Art. 37 of the patent law of Jordan, which reads:

Article 37

. . .

licensee will naturally fear that their investment in the transmission, absorption, and adaptation of the technology will be undermined by parallel imports.

From an economic perspective, international exhaustion of patents also creates serious problems, particularly the increased transaction costs associated with the international trade of patented goods. Parallel imports lead to increased litigation involving patents granted in different countries for the same invention, as patents within the same family rarely cover exactly the same invention. During the prosecution of the patent, applicants often change the content of their claims, or reduce or increase their number. In some countries, which accept the so-called continuation patents, the invention is gradually expanded during prosecution until a final decision is reached. By this point, the invention as initially claimed may have become unrecognizable.

Furthermore, current global chains of value tend to concern complex goods, whose invention, design, and production take place in multiple countries, and involve the coordination of hundreds, if not thousands, of patents. The exhaustion of the rights of one patent can—and usually does—leave the rights arising from the others entirely unaffected.

In a nutshell, international exhaustion leads to increased transaction costs and situations of legal uncertainty—when it is not purely seen as a seemingly legitimate substitute for fraud and counterfeiting.

In turn, the national exhaustion solution is criticized for allowing a practice known as "double dipping." Those who make this type of claim assume that a patent holder should not be permitted to extract "monopoly rent" more than once. Once the article incorporating the patented invention is sold, the holder of the right to the intangible asset will have already been duly "rewarded" by charging a "supracompetitive price." According to this perspective, if the holder could impose restrictions on the buyer's subsequent commercial acts, the patent right would be expanded beyond the scope of the law.

This understanding is profoundly mistaken. Patent rights are not monopolies, nor is the primary purpose of a patent to reward inventors. If the idea of reward were correct, then exhaustion would occur only when the patent holder made a profit from the first sale or other form of assignment of the good. Therefore, the first transfer of the title in the patented goods, when made without a profit—such as a sale at a loss or a donation—could not be considered a "reward" and thus could never lead to exhaustion, whether national or international.

B. *In spite of the inclusions of paragraph (A) of this article* [establishing international exhaustion under certain conditions, which will be discussed infra] *and without prejudice to the provisions of the related International conventions, goods covered by patent of invention may not be imported by any Licensee, if the Licensing contract prohibit him from importation to the kingdom, provided that the patent owner notify in writing the Customs Administration and the Registrar in this respect. The Registrar shall, at the expense of the patent owner, publish this notification in at least one of Local daily gazettes; and the applicable legislations shall apply to this case.*

Patents of Invention Law, Law No. 32 for the Year 1999 (and its amendment by Temporary Law No. 71 for the Year 2001), available at <www.sabaip.com/wp-content/uploads/2018/04/Jordan-Patent-Law.pdf>. This law was amended again in 2017, and is available, in Arabic, in the WIPO Lex database, but Art. 37 has not been modified.

Exhaustion is not an economic concept, but a legal one. Whether or not the holder of an intellectual property right can extend its influence over subsequent acts performed by a legitimate buyer results from the definition of the scope of that right. The amount of income, or "reward," that the holder is able to extract from the commercial exploitation of the intangible asset is irrelevant for this purpose. Furthermore, the reward theory is contradicted by international exhaustion itself. Indeed, one might ask, how can an inventor be rewarded for an invention made, say, in Jordan, through the price of an item manufactured and sold by him or a licensee in Bangladesh? It is not the inventor's desire for reward that dictates prices—it is the amount of money that consumers are willing to pay for the items they acquire. It is the market, not the patent office, that "rewards" patent holders. Without market interest, patents are often very pretty documents, with official seals and bright colors, that inventors can place on their walls, decorating their laboratories, but they are nothing more than pieces of paper.

National exhaustion, therefore, does not lead to "double dipping," but rather to remuneration for the use of distinct rights, arising from distinct property titles, granted under different sovereignties in distinct countries. If the buyer is interested in exploiting price differences in segmented international markets, he/she can negotiate with the patent holder in both countries and obtain special conditions. Note that the situation is exactly the same if the same invention is covered by two patents in two countries, belonging to two different holders. What confers exclusivity (limited by countries' borders) is not the identity of the holder but the right resulting from the patent. Two patents in different territories generate different rights, regardless of their being owned by the same patentee or by two different patentees.

Another criticism addressed to national exhaustion is that if it protects international investors as well as international technology licensors from competition of their own products (imported from another country), in the case the right holder does not exploit his/her intangible asset in a satisfactory manner, a country that adopts national exhaustion has no possibility to remedy the abuse by resorting to importation. In other words, the country lies in the hands of the patentee holder because he/she holds the exclusive right to import. Naturally, such country might prefer to make international exhaustion available in the event the right holder does not make the product available in the country, or where he/she charges prices abusively high (in violation of national price controls, for example), or where he/she engages in antitrust violations (such as anticompetitive market segmentation).

In conclusion, both systems of national and international exhaustion of patent rights have positive and negative consequences. It is possible, however, to find variations, so as to eliminate the disadvantages of the two "traditional" solutions and yet keep their advantages.

2.2 Conditioned Exhaustion

One of such variations is *conditioned* exhaustion. Under such a regime, international exhaustion does not occur automatically upon the first sale (or another sort of transfer of property) of a patented article in another territory. Primarily, exhaustion would occur at the national level only, but it would be converted into international exhaustion in the case of failure to comply with certain conditions. One condition is that the exploitation of the patented invention does not attend the public interest. Therefore, parallel importation would be allowed when its purpose is to remedy an anticompetitive practice, or the abuse of intellectual property rights, or to attend urgent needs of the domestic market when the patentee does not make the patented goods available to customers in fair and reasonable conditions regarding price, quality, and quantity. The other additional condition should be that parallel importation would require prior approval by a public authority or by a court because only that authority could assess in an impartial manner whether the patent owner is not attending the public interest.

Putting it differently, *conditioned* exhaustion is built primarily on the national exhaustion regime. Only if the patent holder does not comply with certain mandatory obligations or conditions that are associated with the economic exploitation of patents, such as those mentioned above, or if reasons of public interest arise, shall the competent authority acknowledge that national exhaustion has been converted into international exhaustion and will issue an authorization for parallel imports to be carried out.

This creative solution can be found in Article 11 of the Industrial Property Act of Oman, as follows:

> *Article 11:*
>
> ...
>
> *(4) (a) The rights under the patent shall not extend:*
>
> *(i) to acts in respect of articles which have been put on the market in Oman by the owner of the patent or with his consent, consequently exhausting the patent owner's rights;*
>
> ...
>
> *(5) Without prejudice to the provisions of subsection 4(a) of this Section, the Minister shall have the authority, ex officio or at the request of any interested party, of declaring the patent rights exhausted, and thus of authorizing others to import the patented product or a product manufactured directly or indirectly by means of the patented invention ("the product") from another territory when that product is not available in the territory of Oman or is available in the territory of Oman with unreasonably low quality standards or in a quantity that is not sufficient to meet the local demand or at prices that the Minister deems abusive or for any other reason of public interest, including anticompetitive practices, provided that:*
>
> *(i) the product has been put in the channels of commerce in the territory from which it will be imported by the owner of the patent or with his consent; and*
>
> *(ii) a patent claiming the product or the process for its manufacture is in force in the territory from which the product will be imported and is owned by the same person who owns the patent in Oman or by a person under his control:*
>
> *(a) If the importer fails to fulfil the purpose that justified the Minister's decision to consider the patent rights exhausted, the Minister shall, ex officio, or at the request of the patent owner, cancel the authorization.*
>
> *(b) If the conditions that gave rise to the Minister's decision to consider the patent exhausted cease to exist, the Minister may, ex officio or at*

> *the request of the patent owner, cancel the authorization, provided that the legitimate interests of the importer are taken into account, including but not exclusively that the importer will retain the right to commercialize the products that remain on stock.*

Let us make it clear: this provision is not about compulsory licenses. Two aspects distinguish the Omani solution concerning exhaustion from compulsory licenses. The first aspect is that, in view of his/her rights having been exhausted through a first sale under a parallel right in another territory, the patent owner would not be entitled to any remuneration. And yet the government would keep control of parallel channels of distribution, particularly in the field of pharmaceuticals.

The second aspect is that the competent authority would have a chance to verify whether the patent owner was making serious efforts to supply the national market, through local exploitation or through imports, at reasonable prices and conditions.

A variation from the Omani solution is found in the Patent Act of the Philippines, under which exhaustion is, in principle, of a national nature, but international exhaustion applies to patents covering pharmaceutical products. The provision in question goes as follows:

> *Section 72. Limitations of Patent Rights.—The owner of a patent has no right to prevent third parties from performing, without his authorization, the acts referred to in Section 71 hereof in the following circumstances:*
>
> *72.1. Using a patented product which has been put on the market in the Philippines by the owner of the product, or with his express consent, insofar as such use is performed after that product has been so put on the said market: Provided, That with regard to drugs and medicines, the limitation on patent rights shall apply after a drug or medicine has been introduced in the Philippines or anywhere else in the world by the patent owner, or by any party authorized to use the invention: Provided, further, That the right to import the drugs and medicines contemplated in this section shall be available to any government agency or any private third party; . . .*

The statute of the Philippines in this regard is compatible with the TRIPS Agreement. In effect, the choice of the exhaustion regime under Article 6 is not limited by the prohibition to discriminate as to the field of technology (Article 27.1). Provided the national and the MFN treatment principles are observed, differentiated treatment concerning exhaustion is indeed possible as regards the nature of the goods covered by the patent in question. Therefore, WTO Members may establish in their law national exhaustion as the generally prevailing regime, but, as regards patented pharmaceutical products, they may apply the international exhaustion regime.

Another variation of the national exhaustion regime is found in the Patent Act of Switzerland. Under Article 9a, national exhaustion applies within the European Economic Area (the territories of European Union Members plus the territories of EFTA Members—Switzerland, Liechtenstein, Norway, and Iceland), but parallel imports are admitted "if the patent protection for the functional characteristics of the goods is only of subordinate importance." The literal translation of this expression from the French, Italian, and German official versions of the Act would read "of less importance," "of secondary importance," and "of minor importance," respectively. The provision (paragraph 4 of Article 9a) adds that "Subordinate importance is presumed unless the proprietor of the patent provides *prima facie* evidence to the contrary."[204]

The Swiss law does not define what "subordinate importance" means, but one may understand it as concerning a complex product, where the patented component is of minor relevance by comparison with the integrality of the article.

The Swiss solution is undoubtedly interesting, but may give rise to uncertainty, given the absence of more precise language defining the secondary importance of the patented article or feature as compared to the whole product.

2.3 Other Approaches to Exhaustion

A country could take another approach: in principle, the law may establish that exhaustion is international (i.e., the patentee's right to oppose the importation of the product is lost when the same product, covered by a patent in another territory, is legitimately transferred by the same patentee or by someone under his/her control). But the right holder would be entitled to block parallel imports if he/she proved (before a court or other competent national authority) that parallel imports offend a number of principles that operate in protecting his/her legitimate interests.

A solution that goes in this direction, although with some variations, is found in the Patent Act of Jordan, as follows:

> *Article 37*
>
> A. *The provisions of this law shall not prevent any person from importing any materials or goods from a third party if that party enjoys the legal protection of the same patent protected in the Kingdom and if that importation is lawful, complies with the principles of commercial competition and fairly takes into account the economic value of the protected patent.*

The particularities in the law of Jordan are three: (i) the importation of the patented good from another country must be lawful; i.e., it may not breach rules dealing, for example, with administrative requirements, such as those that concern the commercialization of regulated products, like pharmaceuticals and agrochemicals; (ii) the importation must comply with the principles of commercial competition, in the sense that the patentee shall not be harmed by the competition he/she suffers from his/her own goods sold in another country; an example already mentioned can be repeated here: the inventor has obtained two patents, one in Jordan, and another in Bangladesh, for the same invention; the inventor sells the patented article on both markets; a third party imports the product from Bangladesh into Jordan and intends to make a profit from the significant difference in prices, given that in Bangladesh costs of production and distribution are much lower than in Jordan; under the law of Jordan, the patentee could oppose the parallel imports, alleging those imports offend "the principles of commercial competition"; in other words, international exhaustion, under the law of Jordan, seems to take place where the price of the imported good is the same or higher than the price that prevails on the market of Jordan; and (iii) parallel imports

204. Federal Act on Patents for Inventions (Patents Act), of June 25, 1954 (as of April 1, 2019).

shall not become so frequent or massive that reduce significantly the legitimate expectations of the patentee as regards the gains he/she would extract from the patented invention.

Therefore, in Jordan, we find a mechanism of international exhaustion that is conditioned by the observation of three requirements that safeguard the legitimate interests of the patentee.

This solution is also acceptable from the perspective of the inventor, but, unlike the Omani solution, it brings an extra burden on the right holder, given that the obligation to prove that parallel imports have taken place in breach of at least one of those three elements falls upon him/her.

Other developing countries have used creativity in order to secure the most positive aspect of national exhaustion—the provision of legal security to foreign direct investors who do not need to worry about the eventual competition of products made by themselves or their licensees in other countries—and yet to some extent avoid excesses that could be instilled by that modality of exhaustion.

One example is Brazil, the Industrial Property Act of which provides in this regard:

> *Art. 43. The provisions of the previous article do not apply to:*
>
> . . .
>
> *IV— a product manufactured in accordance with a process or product patent that has been placed on the domestic market directly by the patent holder or with his consent;*
>
> *Art. 184. A crime is committed against a patent of invention or utility model by anyone who:*
>
> . . .
>
> *II— imports a product that is the subject matter of a patent of invention or utility model or obtained by means or process patented in the country, . . . and that has not been placed on the foreign market directly by the patent holder or with his consent.*

What is of particular interest in the Brazilian act is that primarily it provides for national exhaustion, and therefore the importation of goods patented in Brazil or goods made with a process patented in Brazil constitutes an infringement. It follows that parallel imports may be pursued in a civil court and give rise to injunctive relief and damages. But they do not constitute a criminal offense.

The patent law of Nigeria has taken an approach that takes a stricter approach to national exhaustion. The law provides:

> *Section 6. . . .*
>
> *(3) The rights under a patent—*
>
> . . .
>
> *(b) shall not extend to acts done in respect of a product covered by the patent after the product has been lawfully sold in Nigeria, except in so far as the patent makes provision for a special application of the product, in which*

case the special application shall continue to be reserved to the patentee notwithstanding this paragraph; . . .[205]

This language permits a reading that leads to the understanding that the rights conferred by patents granted in Nigeria are exhausted at the national level only. The transfer of the title of goods in other countries under a patent for the same invention has no consequences within Nigerian territory. Furthermore, exhaustion does not occur as regards special applications of the product, provided those applications are claimed in the patent. This is an invitation for inventors to be precise and specific in drafting the claims, so that they reveal (and claim) the applications possible for the patented product. Where the application is not revealed, the rights in the product shall be exhausted (nationally).

2.4 Discussion

As said, international exhaustion can be seen as a mechanism useful in the prevention of anticompetitive practices on the international market. In the face of the possibility of parallel imports, the right holder would refrain himself/herself from engaging in practices such as international price discrimination. But the first modality suggested above works more as a remedy than a preventive measure because parallel importation would be permitted only where the government authority is satisfied that the patent owner has failed to work the invention in a manner compatible with public interest.

This may give rise to a few questions. Would the remedy of international exhaustion be compatible with the provisions of Articles 31(k) and 32 of the TRIPS Agreement, which seem to impose limits on the kind of remedies that governments can impose in the event of finding anticompetitive practices? Would there be a need for the prior adjudication of the anticompetitive practice, as Article 31(k) says? Are governments requested to give an opportunity for judicial review of a decision permitting the parallel imports as a sanction against the failure to use the patent in a manner compatible with public interest? Should the government first grant a compulsory license, as Article 5(A)(3) of the Paris Convention provides for?

The answer to these questions is that conditioned exhaustion, as adopted by the Omani patent statute, should not be scrutinized vis-à-vis norms that apply to compulsory licenses. As noted above, conditioned exhaustion and compulsory licenses are distinct measures. After all, conditioned exhaustion is a modality of exhaustion for all purposes.

Let us not forget, however, that the introduction of an element that conditions exhaustion would not make it less incompatible with the principle of independence of the Paris Convention, as mentioned above, and as it will be discussed in more detail below. However, eventually, where parallel imports are authorized on a case-by-case approach and with the purpose of sanctioning abuses—in accordance with the Omani statute—the question of territoriality could be put aside.

205. Patents and Designs Act (Chapter 344).

After all, the government would sanction an abuse or address a matter of public interest in the importing country, where the right is in force. In the face of the impossibility of resorting to parallel importation, the government would need to issue a compulsory license. So, one might be tempted to build a case on the compatibility of conditioned exhaustion with the principle of independence. Nevertheless, national exhaustion, whether justified or not by abuses and other serious circumstances in the importing country, arises from sales made in the territory of another jurisdiction where a patent is in force for the same invention (and owned by the same patentee or by another person under the control of the patentee). This idea may never be consistent with the principle of independence.

3 ABOUT THE PRIOR USER EXCEPTION

Although the TRIPS Agreement does not mention the prior user exception, many national patent laws have provisions permitting it.[206] Using the language of the draft Treaty Supplementing the Paris Convention as far as Patents are Concerned, the prior user exception means that:

> *. . . a patent shall have no effect against any person (hereinafter referred to as "the prior user") who, in good faith, for the purposes of his enterprise or business, before the filing date or, where priority is claimed, the priority date of the application on which the patent is granted, and within the territory where the patent produces its effect, was using the invention or was making effective and serious preparations for such use; any such person shall have the right, for the purposes of his enterprise or business, to continue such use or to use the invention as envisaged in such preparations.*

In spite of the fact that negotiations around the draft Treaty have been suspended after 1991 and its provisions have never entered into force, the presence of this provision in itself reveals a generalized acceptance of the exception. It has, however, a problem, which results from its not being "limited," and therefore it is not clearly authorized by Article 30 of the TRIPS Agreement, which provides for the general boundaries within which exceptions to rights conferred must stand. Article 30 reads:

> *Article 30*
>
> *Exceptions to Rights Conferred*
>
> *Members may provide limited exceptions to the exclusive rights conferred by a patent, provided that such exceptions do not unreasonably conflict with a normal exploitation of the patent and do not unreasonably prejudice the legitimate interests of the patent owner, taking account of the legitimate interests of third parties.*

The prior user exception is not "limited" for the purposes of Article 30, in accordance with the interpretation given to this provision by the WTO Dispute

206. Additional grounds for exceptions to rights conferred are found in Art. 5*ter* of the Paris Convention. They concern devices forming part of vessels, aircraft, and land vehicles, that temporarily or accidentally enter the territory of Union country where they are patented.

Settlement Body.[207] The reason is that, in general, the rights acknowledged to the prior user include the making, the using, and the selling of the product. Some laws limit that right to the level or proportion of use that existed prior to the patent application (or publication), thus prohibiting the prior user from increasing the production above the previous levels. But even in that event there are no limits as to the scale of the prior use itself. That is, if the prior user is a large company, and if the patent owner is a small enterprise, probably nothing is left for the patent owner to exploit because the prior user may have prepared itself to supply the entire market.

The prior user exception is also troublesome vis-à-vis the two other conditions set by Article 30 (i.e.: (i) the exception should not "unreasonably conflict with a normal exploitation of the patent" and (ii) it should "not unreasonably prejudice the legitimate interests of the patent owner"). In effect, it is difficult to understand the logic of recognizing inventors who, instead of rushing to the patent office to apply for a patent, thereby disclosing the inventions, prefer to conceal them, with the hope of maintaining their exclusivity for the indefinite term of (indirect) protection of trade secrets. Evidence that the notion of the prior user corresponds to that of a previous inventor is found in the language of Brazil's Industrial Property Act, of 1996, as follows:

> *Prior User*
>
> *Article 45. Any person acting in good faith who, prior to the filing or priority date of a patent application, was exploiting its subject matter in Brazil, shall be guaranteed the right to continue exploiting it, free of charge, in the previous form and conditions.*
>
> . . .
>
> *§ 2. The right referred to in this article shall not be granted to a person who has become aware of the subject matter of the patent through disclosure pursuant to art. 12, provided that the application was filed within 1 (one) year from the disclosure.*

Article 12 is the provision of Brazil's law that addresses the grace period. Combined, the two provisions mean that the person who invokes the prior user exception must not have acquired knowledge of the invention that later becomes the content of the claims of a patent application through any sort of publication, by the applicant, by a patent office, or by an abusive third party. It follows that the prior user is an inventor or has received the invention from an inventor—one who has decided to keep the invention under secrecy, or has neglected to rush to the patent office and file a patent application.

In conclusion, the prior user exception is nothing else than a reward to the earlier inventor and a punishment to the patent applicant (also an inventor). In spite of the generalized practice by WTO Members of adopting the prior user exception, it is difficult to devise its consistency with Article 28.1, in the light of the conditions of Article 30. Furthermore, the language of Article 70.4 seems to indicate that the thrust of the TRIPS Agreement does not admit such an exception to rights conferred.[208]

207. *Canada—Patent Protection of Pharmaceutical Products* (WT/DS114/R, of March 17, 2000, para. 7.25), adopted by the Dispute Settlement Body (WT/DS114//Rev. 1, of April 27, 2000).

208. Article 70.4 of the TRIPS Agreement reads:

Article 70.4 addresses a practical problem that arises from the extension of the terms of patents existing on the date of the application of the Agreement, according to Article 70.2. It is indeed common that a competitor, expecting the expiry of a patent, takes steps in preparation for the exploitation of the invention—steps that may represent significant investments. Article 70.4 recognizes that the extension of the patent term, in consequence of Article 70.2, may come as a surprise to the patentee's competitors. Article 70.4 is not an authorization for those competitors to exploit the patented invention during the extended term. Instead, it permits WTO Members to limit the remedies available to the patent owner to the payment of equitable remuneration. In the absence of such an authorization, the extended patent rights would be fully enforceable against those competitors, under Articles 70.2 and 28.

The analogy of Article 70.4 with situations relating to the prior use seems evident. The prior user is also caught by surprise by the patent application. He/she should not be allowed to exploit the invention without authorization by the patent owner because that would be an act of infringement. At least, the patent owner should be entitled to receive an adequate remuneration, as provided for by Article 70.4.

The prior user exception could have some relevance in the event that the patent applicant, during the prosecution, introduces modifications that expand the initial claims. Actually, as seen above, the patent laws of many countries permit patent applicants to introduce modifications in the claims, provided those modifications are supported by the description. Therefore, in those countries, if the patent application claims less than what it originally describes, it is possible for the applicant, before the patent office makes a final decision, to add to the claims the subject matter not initially claimed (but described). As discussed above, this may give rise to legal insecurity because third parties who take notice of the application as soon as it is published may detect the difference in the scope between the description and the claims and may, eventually, start preparations to use the unclaimed part of the invention. Later, if the claims are expanded, those third parties may be surprised with a complaint of infringement. However, this would require a change in the prior user exception as it is usually adopted. Indeed, generally, the exception applies to those who started exploiting the invention or made serious preparations *before the patent application was filed* (or before the priority date). It would be therefore necessary to apply the exception to those who start using the invention (or making preparations for its use) *before the matter was effectively claimed.*

In respect of any acts in respect of specific objects embodying protected subject matter which become infringing under the terms of legislation in conformity with this Agreement, and which were commenced, or in respect of which a significant investment was made, before the date of acceptance of the WTO Agreement by that Member, any Member may provide for a limitation of the remedies available to the right holder as to the continued performance of such acts after the date of application of this Agreement for that Member. In such cases the Member shall, however, at least provide for the payment of equitable remuneration.

At the end of the day, patent lawmakers have to decide: are they drafting a law for the sake of the protection of the interests and rights of inventors?; do they really believe that the idea of setting the foundations of a strong patent system is more valuable than bending to the imposition of a mere trade-off inserted in a multilateral trade agreement?

If the answer is yes to both questions, the prior user exception should not be inserted in the law, for the reasons explained above: the prior user is someone who either ignored or tried to circumvent the obligation to disclose that is associated with the filing of a patent application. However, if the drafter understands that there may be circumstances that justify a tolerant treatment of the first inventor—because that is what the prior user usually is—and wishes to include the prior user exception, then he/she should make it clear that the prior user, when invoking his/her exceptional right to use the invention in question, has a good explanation for not having sought patent protection earlier.

Before presenting a suggestion for the drafting of a provision on the prior user exception that takes into account the private and public interests involved, let us see some examples.

The WIPO Model Law for Developing Countries on Inventions reads, in this regard:

> *Section 137: Rights Derived from Prior Manufacture or Use*
>
> *Where a person, at the filing or, where appropriate, priority date of the patent application and in the country, (i) was making the product or using the process which is the subject of the invention claimed in that application, or (ii) had made serious preparations toward the working referred to in item (i), that person shall have the right, despite the grant of the patent, to exploit the patented invention, provided that the product in question is made, or the process in question is used, in the country by the said person, and provided that he can prove that his knowledge of the invention was not by reason or in consequence of acts committed by the owner of the patent or his predecessor in title or of an abuse committed with regard to the owner of the patent or his predecessor in title. Such right cannot be assigned or transferred by succession except as part of the establishment of the said person.*

The law of Qatar also contains the prior user exception, as follows:

> *Article 10*
>
> *Whoever manufactures the patented product [,] uses the patent subject technique or undertakes serious arrangements for such manufacturing or usage within the State before the registration [filing?] or priority date shall be allowed to carry on such action on the basis of good faith. Such right shall not be assigned or transferred to others except with the other parts of the enterprise.*

The Patent Act of Nigeria, in this same regard, provides that:

> *Section 6. . . .*
>
> *(4) Where, at the date of the filing of a patent application in respect of a product or process or at the date of a foreign priority validly claimed in respect of the application, a person other than the applicant—*
> *(a) was conducting an undertaking in Nigeria; and*
> *(b) in good faith and for the purposes of the undertaking, was manufacturing the product or applying the process or had made serious preparations with*

a view to doing so, then, notwithstanding the grant of a patent, there shall exist a right (exercisable by the person for the time being conducting the undertaking, and not otherwise) to continue the manufacture or application, or to continue and complete the preparations and thereafter undertake the manufacture or application, as the case may be, and in respect of any resulting products to do any other act mentioned in subsection (1) of this section.

Interestingly, the Patent Act of the United States conditions the acknowledgement of the prior user exception to the observation of a determined time period:

§273. Defense to infringement based on prior commercial use

(a) In General.—A person shall be entitled to a defense under section 282(b) with respect to subject matter consisting of a process, or consisting of a machine, manufacture, or composition of matter used in a manufacturing or other commercial process, that would otherwise infringe a claimed invention being asserted against the person if—
  (1) such person, acting in good faith, commercially used the subject matter in the United States, either in connection with an internal commercial use or an actual arm's length sale or other arm's length commercial transfer of a useful end result of such commercial use; and
  (2) such commercial use occurred at least 1 year before the earlier of either—
    (A) the effective filing date of the claimed invention; or
    (B) the date on which the claimed invention was disclosed to the public in a manner that qualified for the exception from prior art under section 102(b).

The US Patent Act adds that the commercial use by the person benefiting from this exception should not have been abandoned, albeit temporarily:

(4) A person who has abandoned commercial use (that qualifies under this section) of subject matter may not rely on activities performed before the date of such abandonment in establishing a defense under this section with respect to actions taken on or after the date of such abandonment.

Section 273 provides for some examples of prior commercial use covered by the exception, such as the use of the invention for the purposes of premarketing regulatory review and for nonprofit laboratory use. Importantly, the same section clarifies who can invoke the defense, in the following terms:

(e) Limitations and exceptions.—
  (1) Personal defense.—
    (A) In general.—A defense under this section may be asserted only by the person who performed or directed the performance of the commercial use described in subsection (a), or by an entity that controls, is controlled by, or is under common control with such person.
    (B) Transfer of right.—Except for any transfer to the patent owner, the right to assert a defense under this section shall not be licensed or assigned or transferred to another person except as an ancillary and subordinate part of a good-faith assignment or transfer for other reasons of the entire enterprise or line of business to which the defense relates. . . .

(2) *Derivation.—A person may not assert a defense under this section if the subject matter on which the defense is based was derived from the patentee or persons in privity with the patentee.*

Both the WIPO Model Law and the US Patent Act very wisely make it clear that the person who benefits from the prior user exception should not have acquired knowledge of the invention from the patentee or because of his/her proximity with the patentee, thus implying an abusive or bad-faith manner of acquiring such knowledge, such as breach of trust.

Moreover, the general understanding that buttresses the prior user exception in patent laws is that it constitutes a defense to be used in the case the patent owner sues the user on grounds of infringement. The operation, therefore, operates as a prerogative established directly by law, without the need for any formality. However, the patent law of Indonesia has followed a different path. The relevant provisions read:

Article 14

(1) *A party who exploits an Invention at the same time that Invention is filed for a patent is still entitled to exploit the Invention even though that similar Invention is then granted the Patent.*
(2) *The party who exploits the Invention as referred to in section (1) is recognized as the prior user.*
(3) *The provisions as referred to in section (1) are not applicable when the party who exploits the Invention as the prior user uses the knowledge about the Invention from the description, drawings, samples, or claims from the Invention for which the Patent is requested.*

Article 15

(1) *The party who exploits an Invention as referred to in Article 14 is only recognized as the prior user if after the Patent has been granted for a similar Invention, he/she files an application as the prior user to the Minister.*
(2) *Recognition as the prior user is issued by the Minister in the form of a letter of statement as the prior user upon fulfillment of requirements and payment of a fee.*
(3) *The right of prior user expires at the same time as the expiry of the Patent for the same invention.*

Article 16

(1) *Prior user cannot transfer his/her right as the prior user to other party, by Licensing or transfer of right, except because of inheritance.*
(2) *Prior user may only use his/her right to exploit the Invention.*
(3) *Prior user is not entitled to prohibit other parties from exploiting the Invention.*

Article 17

In the event that a prior user violates provisions as referred to in Article 16 section (1), the Minister may revoke the letter of statement as a prior user.

Article 18

Further provisions regarding prior user are regulated by a Ministerial Regulation.

3.1 *Dos and Don'ts* Concerning the Prior User Exception

We have seen that the prior user exception, in spite of its general acceptance by WTO Members, generates more inconveniences than advantages: not only it opens the door for a very extensive exception to the rights conferred by the patent, in conflict with Article 30 of the TRIPS Agreement, but also it tends to reward an inventor who has not submitted his/her invention to the scrutiny of the patent office and society as a whole, preferring to keep it secret. Moreover, the prior user exception can be used, if the law is not well drafted, to suffocate the legitimate interests of the inventor who has applied for the patent. In effect, when the prior user is a large company, it may use the invention in a way that pushes the patentee out of the market.

However, developing countries, and in particular those that are poorer, may have good reasons for adopting the prior user exception, in the sense that it protects naïf inventors who, unaware of or less familiar with the patent system, keep the invention to themselves and are later surprised by a patent filed by an independent inventor.

The balance can be obtained through a provision that accepts the prior user exception but submits it to three conditions: first, the prior user needs to provide a reasonable justification for not having been diligent in filing his/her own patent application expeditiously;[209] second, the prior user shall confine the future use of the invention to the same dimension and quantities it had in view until the patent application that took him/her by surprise was published; and, third, the prior user shall pay the patentee an adequate remuneration for his/her use of the invention.

It should be emphasized, however, that the exception that benefits the prior user, when accepted by the lawmaker, should constitute a defense to be used by the defendant in an infringement lawsuit and to be acknowledged by the court upon the evidence submitted by the prior user. The formal procedure adopted by the patent law of Indonesia should be avoided, not only because it gives rise to an unnecessary formal procedure, which takes time and resources in order to be successful, but also because it is difficult to access in the event the infringer/prior user was not aware of the infringement. Admittedly, in this case, the court will have to suspend the lawsuit until the defendant obtains the certificate from the Registrar. It saves time and money for the court to handle that exception directly.

---

209. The lawmaker may not see interest or convenience in entering into the detail of identifying the justifications that the patent office will accept as reasonable, thus leaving that matter to the courts, but we can indicate at least three: (i) in the industrial field where the invention applies, counterfeiting is rampant, and thus the prior user preferred, for better protecting his/her investment, to keep the invention secret; (ii) the prior user, while already using the invention, wished to submit it to thorough testing and experimenting, in search for improvements; therefore, the fact that he/she did not apply for the patent was not a matter of neglect, but of commercial wisdom; (iii) the prior user, based on sound and demonstrable reasons, believed the invention was not patentable. In the last case, a wise prior user will prefer to share the market with the patent owner than challenging the patent and eventually causing its invalidation—when he/she would face the unlimited competition by anyone interested in using the invention.

Here is the suggested language:

Article . . .

Defense to infringement based on good faith prior commercial use

(a) *A person (the "prior user") shall be entitled to a defense under section . . . with respect to subject matter that would otherwise infringe a patented invention being asserted against the person if such person, acting in good faith, commercially used, or took serious preparations aimed at using the subject matter in the . . . [name of the country] before the effective date on which the patent application was filed or the claimed invention was disclosed to the public.*
(b) *This defense only applies to the prior user who has become aware of the patented invention because he/she has reached the same inventive result through his/her own efforts or has acquired the knowledge legitimately from another person who has reached the same inventive result through his/her own efforts.*
(c) *The prior user needs to provide a reasonable justification for not having filed his/her own patent application expeditiously.*
(d) *The prior user shall confine the future use of the invention to the same dimension and quantities he/she had in view until he/she became aware of the claimed invention.*
(e) *The prior user shall pay the patentee adequate remuneration for the use of invention.*
(f) *Failure to comply with any of the conditions established in this Article will cause the prior use not being acceptable as a defense.*

4 LICENSES OF RIGHT

Licenses of right are mechanisms through which patent owners offer publicly their patents for licensing to anyone interested, under reasonable conditions. In return, patentees pay lower maintenance fees and are exempted from having their patents compulsorily licensed on grounds of failure to work.

Today, a variant of licenses of right is being offered in abundance in the field of technical standards. The variation stands in the fact that these licenses of right are offered to the entities engaged in developing and organizing technical standards (known as Standard-Setting Organizations, or SSOs) and are celebrated with implementers through private contracts, not through the law of patents. These licenses usually concern SEPs and involve contractual conditions that must be fair, reasonable and nondiscriminatory (FRAND), in favor of implementers.

A number of countries submit licenses of right to terms and conditions that could vaguely evoke FRAND terms. One example is Guyana, the patent law of which contains a clause that explicitly addresses the topic of nondiscriminatory treatment of licensees of right:

Section 28

(1) *At any time after the sealing of a patent the Registrar shall, if the patentee so requests, cause the patent to be endorsed with the words "licence of right," and a corresponding entry in the register, and thereupon—*

. . .

> (b) *in settling the terms of any such licence, the Registrar shall be guided by the following considerations—*
>
> . . .
>
> (iii) *he shall also endeavour to secure equality of advantage among the several licensees, and for this purpose may, on due cause being shown, reduce the royalties or other payments accruing to the patentee under any licence previously granted;*
>
> *Provided that, considering the question of equality of advantage, the Registrar shall take into account any work done or outlay incurred by any previous licensee with a view to testing the commercial value of the invention or to securing the working thereof on a commercial scale in Guyana; . . .*

Licenses of right, although very rarely used in practice (except in the case of SEPs), are an interesting measure to be included in the patent law of developing countries. By a simple mechanism, licenses of right increase legal security in transactions dealing with technology transfer and, if well utilized, can facilitate the emergence of technological clusters in the country.

CHAPTER 8

On the Independence of Patents and of the Rights They Confer

Extraterritoriality in the context of SEPs has been a topic of growing concern, especially in lawsuits involving the determination of global royalty rates and the application of anti-enforcement measures such as interim licenses. In essence, these measures seek to (i) prevent the effectiveness of decisions handed down by a foreign court or (ii) judicially define the amount for the payment of global royalties under F/RAND conditions,[210] regardless of the private negotiations carried out between the parties. These practices, adopted mainly by courts in the United States, the United Kingdom, and China, have directly impacted the sovereignty of other nations, whose judiciary branches see their autonomy threatened by undue interference from foreign jurisdictions.

Taking into account the current trend in some jurisdictions in the sense of attributing extraterritorial effects to judicial opinions and orders, either concerning the enforcement of those patents or in relation to the setting of licensing conditions, one may ask whether the time has come for national patent laws to assert the independence of patents granted under those same laws. The main factor that would justify such an

210. FRAND is the acronym used in Europe (and the world in general) for Fair, Reasonable and Non-discriminatory terms offered by the owner of a standard essential patent to the members and users (implementers) of a technical standard elaborated by an SSO. In the United States, the acronym used is RAND. The patent owner may be a member of the SSO (and, thus, may have participated in the elaboration of the standard in question) or not (and may have offered the license to the SSO). But if the patent owner is not a member of the SSO and has not participated in the elaboration of the standard, he/she is not obliged to offer a license under F/RAND conditions. When he refuses to offer a voluntary license and the standard becomes (under a law or a regulation) of mandatory observation by implementers, the grant of a compulsory license may ensue—provided that the implementer has not started using the invention without authorization. In the case of technical standards that are not mandatory, the patent owner who is not an SSO member is not compelled to offer a voluntary license under any conditions whatsoever. *See* Nuno Pires de Carvalho, Technical Standards, Intellectual Property, and Competition: A Holistic View, 47 Journal of Law Policy 61 (2105).

assertation by developing countries is the interest of those countries in keeping an eye on the contractual terms of patent licensing agreements, as we will discuss below. Global licensing agreements that do not take the local interests of developing countries into account may be inconvenient to them, besides denying the public administration—both the patent office and the competition authority—the competence to have a final word on the contents of those contracts.

What is proposed here is that the lawmaker should clearly acknowledge the independence of national courts as regards decisions taken by courts that belong to other jurisdictions.

The principle of independence of patents has been unequivocally established in the Paris Convention since 1900 (with an important addition in 1911). The relevant provisions read:

> *Article 4bis*
>
> *(1) Patents applied for in the various countries of the Union by nationals of countries of the Union shall be independent of patents obtained for the same invention in other countries, whether members of the Union or not.*
>
> *(2) The foregoing provision is to be understood in an unrestricted sense, in particular, in the sense that patents applied for during the period of priority are independent, both as regards the grounds for nullity and forfeiture, and as regards their normal duration.*

It is worth noticing that the independence of patents, as defined in an *absolute manner* ("d'une façon absolue," in the original French version), is a principle, more than a rule. Being an absolute principle, it does not admit exceptions or divergent approaches to its meaning and application.

Despite the principle of patent independence, so clearly stated by the Paris Convention, we must recognize that it generates some tension with the commercial and economic reality that today surrounds this type of intangible property. We can point to at least two factors that contribute to this tension.

First, since the decentralization of production centers and international trade flows intensified in the 1950s, more and more global chains of value have been established. These chains refer to sequences of invention, manufacture, and marketing of complex products that are not restricted to the territory of a single country. On the contrary, these three components come together to form an international chain, from the moment the product is conceived to the moment it reaches the buyer. If we think of complex products—understood as products made up of a relatively large number of elements—such as aircraft, computers, and mobile phones, it is easy to conclude: (i) that, in their overwhelming majority, these products are made up of inventions made by several companies, located in different parts of the world; (ii) that these products embrace parts manufactured in different countries; (iii) that the various parts are assembled in another country that offers better conditions in terms of human resources and tax treatment; and (iv) that, finally, they are marketed all over the world. These products thus form a global chain in which each phase corresponds to an increase in value. They are covered by patents and families of patents that are enforceable in a multitude of countries, as well.

As regards the products resulting from these chains, their operation must often comply with technical standards that require their interoperability, so that components manufactured in one country do not compromise the efficient operation of the final product in any country where it is put into use by the end consumer. In other words, the rules—some of which are patented—that determine how the product operates (and, often, how it is manufactured) tend to be the same throughout the world. This dissolves technical and commercial boundaries. It is not surprising that there is a tendency, in some cases at least, to also dissolve the normative boundaries that govern the rights applicable to the technological content of standards.

Second, intellectual property assets are intangible and immaterial. They move from country to country imperceptibly—often through digital transfer. If a few centuries ago technology was transferred through personal contact between master and apprentice, today, through the reading of a patent, even if granted in one single country, knowledge is acquired anywhere in the world by those skilled persons with sufficient experience to read and understand its specifications.

Nevertheless, developing country lawmakers may be justifiably worried about the loss of independence of their courts and executive branches of government, at least as far licensing and enforcement of patents are concerned. What may sound as a fair licensing clause in one country may not be so in another. Harmonized royalty rates may seem a good idea for complex products that are sold worldwide, but exactly in the same manner as those products will not be sold under the same price in every country, the corresponding royalties should not be necessarily identical either.

Below, we will make some comments on the convenience of developing countries keeping control over the contents of patent licensing agreements, at least to some extent. But, for now, here is a suggestion on language that a lawmaker could include in the patent statute:

Article . . .

Independence of patents

1. *Patents granted under this law and the rights thereby conferred shall be absolutely independent of patents for the same invention obtained in other countries, including as regards their validity, maintenance, licensing, assignment, and enforcement.*
2. *For the purposes of this section, the term "for the same invention" shall be understood in a broad sense, and includes patents the corresponding applications of which have been altered, or amended after their filing in other countries.*

In view of this language, the courts of a developing country would not be required to respect the terms of contracts signed by patentees in other countries, in the case the latter sue on allegations of infringement in that country. This will protect patentees that are compelled by foreign courts to accept licensing conditions that they would not willingly offer to licensees.

However, in spite of this clear statement of the principle of independence, the problems caused by those anti-suit injunctions issued in other jurisdictions, associated with threats of retaliation against those companies that might enforce their patent rights in other territories, require an international solution, which can only be negotiated in a way that restores the integrality of territorial protection for patents, as per Article 4*bis* of the Paris Convention—or that puts it aside, in part or totally.[211]

211. Recently, a WTO Panel, upon a complaint lodged by the European Union, examined a policy adopted by Chinese courts, in the context of litigation involving FRAND commitments for the licensing of standard-essential patents. The Panel held that there was nothing in the TRIPS Agreement that could prevent those courts from issuing anti-suit injunctions, prohibiting non-Chinese patent holders to sue Chinese companies on allegations of infringement in other jurisdictions, grounded on non-Chinese patents. The EU appealed to a board of arbitrators (replacing temporarily the WTO Appellate Body, which is currently in a nonfunctional standing due to the U.S.'s blockage of the designation of its Members), and the arbitrators reversed. In the arbitrators' decision, three points should be emphasized:

- "[. . .] we [. . .] find that the corollary of the obligation in Article 1.1, first sentence of the TRIPS Agreement to 'give effect' to the provisions of that Agreement in a WTO Member's territory is to do so without frustrating the functioning of the systems of protection and enforcement of IP rights implemented by other Members in their respective territories."
- "In this context, and considering that the factors for granting an A[anti]-S[uit] I[njunction] and the policy objectives underlying the ASI policy bear no relation to the SEP holder's ability to exercise the exclusive rights conferred on it by another WTO Member by means of infringement proceedings, the ASI policy affects the patent owner's right to prevent third parties not having its consent from making, using, offering for sale, selling, or importing the patented product."
- "For the reasons described in this section, we consider that the ASI policy does indeed contribute to the non-fulfilment of the central condition on which a SEP holder has predicated the exercise of its 'right . . . to conclude licensing contracts', namely on the engagement of SEP implementers in good faith negotiations to arrive at mutually-agreeable FRAND terms."

See China—Enforcement of Intellectual Property Rights, Arbitration under Article 25 of the DSU, Award of the Arbitrators, WT/DS611/ARB25, July 21, 2025, at 26, 33, and 44. The bottom line of the arbitrators' decision is that the Panel had failed to give due consideration to the principle of independence of patents, from which the notion of extraterritoriality derives, and which enables the holder of patents in different jurisdictions to seek the judicial protection of his/her rights in each one of the territories where he/she holds a patent. Unfortunately, the arbitrators failed to mention this fundamental principle, which, eventually without their knowing it, buttresses their decision. Both in the Panel report and in the Arbitrators award, there is not a single mention of Art. 4*bis* of the Paris Convention.

CHAPTER 9

On the Terms of Patents and Their Extension

The term of patents has been standardized across the world under the TRIPS Agreement, regardless of the countries' level of development. The reason for setting a uniform term of protection lies in the globalization of markets and the increasing eruption of the already mentioned global chains of value, under which complex products are the result of the combination of a variety of technological components, each being produced and/or assembled (and patented) in different countries. The rationale is that those components combine harmoniously not only from a technical point of view but also from a legal one. Ideally, a patent granted in China should have the same value as in the United States or in Germany. This sort of consistency implies that patent applications have undergone prosecution proceedings obeying similar strict requirements; that the resulting patents are protected under similar criteria by courts; and, of course, that patent protection ends at about the same time.

Therefore, in a globalized economy, the fact that LDCs, developing countries, and the most industrialized countries grant patents with the same duration—twenty years counted from the date of filing—should not come as a surprise.

1 THE EXTENSION OF THE TERM OF PATENTS: DOS AND DON'TS

Patent rights can be enforced against infringers only after the corresponding titles are issued, even when those patents generate retroactive effects. The question in this regard that developing country lawmakers have to address—in particular, if their countries have joined free trade agreements, under which that commitment is usually included—is whether the terms of patents should receive extensions in order to compensate for certain factors that reduce the practical significance of those terms.

Three factors may be identified in this context:

(i) the patent office takes a long and unjustifiable time in granting the patent for reasons that are not attributed to the applicant;
(ii) the patent takes an exceptionally long period for it to start producing economic effects in view of the delays necessary for the inventor to obtain marketing approval for the (regulated) patent products, delays which are caused by the necessity of the inventor to provide data that prove the efficacy of those products and of following a more or less complex administrative procedure; and
(iii) the market has taken a long time to accept the inventive concept offered by the patented product, which means that the inventor has spent part of the period corresponding to the term of the patent advertising the product, so as to create demand for it; this may have left a short period for the patentee to be able to recover the costs sunken into inventing and extracting a profit; the feeling of injustice may be aggravated when the invention is of great significance socially, economically, and technically.

1.1 Compensating for Unreasonable Delays in Examining Patent Applications

No international agreement defines the amount of time that should be necessary for ensuring the expeditious prosecution of a patent application. No WIPO Treaty deals with that (crucially important) matter. And the TRIPS Agreement does not go beyond suggesting that patent applications should be prosecuted expeditiously. In this regard, Article 62.2 of the TRIPS Agreement provides:

> *Where the acquisition of an intellectual property right is subject to the right being granted or registered, Members shall ensure that the procedures for grant or registration, subject to compliance with the substantive conditions for acquisition of the right, permit the granting or registration of the right within a reasonable period of time so as to avoid unwarranted curtailment of the period of protection.*

This language should be read in association with Article 33, which establishes that the terms of patents are to be counted from the date of filing. Combined, the two provisions reflect the trend of the vast majority of WTO Members' patent laws, under which the rights conferred by the patent can be exercised after the grant only. This means that delays in that grant will necessarily curtail the period of protection.

However, for those WTO Members that grant retroactive protection as from the filing date, or from the publication date, the impact of eventual delays by the patent office is of less importance. We find examples of these solutions in the law of Brazil, for example, as follows:

> *Article 44. The patent holder is guaranteed the right to obtain compensation for the undue exploitation of its object, including in relation to exploitation that occurred between the date of publication of the application and the date of granting of the patent.*

§1 If the infringer obtained, by any means, knowledge of the content of the filed application, prior to publication, the period of undue exploitation for the purposes of compensation shall be counted from the date the exploitation started.

A similar orientation, but with a major (and inconvenient) difference, is found in the Patent Act of Tunisia:

Article 82

...

Acts performed prior to the publication of the patent application shall not constitute the offense of infringement and shall not give rise even to an adverse civil judgment except where they occur subsequently to the serving on the presumed infringer of an official copy of the patent application.[212]

The Brazilian solution is better devised than that of Tunisia. Under the Brazilian statute, the early acquisition of knowledge of the invention (before the publication) by the infringer can be acquired through any means, whereas the Tunisian law links that knowledge to a formal notice given by the applicant. In the absence of such notice, apparently, there is no retroactive protection.

Lawmakers may feel reluctant to move along this avenue, given that the perspective of retroactive protection increases the threatening power of patent applications, when inventors are not yet sure of the merits of their inventions. And yet the availability of retroactive protection constitutes a powerful incentive for local inventors to file for patent protection even when the patent office deals with serious backlogs. It should be noted, however, that making retroactive protection available does not discharge the WTO Member from its obligation to ensure an expeditious prosecution process. Retroactive protection may reduce the harm caused to patent applicants by long delays, but it does not eliminate the delays and does not compensate for the totality of the harm suffered by them.

Moreover, the availability of retroactive protection enables the (future) patentee to ask from a court that it authorizes the acquisition of evidence of infringement even before the patent is granted—evidence which may become difficult to obtain as time goes by. Therefore, patent applicants, in those countries that allow for retroactive protection, should stay attentive to eventual acts of potential infringement by competitors since the filing date. They may even issue legal notices to potential infringers, alerting them for the possibility that later, once the patent is granted, they will be sued, without fearing being charged with anticompetitive threats.

A variant of retroactive protection that follows the same orientation found in the law of Tunisia is proposed by the patent law of Botswana, as follows:

Section 21

...

(3) *The applicant shall be entitled to claim compensation from any person who, after the publication of the application and before the grant of the patent, performs without authorisation from the applicant in respect of the claimed*

212. Law No. 2000-84 of August 24, 2000, on Patents.

> *invention any act that would be regarded as an infringement of a patent granted on the invention.*
>
> *(4) An applicant may claim compensation referred to in subsection (3) where the applicant gives notice to the person concerned and the claim deals with only those acts covered by the patent as published.*

This is a sort of an innocent infringement exception that applies only before the patent is granted, with a major difference: in Botswana, as in Tunisia, the presumption of knowledge of the contents of a patent application upon their publication is not accepted; the applicant needs to give notice to the unauthorized user. In practice, this provision may reduce the cases of retroactive protection.

Another example of retroactive protection found in the law of Uruguay is worth noticing because it breaches the country's TRIPS obligations not once, but twice—it is Article 99, which reads:

> *Article 99*
>
> *The patentee may start appropriate legal actions against anyone who commits acts that violate the rights resulting from the patent, and may even claim compensation for acts committed between the publication of the application and the grant of the patent. . . .*
>
> *The possibility of claiming compensation for acts committed between the publication of the application and the grant of patents shall not apply in the case of the patenting of pharmaceutical products, with the exception of those cases in which it is sufficiently demonstrated that a substantial part of their development has actually been carried out in the country.*

The exclusion of pharmaceutical patents from the possibility of benefiting from retroactive protection is an obvious breach of the rule of nondiscrimination against technological fields, as set in Article 27.1 of the TRIPS Agreement. Moreover, the admission of an exception as regards products substantially invented in Uruguay is a clear breach of the principle of national treatment.

Anyway, the determination of what should be the reasonable delay for a patent office to decide on the grant or the refusal of a patent is one of the points where TRIPS negotiators have abdicated from reaching a practical solution. Indeed, they could have determined that the term of the patent should be counted from the day of grant, as it happened in some GATT Contracting Parties before the entry of the TRIPS Agreement into force, such as Canada and the United States. Or they could have set the term of the patent as being counted from the date of filing, as Article 33 does, but with the guarantee that the term of the patent would be no less than fifteen (or sixteen, or seventeen) years from the date of grant. And, additionally, the TRIPS Agreement could have kept the obligation for patent offices to be rapid and efficient because for some technologies a delay of five years may prove to be excessive.

Some patent offices, like those of the Republic of Korea and of Colombia, are known for their efficiency in examining patent applications. In normal circumstances, those two patent offices take around nine months to issue a decision on the grant or denial of applications. And yet, their laws do not set a time limit for a decision to be issued by the Office.[213]

The patent law of Indonesia is one of the few statutes that determines a period for the patent office to decide on granting the patent or denying the application. That rule is found in Article 57, which reads:

> *Article 57*
>
> *The Minister decides to grant or refuse an Application not later than 30 (thirty) months as from:*
>
> a. *the date of receipt of the request for substantive examination if the request for substantive examination is submitted after the expiry of the announcement period; or*
> b. *the expiry of announcement period*[214] *as referred to in Article 48 section (1) if a request for substantive examination is filed before the expiry of announcement period.*

Another country that imposes a limited period for the patent office to carry out the examination of the application is Costa Rica. Its patent law provides as follows:

> *Article 13.—Substantive examination*
>
> . . .
>
> 2. . . . *Reports submitted by the centers, entities or experts consulted shall be issued within the period set by the Industrial Property Registry, depending on the complexity of the subject, and shall contain a detailed justification of the conclusions. . . .*
> 6. *The technical reports referred to in paragraph 2 of this Article shall be concluded within the non-extendable period of two years, computed from the receipt of the application for study by the corresponding body. Substantive examinations shall be concluded within the period of 30 months, beginning from the receipt of the application for study by the corresponding entity.*

Of course, in the case of Costa Rica, to keep the periods for the substantive examination under predetermined limits is easier than in other countries for the single reason that the patent office of Costa Rica, as noted above, relies on the work of outside organizations and experts to perform that task. It is in the hands of the patent office, therefore, to delegate the examination tasks to entities that are not overwhelmed with pending work and can perform the examinations speedily.

Anyway, in spite of the lack of clarity of the TRIPS Agreement, which has left WTO Members without a precise guidance on how to avoid the undue curtailment of the protection of the inventor's rights, among the three factors that justify the admission by national laws of the extensions to the term of patents, the one that is more usually invoked in patent laws is that of the unreasonable delays by patent offices. It

213. An English version of the Korean patent law (Act No. 18505, October 19, 2021) is available at < elaw.klri.re.kr/eng_service/lawView.do?lang = ENG&hseq = 59876 >. Colombia, as a Member of the Andean Community of Nations, follows the patent regime set by Decision No. 486, of 2000, on industrial property.
214. The term "announcement period" means the publication of the application once the Minister (i.e., the patent office's Registrar) is satisfied that all formalities have been complied with.

constitutes a response to the almost inevitable inefficiency of patent offices in prosecuting applications with speed and quality, in view of their being frequently overwhelmed with unexpected high levels of patent filings.

The extension of patent terms for compensating for unreasonable delays in the prosecution of applications that are not attributable to the applicants[215] should be limited. As discussed above, securing an expeditious outset for the prosecution of patents is not only a matter of interest for diligent inventors—it is also a question of legal security for third parties. It is, therefore, a matter of interest to society. It follows that, taking into account that the average period required for an adequate examination of the patent application should take no longer than two years from the date of the request for examination, the law should define that the unreasonable delays that deserve a compensatory extension are those that take more than three years from the filing date or two years from the date of the beginning of the examination.

It is common to see periods set in the laws of developing countries that are longer than those that were suggested above, but those periods correspond to the peculiarities of the administrative procedure, such as the adoption of a fixed period for the publication of the application, and of an additional period for the request for the examination to be submitted. These are periods in which the patent applications stay *idle*, if we can use a force of expression to designate the period in which the application is not being examined.

Also, longer are the compensatory periods adopted by a number of developing countries that have signed free trade agreements with the United States. Just to give one example, the free trade agreement signed with Bahrain contains the following clause:

> *Annex 14, Article 8*
>
> . . .
>
> *(6) (a) Each Party, at the request of the patent owner, shall adjust the term of a patent to compensate for unreasonable delays that occur in granting the patent. For the purposes of this paragraph, an unreasonable delay shall at least include a delay in the issuance of the patent of more than four years from the date of filing of the application in the Party, or two years after a request for examination of the application has been made, whichever is later, provided that periods attributable to actions of the patent applicant need not be included in the determination of such delays.* [216]

These periods have been adopted as a standard in FTAs signed by the United States with a significant number of developing countries. This means that a significant number of developing countries have established periods of compensation for unreasonable delays by patent offices that are longer than those suggested above. But those countries are not prohibited from including in their laws a sort of compensatory measure, by defining a limit to the extensions given.

215. Examples of delays attributable to the applicant are his/her repeated requests for amending or correcting the application by his/her own initiative, not in response to actions by the patent examiner.

216. The text of the free trade agreement signed by the United States with Bahrain is available at < ustr.gov/sites/default/files/uploads/agreements/fta/bahrain/asset_upload_file2116293.pdf > .

For example, the law of the Sultanate of Oman (which, like Bahrain, has signed an FTA with the United States) reads:

> *Article (12):*
>
> *1— . . .*
>
> *(B)— In the event a patent is granted more than four years after the filing date, or two years from the request for examination, whichever is later, and for reasons outside the applicant's control, the term of protection of that patent shall be extended so as to compensate for any period of time in excess of four years from the filing date,* but shall not exceed five years from the normal expiry date. *Extensions shall be granted upon request by the patent owner and the payment of the prescribed fee* (emphasis added).

As regards this topic, and as a striking example of a *don't*, we should bring here the example of the derogated sole paragraph of Article 41 of the Brazilian Industrial Property Act, of 1996. Its language goes (or, rather, went) as follows:

> *The term of validity [of 20 years from the filing date] shall not be less than 10 (ten) years for the utility patent . . ., counting from the date of the grant, except in the event that the [patent office] is prevented from examining the merits of the application, due to a proven pending lawsuit, or [for reasons] of force majeure.*

This provision had a shocking implication: the application for a patent could require more than ten years from the date of filing to the date of granting.

Anyway, even in the absence of a clear international rule setting the reasonable period for a patent office to decide on the patentability of a submitted invention, ten years is too long. And yet, the Brazilian patent office, for a long period, was taking twelve, even fifteen years, for granting a patent. That delay, as of the time of writing, has been reduced, but INPI continues to be an office that does not give good assurance to inventors that their demands will be examined expeditiously and carefully. This, among other reasons that have to deal with disinvestment in research-based industry in Brazil in recent years, explains why, by shocking contrast with other developing economies, such as China and Saudi Arabia, patent applications in Brazil have been significantly reduced.[217]

But if the solution provided by the sole paragraph of Article 41 of the Industrial Property Law of Brazil implied a dysfunctional situation, the solution was even worse. In 2021, upon request by the Republic's General Attorney, the Supreme Court decided that the provision was unconstitutional. The basic reason for such a decision was that the provision generated imprecision and unpredictability as far as the terms of patents were concerned. In holding that all patents whose terms had been automatically

217. For the sake of comparison, and as a powerful message that wrong or good policies by patent offices do have an impact on the luring of inventors (both residents and nonresidents), in search of legal security for their inventions, the WIPO statistical database shows that, between 2015 and 2023, in Brazil, the number of patent applications fell about 21%; in China that number grew 52%; and in Saudi Arabia—as a response to the impressive changes made to the country's economy, under the guidance of the Saudi Vision for 2023, and the efforts of modernization of its patent office—that number grew 94% (from a total of 2,406 patent applications to 7,084).

extended by the patent office (which had accorded that extension to several thousands of patents) should be revoked, the Supreme Court of Brazil revealed their subjacent intention—and bias: those patents granted for pharmaceutical inventions would cease to produce effects immediately, whereas patents for other inventions would remain in force until the end of the extended terms. No other extensions were to be given (at least, automatically).[218]

In other words, the Supreme Court of Brazil (acting on the majority, not on consensus, because there were two dissenting votes as regards the infringement of Article 27.1 of the TRIPS Agreement) gave a blatant display of their disliking of pharmaceutical patents, thus rejecting Brazil's decade-long support for the building of consensus in the WTO in favor of rules promoting the harmonization of rules that sustained free and balanced trade, including the abandoning of the negative treatment of special classes of inventors, in accordance with their field of research and work.[219]

Anyway, the lawmaker of a developing country should consider whether to offer compensation for undue delays by the patent office or to prevent those delays from occurring is the best solution for inventors, with a view to encouraging them to file for patent applications. If the lawmaker prefers the second option, then the following suggested language aims at solving the complex issues that result from undue delays by the patent office when the law requires it to carry out the pre-grant substantive examination of applications:

Article . . .

Period for the examination

1. *The patent office shall make its decision to grant or reject the patent public within a period of two years from the date of request of examination has been filed.*

   [Alternative for those countries where the examination procedure starts automatically, once the formal examination is satisfactorily completed, and there is no need for the applicant to request the substantive examination] (i) The patent office shall make its decision to grant or reject the patent public within a period of three years from the date of filing of the patent application.
2. *When the period determined in paragraph 1 has expired and the patent office has not published the decision to grant or reject the patent application, and when the delay has not been caused by reasons exclusively attributed to the applicant, the patent shall be granted and the patent office will publish the corresponding notice in the official gazette within sixty (60) days counted from the date that period expired.*
3. *A patent granted in accordance with the provisions of paragraphs 1 and 2 shall not lose its presumption of validity.*

218. *See* Direct Action of Unconstitutionality No. 5,529, opinion and documents available at <portal.stf.jus.br/processos/detalhe.asp?incidente=4984195> [access June 2025].

219. Subsequently to the Supreme Court decision, the sole paragraph of Art. 41 of the law of industrial property of Brazil was revoked in 2021, by Law No. 14,195. Unfortunately, Brazilian Congress could have replaced the banned provision with one drafted in more rational terms, but it has opted for simply revoking it. The Brazilian patent system, which in the course of the last years has shown evident signs of loss of credibility from the perspective of not only foreign investors but also national inventors, has become less significant as an element of economic and technological development. The figures provided in the previous note are unambiguous.

4. *In the event a patent granted in accordance with the provisions of paragraphs 1 and 2 is invalidated by the court, whether in invalidation or in infringement proceedings, the patent office shall be liable for the damages caused to both the patentee and third parties.*

1.2 Compensating for Delays in Obtaining Marketing Approval for (Regulated) Patented Products

The grant of extension to patents covering regulated products, the commercialization of which depends on their being previously approved by some governmental authority, is a measure that is relatively common, especially in the fields of pharmaceutical and agrochemical (or plant protection) inventions.

Under the name of Supplementary Protection Certificates (SPCs), the European Union has enacted two separate regulations dealing with the extended protection of plant protection and of pharmaceutical products. The first, concerning plant protection products, is Regulation (EC) No. 1610/96 of the European Parliament and of the Council of July 23, 1996, concerning the creation of a supplementary protection certificate for plant protection products. It provides:

Article 2

Scope

Any product protected by a patent in the territory of a Member State and subject, prior to being placed on the market as a plant protection product, to an administrative authorization procedure as laid down in Article 4 of Directive 91/414/EEC (6), or pursuant to an equivalent provision of national law if it is a plant protection product in respect of which the application for authorization was lodged before Directive 91/414/EEC was implemented by the Member State concerned, may, under the terms and conditions provided for in this Regulation, be the subject of a certificate.

. . .

Article 4

Subject-matter of protection

Within the limits of the protection conferred by the basic patent, the protection conferred by a certificate shall extend only to the product covered by the authorizations to place the corresponding plant protection product on the market and for any use of the product as a plant protection product that has been authorized before the expiry of the certificate.

Article 5

Effects of the certificate

Subject to Article 4, the certificate shall confer the same rights as conferred by the basic patent and shall be subject to the same limitations and the same obligations.

. . .

Article 13

Duration of the certificate

1. *The certificate shall take effect at the end of the lawful term of the basic patent for a period equal to the period which elapsed between the date on which the application for a basic patent was lodged and the date of the first authorization to place the product on the market in the Community, reduced by a period of five years.*
2. *Notwithstanding paragraph 1, the duration of the certificate may not exceed five years from the date on which it takes effect. . . .*[220]

The second regulation, dealing with pharmaceutical products, is Regulation (EC) No. 469/2009 of the European Parliament and the Council, of May 6, 2009, concerning the supplementary protection certificate for medicinal products (amended in 2019).[221] Its relevant provisions are, *mutatis mutandis*, the same as the Regulation that applies to plant products, with the exception that the duration of the SPC shall be extended by six months in the case the product in question has a pediatric indication (Article 13(3), combined with Article 36 of the Regulation (EC) No. 1901/2006).

In its FTAs celebrated with developing countries, the United States also has inserted certain provisions dealing with compensatory extensions of the terms of patents in view of the time required for obtaining marketing approval. However, by contrast with the EU Regulations, the U.S. FTAs provide for the mandatory extension of patents for pharmaceutical products only. Moreover, the U.S. FTAs require that patent terms be extended in view of the "unreasonable curtailment of the effective patent term." There is here, therefore, an element of evaluation of the nature of the delay, whereas under EU law, the extension is automatic.

In this respect, the U.S.-Bahrain FTA reads:

Article 14.8: Patents

. . .

6. . . .

(b) *With respect to any pharmaceutical product that is covered by a patent:*

(i) *each Party shall make available an extension of the patent term to compensate the patent owner for unreasonable curtailment of the effective patent term as a result of the marketing approval process related to the first commercial use of the product in that Party; and*

(ii) *where a Party approves the marketing of a new pharmaceutical product on the basis of information concerning the safety or efficacy of a same or a similar product in another territory, such as evidence of prior marketing approval, the Party shall make available an extension of the patent term to compensate the patent owner for unreasonable curtailment of the effective patent term in the Party as a result of the marketing approval process in the other territory and in the Party.*

For purposes of this paragraph, effective patent term means the period from the date of approval of the product until the original expiration date of the patent.

220. Available at <eur-lex.europa.eu/legal-content/EN/TXT/HTML/?uri=CELEX:31996R1610>.
221. Available at <eur-lex.europa.eu/legal-content/EN/TXT/HTML/?uri=CELEX:32009R0469>.

The *don't* in this sort of justification for extending the terms of patents is that it contradicts the already mentioned provisions of the TRIPS Agreement (Article 1.1 in combination with Article 27.1) that prohibit positive discrimination when it is based on a selective approach of the technological fields covered. It would be difficult to object, and actually it should be commendable, that patentees be compensated for delays in bringing their inventions to the market because of governmental interference, which prevents those patentees from selling their products until an authority decides they may do so. However, such compensation should not be confined to one or two classes of products whose commercialization is regulated, such as pharmaceuticals and agrochemicals. Patents for transport equipment, medical devices, food additives, and other regulated products should also receive the same treatment.

Unfortunately, this is a *don't* that a significant number of WTO Members overlook, including the patent law of the United States. Interestingly, paragraph (a) of section 156 seems to indicate a reasonably wide coverage of the extension, but paragraph (f) reduces it significantly, as follows:

Section 156. Extension of patent term

(a) The term of a patent which claims a product, a method of using a product, or a method of manufacturing a product shall be extended in accordance with this section from the original expiration date of the patent, which shall include any patent term adjustment granted under section 154(b), if—

...

(f) For purposes of this section:
  (1) The term "product" means:
    (A) A drug product.
    (B) Any medical device, food additive, or color additive subject to regulation under the Federal Food, Drug, and Cosmetic Act.
  (2) The term "drug product" means the active ingredient of—
    (A) a new drug, antibiotic drug, or human biological product (as those terms are used in the Federal Food, Drug, and Cosmetic Act and the Public Health Service Act), or
    (B) a new animal drug or veterinary biological product (as those terms are used in the Federal Food, Drug, and Cosmetic Act and the Virus-Serum-Toxin Act) which is not primarily manufactured using recombinant DNA, recombinant RNA, hybridoma technology, or other processes involving site specific genetic manipulation techniques, including any salt or ester of the active ingredient, as a single entity or in combination with another active ingredient.

However, the United States Code contains a *do*: it admits the grant of *interim extensions*, which the patentee can apply for if the term of the patent is expected to end before the patented product obtains the regulatory approval.

In 1998, Canada requested consultations with the (then designated as) European Communities, under the WTO Dispute Settlement Mechanism, alleging that the patent term extension scheme conferred by several European regulations to pharmaceutical and agricultural was inconsistent with the EC's obligation not to discriminate on the basis of the field of technology. Canada has decided not to pursue the consultations and has never requested the establishment of the Panel.[222] Eventually, the reason for having dropped the case against the EC, which it would have very much probably won, was that Canada saw in the EC's breach of their WTO obligations a minor, if any, impact on its trade-related interests.

1.3 Compensating for the Insufficient or Late Recognition by Society of the Inventors' Efforts and/or for the Invention's High Social and Technical Value

The third option is definitively an important one, which developing countries should have in their laws, but with an important caveat: in requesting the extension of the term, the patentee must give evidence not only of the facts that justify the extension (i.e., that the market has taken a long period in responding positively to the product, in spite of the patentee's efforts in advertising the invention and educating the public about its benefits) but also of the particular significance of the product in question, in technical, economic, or social aspects. In other words, there is no point in offering the extension of terms for patents that cover trivial inventions.

This is the solution provided by the patent statute of Guyana, which establishes a mechanism through which the request for extension is examined by a court, and is subject to an *inter partes* procedure:

> *Section 22.*
>
> *(1) A patentee may, after advertising, in a manner provided by rules of the High Court his intention to do so, present a petition to the Court praying that his patent may be extended for a further term, but such petition must be presented at least six months before the time limited for the expiration of the patent;*
>
> . . .
>
> *(2) Any person may give notice to the Court of objection to the extension.*
>
> *(3) On the hearing of any petition under this section the patentee and any person who has given such notice of objection shall be made parties to the proceeding, and the Registrar shall be entitled to appear and be heard, and shall appear if so directed by the Court.*
>
> *(4) The Court, in considering its decision, shall have regard to the nature and merits of the invention in relation to the public, to the profits made by the patentee as such and to all the circumstances of the case.*
>
> *(5) If it appears to the Court that the patentee has been inadequately remunerated by his patent, the Court may by order extend the term of the patent for a further term not exceeding five years, or in exceptional cases, ten years, or may order the grant of a new patent for such term as may be specified in the order and containing any restrictions, conditions and provisions the Court may think fit.*
>
> . . .

A particularly positive *do* in Guyana's law is the necessary publicity given to the patentee's intention to have the term of his/her patent extent before he/she applies for it. With this simple but important move, competitors and society as a whole will be

222. *See* <www.wto.org/english/tratop_e/dispu_e/cases_e/ds153_e.htm>.

protected against future surprises and may consider the submission of objections to such an extension.

The *don't* in Guyana's law is the possibility of a new patent being granted instead of a simple extension of up to five years or up to ten years of the original patent. If the intention of the lawmaker was to allow for an extension of up to twenty years (of course, in extremely rare circumstances), it would have been much easier and more straightforward to grant an extension than issuing a new title that necessarily fails to comply with any of the substantive conditions that buttress the patent. By referring to restrictions, conditions, and provisions that the court may impose on this new/old patent, one understands that the lawmaker was thinking that the new patent would be unenforceable against certain uses of categories of users. But the same restrictions, conditions, and provisions should also be applicable to shorter extensions, eventually with a level of strictness in conformity with the size of the extension accorded.

A different approach to this justification for the compensation of the terms of patents is found in the Patent Act of The Gambia, as follows:

> *Section 13.*
>
> (1) *Subject to the provisions of subsection (2) of this section, a patent shall expire fifteen years* [223] *after the date of the application for the patent.*
>
> (2) (a) *Upon request, made not more than twelve months and not less than one month before the expiration of the period provided for in subsection (1) of this section, and on payment of the prescribed fee, the Registrar General shall extend the duration of that patent for a period of five years, provided that the person making the request proves, to the satisfaction of the Registrar General, either that the invention is being worked sufficiently in The Gambia at the date of the request or that there are circumstances (other than importation) which justify the failure so to work the invention.*

The problem with this provision is the mention of the sufficient working of the invention in The Gambia. As discussed above, this is an infringement of the principle of national treatment of goods, under the GATT 1947. Moreover, this provision seems to be in conflict with section 12(4) of the law, which establishes national exhaustion.[224] But the main problem is that there is no indication of additional conditions for granting the extension, such as that the work of the invention did not last for a period sufficient to reward the inventor, or that the invention acquired social relevance that it did not have at the time the patent was granted. It seems that the extension in The Gambia appears to be a prize for a successful patentee—idea that may raise contrary reactions by those who defend that the patent should expire at the end of its normal term so that competitors can use the invention.

In any event, the great merit of extending the term of patents on grounds of their merits and/or on the patentee's inability to get a remuneration from the market

223. Amended to twenty years as per the revision of 2015.

224. Section 12(4) of the Industrial Property Act of The Gambia reads:

> (4) *The rights under the patent shall not extend*
>
> (a) *to acts in respect of articles which have been put on the market in The Gambia by the owner of the patent or with his consent; . . .*

commensurate with the invention's social value is that it encourages inventors to face the risks of unresponsive markets. Those extensions may stimulate inventors to invest their time and resources in creating useful inventions in new fields of technology not yet accepted by the market, by giving them the assurance they will have additional time to persuade consumers of the invention's value.

Chapter 10
On the Use of Patent Rights: Licensing and Enforcement

1 PATENT LICENSING AND THE ROLE OF PATENT OFFICES AND COMPETITION AUTHORITIES

The first aspect to notice in the matter of patent licensing is that patent letters are public documents that produce effects *erga omnes*, and therefore any changes in those titles and/or in the rights they confer must be publicized through documents of an equally public nature, in order to inform the public. The publicity of licensing and assignment contracts is of crucial importance to the patentee's competitors and to society as a whole.

This said, the essence of the rights accorded by patents is the right to say "no" against any third parties that may be interested in exploiting the claimed inventions commercially. It is for this reason that, as said above, in the absence of other elements, the refusal by patentees to license their inventions is never unlawful. In this regard, a number of patent laws of developing countries should be revised, such as that of Uruguay, which provides:

> *Article 64*
>
> *Any interested party may obtain a compulsory license or other uses without the owner's authorization if he/she has requested a contractual license from the patent owner and has been unable to obtain it under commercially reasonable conditions appropriate to the country within ninety days from his/her request.*
>
> *In all cases, the National Directorate of Industrial Property must grant the compulsory license or other uses without the owner's authorization when the interested party demonstrates that:*

This language may be the consequence of poor drafting, but the term "other uses" does not have any meaning. In the TRIPS Agreement, the term "other uses" (in Article 31) means those uses of the invention made by third parties that do not fall under the exceptions and limitations of Article 30, which is not the case in the Uruguayan legal provision. Following the legal tradition of Roman law, in Uruguay, the unauthorized use by a governmental entity requires the issuance of a compulsory license, under the same format (but not necessarily the same substantive conditions) as a compulsory license granted in favor of a private undertaking. Moreover, the combination of the language of paragraphs 1 and 2 of Article 64 of Uruguay's law can be read as meaning that the simple refusal by the patentee of granting a license is sufficient ground for the issuance of a compulsory license, whereas the TRIPS Agreement, in Article 31(b), just requires that the attempt to obtain a voluntary license be seen as formal condition in order for a request for a compulsory license, on acceptable grounds, to be accepted. The refusal to grant a voluntary license is not a ground for the compulsory license—it is just a formal requirement, which must precede, for example, the request for a compulsory license on grounds of lack of sufficient exploitation. Once again, the law of Uruguay, in this article, seems to have been poorly drafted and could even be construed differently, but it should nevertheless be revised, so as to avoid future mistaken interpretation.[225]

Anyway, developing countries tend to show concern with the impact of patent licensing, in particular when the patent owners are foreign companies. In the 1970s, that concern led UNCTAD (the United Nations Conference on Trade and Development) to discuss an international instrument that dealt with the most common abusive aspects that licensing agreements contained.[226] With the advance of globalization and the increase in the number of global chains of value, that were discussed above, that sort of debate seemed outdated, but in 2007, with the Agenda for Development approved in WIPO, it resurfaced.[227]

The question is: should the patent office or another public office preventively examine the contents of patent licensing (and assignment) agreements, in order to verify their compliance with antitrust laws?

---

225. Actually, it seems that Art. 64 of the law of Uruguay is contradicted by Art. 71, which reads:

> *Anyone interested in obtaining a compulsory license or other uses must prove that he/she has requested a contractual license from the patentee and has been unable to obtain it under commercially reasonable conditions appropriate to the country, within ninety days from his/her request.*
>
> *This requirement may be waived in circumstances of national emergency, extreme urgency, and in cases of non-commercial public use and anti-competitive practices.*

226. In 1974, under the aegis of UNCTAD, an initiative aiming at developing an International Code of Conduct on the Transfer of Technology was launched. Even though the Code of Conduct was never formally accepted because of lack of consensus, it nevertheless had great influence in the laws and attitudes of a number of governments.

227. One of the forty-five recommendations of the WIPO Development Agenda reads:

> 29. To include discussions on intellectual property-related technology transfer issues within the mandate of an appropriate WIPO body.

One of the purposes of Argentina and Brazil, when they submitted a proposal for the Development Agenda in WIPO, in 2004, was indeed to revive the debates previously held in UNCTAD.

To find the correct answer to this question is more important than it seems, given that this discussion does involve much more than a matter of more or less bureaucracy and (avoidable) formalities. What is at stake here is ensuring, on the one hand, that patent owners will enjoy freedom in exercising their rights, and, on the other, more or less fragile economies and vulnerable industrial sectors will be protected from abusive conduct by patent licensors—when abusive conduct is effectively in question.

The answer to that question is therefore multifaceted: the freedom of patentees in engaging in private contracts should be respected, on the one hand, but the social interests in keeping abusive licensing practices under control should not be put aside, on the other hand. It follows that the lawmaker of a developing country should orient the parties involved, as well as the administration, in a way that conserves the two equally important sides of the equation.

An example of this sort of guidance can be found in a number of patent laws, such as that of Indonesia, whose relevant provisions read:

> *Article 78*
>
> *A Licensing Agreement is prohibited from containing provisions that may damage the Indonesian national interest or to contain restrictions which obstruct the abilities of Indonesian people to transfer, master and develop technology.*
>
> . . .
>
> *Article 80*
>
> *Further provisions regarding recording of Licensing agreement are regulated by a Ministerial Regulation.*

The law of Uruguay also lists (although not exhaustively) a few clauses that are not acceptable in licensing agreements, as follows:

> *Article 51*
>
> *Unless otherwise provided, the following rules [concerning patent licensing agreements] shall apply:*
>
> . . .
>
> *It is prohibited to establish in contractual licenses clauses or conditions that result in a negative effect on competition, constitute unfair competition, or allow an abuse by the owner of the patented right or of its dominant market position.*
>
> *Among such clauses or conditions, it is worth noticing those that result in:*
>
> *A) Harmful effects on trade.*
> *B) Exclusive grant-back conditions.*
> *C) Impediments to challenging the validity of patents or dependent licenses.*
> *D) Limitations on the licensee at the commercial or industrial level, when this does not derive from the rights conferred by the patent.*
> *E) Limitations on the exportation of the product protected by the patent to countries with which an agreement exists to establish an economic and trade integration zone.*

The same law, in Article 60, adds a few examples of practices deemed to be anticompetitive or unfair and which may serve as justifications for the grant of compulsory licenses. Those examples correspond mainly to unilateral abuses, but one or two of them may result from a collusive practice between licensor and licensee.

Just to resort to one additional example, we find in the law of Namibia the following provisions concerning patent licensing agreements:

> *Section 52. Prohibited terms in licences*
>
> *(1) Any condition in a contract relating to the sale of a patented invention or to a licence under a patent of which the effect will be—*
> *(a) to prohibit or restrict the purchaser or licensee from purchasing or using any product or process or class of products or processes, whether patented or not, supplied or owned by any person other than the seller or licensor or his or her nominee;*
> *(b) to prohibit or restrict the purchaser or licensee from using any product or process not protected by the patent;*
> *(c) to require the purchaser or licensee to acquire from the seller, licensor or his or her nominee any product or process or class of products or processes not protected by the patent;*
> *(d) to require or induce the purchaser or licensee to observe a specified minimum resale price in respect of any article or class of articles protected by the patent; or*
> *(e) to prohibit or restrict the making, using, exercising or disposing of the invention concerned in any country in which the invention is not patented, is invalid.*
>
> *(2) Nothing in this section affects any condition in a contract—*
> *(a) whereby a person is prohibited from selling any goods other than those of a particular person; or*
> *(b) for the lease of or a licence to use a patented article, whereby the lessor or licensor reserves to himself or herself or his or her nominee the right to supply such new parts of the patented article, other than ordinary articles of commerce, as may be required to put or keep it in repair.*
>
> *(3) The Board may, after consultation with the Registrar, by notice in the Gazette declare any other condition in a licence to be a condition to which subsection (1) applies and that condition if contained in a licence is invalid for the purposes of subsection (1).*

As useful as this sort of provision may be, in the sense they provide guidance to prospective licensors and licensees, there is a great risk that they put the parties (and the public administration, as well) in a straitjacket, given the mandatory nature of the law. It is advisable that the *dos* and *don'ts* in licensing agreements be set out in a directive or regulation, given the flexibility that is inherent in this type of legal norm, by contrast with a statute that, when it proves to be inconvenient, requires the action by parliament or other legislative body, with all the political implications (and natural delays) of such an initiative.

For example, there are some points in the laws of Uruguay and Namibia that would need to be revised, such as:

- to impose on the licensee the obligation to acquire ingredients and materials necessary to put the licensed invention into practice is not necessarily wrong, even when those ingredients are not patented; this sort of *tie-in* clauses may be justified on a number of grounds, such as that the licensor would not be able to provide for a guaranty of quality of a sophisticated product unless it controls the whole process of making it, including the choice of ingredients and materials;

- to restrict the exportation of the patented product should also be seen with prudence because the licensor may follow a specific commercial policy in terms of market segmentation; the restriction involving exports may be, after all, reflected in the price that the licensee will pay; there is nothing anticompetitive or unfair in that;
- to impose exclusivity in grant-back, i.e., on the transfer of improvements introduced in the patented invention by the licensee, is not, per se, unlawful, provided that the grant-back is subject to the payment of remuneration and is established on a basis of reciprocity.

It is therefore suggested that the provision of a patent statute of a developing country dealing with patent licensing could be as follows:

Article ...

Licensing and assigning the patent

1. *Any instruments that cause changes in the patentee's rights and their exclusivity, such as licensing, assignment, and succession, shall be registered with the patent office.*
2. *Until their registration is published in the official gazette, no instruments mentioned in the previous paragraph shall produce any effect against third parties.*[1]
3. *The patent office shall publish in the official gazette information concerning:*
   (i) *the names of the parties;*
   (ii) *the tile and number(s) of the patent(s) concerned;*
   (iii) *the exclusive or non-exclusive nature of the license; and*
   (iii) *the duration of the agreement.*
4. *The patent office shall keep confidentiality over all clauses and other information associated with the contract.*
5. *When the agreements are celebrated under circumstances and/or contain clauses that are prima facie susceptible of producing anticompetitive effects, and/or have an abusive nature, the patent office shall refer it to the competition authority.* [2/3]
   (a) *Without prejudice to the applicable law and regulation, the following circumstances and clauses are deemed to produce prima facie anticompetitive effects and/or having an abusive nature:*
      (i) *the licensor/assignor and the licensee/assignee are competitors on the same relevant market;*
      (ii) *the agreement(s) lead(s) to the concentration of ownership of patents concerning one technology that has no alternatives on the market;*
      (iii) *the agreement(s) concern(s) the cross-licensing of one or more patents for inventions that provide solutions for the same technical problem, and excludes one or more of the licensors/licensees from the use of the patented inventions;*
      (iv) *the licensee(s) is(are) obliged to continue paying royalties beyond the term of term of the contract;*

(v) *the licensor(s) agree(s) to pay remuneration to the licensee(s) in return for the licensee(s) obligation to drop its(their) product from the market;*
(vi) *the licensee is obliged to assign to the licensor with exclusivity and with no remuneration or any sort of reciprocity, any improvements it will find and/or invent while exploiting the licensed invention;*
(vii) *the licensee(s) agree(s) to acquire from the licensor(s) ingredients and components that are not covered by the patent(s) and/or to pay for the license(s) of other patent(s) that cover technical aspects unrelated to or unnecessary for the exploitation of the patented invention(s).*[4]

6. *This article shall not apply in the case the licensing or assignment contract is part of a settlement in a court dispute. In that case, the contract shall be recorded by the patent office following instructions by the court.* [5]

Notes:

1. Patentees and licensees are entitled to keep the contracts undisclosed, but if they wish that the contracts produce effects against third parties, they must publicize them. This is important particularly when the contracts empower the licensees to sue infringers and to sublicense.
2. To scrutinize eventual anticompetitive aspects of an agreement involving the assignment or the licensing of patents should not be the job of the patent office, but rather of the competition authority. Should this scrutiny be preemptive? The answer depends on the level of education of national entrepreneurs concerning the harm that engaging in anticompetitive agreements as licensees can cause to them (and, eventually, to the national economy). As noted, it is of interest that the two agencies discuss and agree on a joint directive or regulation setting the procedures (and the criteria) that will be used in scrutinizing patent licensing agreements so as to avoid anticompetitive abuses.
3. Agreements may constitute and/or produce abusive effects that do not reach the level necessary for triggering antitrust concerns, namely because the volume of market share involved is not sufficiently significant. Those abuses, unless the lawmaker decides to accord extraordinary powers to the patent office—the topic which will be briefly discussed in the next chapter—should stay under the supervision of courts.
4. As noted, the definition of the criteria for determining when a licensing agreement may produce anticompetitive or abusive effects, supplemented by a list of examples of anticompetitive and abusive clauses, should be covered by a directive jointly elaborated by the patent office and the competition authority. The purpose of this list is not to replace such a directive, but simply to provide for a list of clauses that, depending on the circumstances, even under the *rule of reason* approach, seem to produce potential anticompetitive effects. The list here suggested reproduces the facts of some notorious antitrust cases that have been discussed in courts and in competition authorities in various countries, but it is not intended to exhaust the cases. Indeed, human imagination is too powerful so as to keep finding new ways of acquiring gains against competitors in manners that the lawmaker would never be able to confine into a list. As the Supreme Court of California once said:

> It has been said by some judge or law-writer that "no fixed rules can be established upon which to deal with fraud, for, were courts of equity to once declare rules prescribing the limitations of their power in dealing with it, the jurisdiction would be perpetually cramped and eluded by new schemes which the fertility of man's invention would contrive."[228]

228. *Weinstock, Lubin & Co. v. H. Marks*, Supreme Court of California, 109 Cal. 529 (1895).

5. Courts should be aware that competitors may try to obtain from them the approval of unlawful licensing agreements. Those are cases of frivolous litigation and abuses of process. Courts should be ready to not only reject that kind of settlement but also to sanction the abusive parties. Anyway, this paragraph excludes the authority of the patent office or of the competition authority from scrutinizing the merits of a court decision. It is not for administrative authorities to control court decisions—but exactly the opposite.

2 ON INFRINGEMENT

2.1 The Various Modalities of Infringement

Except for one aspect of enormous importance—injunctions, preliminary and definitive—that will be discussed below, developing country patent lawmakers do not have much leeway in regulating the sanctions and the prosecution of patent infringement cases. Usually, enforcement is dealt with by the laws of civil and criminal process, with some particularities concerning patents, which are defined by Part III of the TRIPS Agreement with clarity and detail.

Infringement may be direct or indirect (or contributory). Direct infringement may affect the totality of the claims or only part of the claims of the patent. In any event, in the case of a patent including more than one independent claim, infringement only occurs when at least one of the independent claims is entirely infringed. The use by a third party of the subject matter of one or more dependent claims that do not represent the total of dependent claims under one independent claim is not infringement.

Infringement is indirect or contributory when a third party, knowingly, sells materials, ingredients or components necessary for exploiting a patented invention to a person who is infringing or will infringe that patent. The notions of direct and contributory infringement are the two sides of the same coin, and there is no need for the lawmaker to insert a special reference to them into the statute. Nevertheless, many patent statutes define indirect infringement, such as the patent laws of Dominica and Trinidad and Tobago.[229]

229. The patent law of Dominica provides:

Section 36.

(1) *While in force, a patent shall confer, on its owner, the right to prevent all persons not having his authorisation, from supplying or offering to supply in Dominica, a person (other than a person entitled to engage in commercial working of the patented invention) with means relating to an essential element of that invention, for putting it into effect therein, provided that the person knows, or it is obvious to a reasonable person in the circumstances that those means are suitable for putting, and are intended to put, that invention into effect.*

(2) *Subsection (1) shall not apply where the means referred to therein are staple commercial products, except where the person induces the person supplied to commit acts which the owner of the patent is entitled to prevent by virtue of section 33.*

The same language can be found in section 41 of the patent law of Trinidad and Tobago.

But the same cannot be said of two other modalities of infringement, which require statutory intervention, except in common law countries, where, through application of principles of equity, courts may integrate some legal loopholes: cooperative or divided infringement and innocent infringement.

Cooperative or divided infringement occurs when two or more undertakings concertedly perform acts that are partly claimed and, together, infringe one or more claims of the patent, but without, individually, reaching the level of infringement in view of the fact that no one of those undertakings performs all the acts covered by one complete independent claim. Given the legal precept *nullum crimen sine lege*, only those acts that the law defines as prohibited (in particular, those acts that are qualified as crimes) can be sanctioned. It follows that, without the legal setting of cooperative infringement, the undertakings that coordinately and in an agreed-upon manner engaged in infringing a patent might be immune against liability.[230]

A reference to cooperative infringement seems to be present in the Patent Act of Lebanon, as follows:

> *Article 43:*
>
> *Persons instigating, sharing or participating in the counterfeit crime shall be penalized according to the stipulations of Article 42 herein.*

Lebanese courts may have a different understanding, but the term "sharing," not being followed by any qualification or restriction, would admit the notion of cooperative infringement. After all, criminal law does not accept construction by analogy, but it accepts extensive interpretation.

The other modality—innocent infringement—is accepted by a number of laws of developing countries, such as the law of Guyana:

> *Section 38.*
>
> *A patentee shall not be entitled to recover any damages in respect of any infringement of a patent granted after the commencement of this Act from any defendant who proves that at the date of the infringement he was not aware, nor had reasonable means of making himself aware, of the existence of the patent and the marking of an article with the word "patent," "patented," or any word or words expressing or implying that a patent has been obtained for the article, stamped, engraved, impressed on, or otherwise applied to the article, shall not be deemed to constitute notice of the existence of the patent unless the word or words are accompanied by the number of the patent:*
>
> *Provided that nothing in this section shall affect any proceedings for an injunction.*

The patent laws of a number of Caribbean countries, such as Dominica (section 42(1)),[231] Trinidad & Tobago (section 51(1)),[232] and Belize (section 42(1)),[233] also

230. Eventually, even in the absence of statutory language, under some very special circumstances, namely if the intent of coordination was proved, the undertakings involved might respond for unjust or causeless enrichment. But that would not be certain.
231. Patents Act, 1999 (Act No. 8 of 1999).
232. Patents Act, 1996 (Act No. 21 of 1996, as amended by Act No. 18 of 2000).
233. Patents Act (Chapter 253, Act No. 14 of 2000, Revised Edition 2020).

provide for the scheme of innocent infringement, with language very similar to that of Guyana, thus suggesting that their lawmakers have followed a common model.

In the same token, and also with very similar language, the Patent Act of the Cook Islands provides:

Section 68

Restrictions on recovery of damages for infringement

(1) *In proceedings for the infringement of a patent, damages or account of profits shall not be awarded against a defendant who proves that at the date of the infringement he was not aware, and had no reasonable ground for supposing, that the patent existed; and a person shall not be deemed to have been aware or to have had reasonable grounds for supposing as aforesaid by reason only of the application to an article of the word "patent", "patented", or any word or words expressing or implying that a patent has been obtained for the article, unless the word or words are accompanied by the words "New Zealand" or the letters "NZ" and by the number of the patent.*

It should be noted that the statutes above quoted were both enacted before the entry of the TRIPS Agreement into force—which, as it will be briefly discussed below, does not accept the idea of innocent infringement, with one single exception. As far as the Cook Islands are concerned, the fact that the TRIPS Agreement does not allow for the innocent infringement scheme (with the single exception that we will mention next) is not a problem because the country is not a WTO Member. But Guyana is, and therefore section 38 of its patent law is in breach of the country's international commitments.

A variation of the innocent infringer scheme, as adopted by a developing WTO Member, can be found in the law of Namibia, as follows:

Section 72. Declaration of non-infringement

(1) *In proceedings between any person and the patent owner the Tribunal may, despite that no assertion to the contrary has been made by the patent owner, make a declaration that the use by that person of any process or the making or use or offer to dispose or disposal or importation of any product by that person, does not or would not constitute an infringement of a patent, if it is proved—*
   (a) *that such person has applied in writing to the patent owner for a written acknowledgement to the effect of the declaration claimed, and has furnished the patent owner with full particulars of the process or article in question; and*
   (b) *that the patent owner has failed to give such an acknowledgement. . . .*

This scheme seems to take place in an ordinary declaratory action. It also seems that the lawmaker is suggesting that in the case of neglect by the patent owner in answering the infringer, some sort of latches apply. Otherwise, the provision eventually will have no strong impact, because what it suggests is that the infringer confesses his/her illegal practice to the patentee, thus making him/herself vulnerable to a subsequent infringement lawsuit. Section 72 would only make sense if the infringer's acknowledgment of the infringement was made in preparation for the request for a voluntary license.

As another example of a law providing for the innocent infringement that has been enacted after 1995 by a WTO Member, here is the text of Article 100 of the law of Uruguay:

> *Article 100*
>
> *Those who commercialize or distribute products infringing goods shall only be liable for damages caused when there is certain and determined evidence that they were in a position to know of the infringement.*

Of course, the fact that the infringer will not be liable for the payment of damages does not mean that the court will not be able to issue an injunction, preliminary and/or definitive, with a view to cease the infringement. Anyway, the principle of publicity of patents does not authorize that an infringer be deemed innocent. There is no innocent infringement of patents upon their publication (or upon the acquisition of the knowledge of the invention by any other means), except in the case of Article 37.1 of the TRIPS Agreement.

Article 37.1 of the TRIPS Agreement admits the innocent infringer defense in the case of patents (or other forms of intellectual property) for integrated circuits incorporating unlawfully reproduced layout-designs, as follows:

> *Article 37*
>
> *Acts Not Requiring the Authorization of the Right Holder*
>
> 1. *Notwithstanding Article 36, no Member shall consider unlawful the performance of any of the acts referred to in that Article in respect of an integrated circuit incorporating an unlawfully reproduced layout-design or any article incorporating such an integrated circuit where the person performing or ordering such acts did not know and had no reasonable ground to know, when acquiring the integrated circuit or article incorporating such an integrated circuit, that it incorporated an unlawfully reproduced layout-design. Members shall provide that, after the time that such person has received sufficient notice that the layout-design was unlawfully reproduced, that person may perform any of the acts with respect to the stock on hand or ordered before such time, but shall be liable to pay to the right holder a sum equivalent to a reasonable royalty such as would be payable under a freely negotiated licence in respect of such a layout-design.*

One may argue that Article 37 aims at those forms of intellectual property that, under Article 4 of the Treaty on Intellectual Property in Respect of Integrated Circuits, of 1989 (the IPIC Treaty), the lawmaker chooses for the protection of layout-designs, which, unlike patents, are not subject to publicity, such as copyright and unfair competition. Therefore, there may not be innocent infringement of patents, or of utility models, covering layout-designs. However, one may counterargue that the innocent infringer scheme applies in the field of layout-designs in situations in which it is materially impossible for the purchaser to verify the lawful origin of the layout-designs—when, for example, the integrated circuit is embedded into a complex product, such as a cell phone, a TV set, or an automobile. So, innocent infringement in the field of layout-designs is a matter of legal realism, i.e., of accepting the inevitability of a factual situation.

This matter has not been the subject of a dispute under the WTO Dispute Settlement or of a Ministerial Decision, and therefore WTO Members may hold divergent views. But as regards all other fields of technology, there should be no divergence—innocent infringement is prohibited by the unequivocal language of Article 41.1 of the TRIPS Agreement:

Article 41

1. *Members shall ensure that enforcement procedures as specified in this Part are available under their law so as to permit effective action against any act of infringement of intellectual property rights covered by this Agreement, including expeditious remedies to prevent infringements and remedies which constitute a deterrent to further infringements.*

Nevertheless, according to Article 1.1, WTO Members are free to determine the appropriate method of implementing TRIPS provisions within their own legal system and practice. In this token, they may take measures to distinguish innocent from willing (or knowing or intentional) infringement. For example, the Industrial Property Act of Brazil, as already noted, distinguishes between those two sorts of infringement for the purposes of setting the liability in the case of retroactive enforcement: before the application is published, only the infringer who had knowledge of the application will be liable for infringement.

The patent law of China has adopted the same distinction but with different consequences: the amount of compensation to be paid by the innocent infringer is lower than that paid by the willing infringer:

Article 71.

The amount of compensation for patent right infringement shall be determined on the basis of the actual losses suffered by the right holder as a result of the infringement or the profits earned by the infringer as a result of the infringement. Where it is difficult to determine the losses suffered by the right holder or the profits earned by the infringer, the amount shall be reasonably determined by reference to the multiple of the amount of the royalties for the patent license. For intentional infringement of a patent right, if the circumstances are serious, the amount of compensation may be determined at not less than one time and not more than five times the amount determined in accordance with the above-mentioned method.

The solution of China is a *do* for developing countries, where undertakings are less familiar with the patent system and less aware of their responsibility for doing regular searches in the relevant patent databases with the defensive purpose of avoiding infringement. But, once this is said, the developing country lawmaker has no choice but to ensure that patent rights are effectively enforceable and in a manner that creates a deterrent for potential infringers. The price for the unavailability of enforcement mechanisms is the loss of credibility of the patent system.

This said, and insisting on the very narrow leeway that the patent lawmaker has in the field of enforcement, national authorities should not neglect the role that the discretionary authority of courts has in determining certain elements of enforcement. In this token, the competent authorities of developing countries should take very seriously the task of having judges thoroughly educated in the principles, norms, and public interests that preside over the law of patents.

2.2 On Remedies (and the Relative Freedom of WTO Members to Adopt Their Own Rules, Including Making Injunctions Dependent on the Protection of Public Interest)

One of the remedies that applies in the event of patent infringement is the injunction, or *cease-and-desist* order, which may be of a preliminary, interim nature and/or definitive. More than the ascertaining and levying of compensatory damages, the issuance of injunctions is the essence of enforcement of patentee's rights, to the extent it prohibits rivals from using the invention.

It follows that injunctions seem to be a natural, automatic component of any court decision acknowledging the infringement of the plaintiff's patent. This understanding results from the combined language of the two paragraphs of Article 42 of the TRIPS Agreement, which apparently indicate that the judge must invariably issue an injunction to force the plaintiff to stop the infringement, except where the infringer is a governmental authority or an entity working for the government. This is how Article 44 reads:

> *Article 44*
>
> *Injunctions*
>
> 1. *The judicial authorities shall have the authority to order a party to desist from an infringement, inter alia to prevent the entry into the channels of commerce in their jurisdiction of imported goods that involve the infringement of an intellectual property right, immediately after customs clearance of such goods. Members are not obliged to accord such authority in respect of protected subject matter acquired or ordered by a person prior to knowing or having reasonable grounds to know that dealing in such subject matter would entail the infringement of an intellectual property right.*
> 2. *Notwithstanding the other provisions of this Part and provided that the provisions of Part II specifically addressing use by governments, or by third parties authorized by a government, without the authorization of the right holder are complied with, Members may limit the remedies available against such use to payment of remuneration in accordance with subparagraph (h) of Article 31. In other cases, the remedies under this Part shall apply or, where these remedies are inconsistent with a Member's law, declaratory judgments and adequate compensation shall be available.*

However, the last sentence of Article 1.1 ("Members shall be free to determine the appropriate method of implementing the provisions of this Agreement within their own legal system and practice") should not be ignored: WTO Members may adopt different rules in their laws from those that are specified in the Agreement, except those that are established in a mandatory manner. In other words, the TRIPS Agreement permits that WTO Members establish remedies against infringement that are not necessarily the same as those of the Agreement, provided that the basic principles and the guidance found in the Agreement are observed.

However, this said, all rules on enforcement must comply with two fundamental, interrelated principles: although they may show aspects of flexibility, they cannot deny the patentee's right to exclusivity in the exploitation of the claimed invention; and they may not convert the remedies for infringement into licensing agreements. Enforcement should lead to the infringers being excluded from using the patented invention without the patentee's authorization. This is the bottom line of the entire patent system.

By referring to "their own legal system and practice," Article 1.1 acknowledges that the TRIPS Agreement represents a major effort by GATT Contracting Parties in introducing consistency into distinct legal systems. Indeed, the Agreement admits the coexistence of legal regimes that follow the civil code system with those that follow the common law, each with different perspectives on law enforcement. WTO Members are not compelled to abandon their own legal practices and systems in order to comply with TRIPS obligations. They may, therefore, apply the TRIPS rules on enforcement in a flexible manner so as, respecting their own systems, to make available to rights holders the necessary enforcement mechanisms.

As noted above, in terms that are unequivocally addressed to developing and least-developed countries, Article 41.5 provides that WTO Members are not required "to put in place a judicial system for the enforcement of intellectual property rights distinct from that for the enforcement of law in general, nor does it affect the capacity of Members to enforce their law in general." The creation of new judicial and customs structures requires resources that many small WTO Members do not have. However, this language should be seen as a flexibility, not a waiver, this meaning that Article 41.5 may not be used as a justification for the failure in making enforcement measures available to intellectual property rights holders. What the Agreement admits here is a balance between the means made available to the general enforcement of law and the means to the enforcement of intellectual property.

Moreover, the TRIPS Agreement represents a very strong commitment by Members toward an accommodation of different legal regimes. As said, it permits the coexistence of the civil code and the common law regimes, which entail different approaches to the enforcement of law. Those differences in approach may be exploited by WTO Members without fear of infringing their TRIPS obligations. However, it should be noted that, in contrast with TRIPS language concerning standards of protection—which are generally enunciated as *minimum standards*—several provisions in Part III of the TRIPS Agreement are phrased in a way that do not permit WTO Members to provide for measures stronger than those established, and therefore do not provide for *minimum standards*, but provide instead for *mandatory standards*. The reason for this is, as enunciated in the first paragraph of the Preamble of the TRIPS Agreement as well as in Article 44.1, to avoid that enforcement measures become abusive and constitute themselves barriers to legitimate trade.

The patentees' right to say "no" is expressed by their right to obtain injunctions and damages from courts. Articles 44 and 45, however, are formulated in a manner that reflects the possibility—raised by the TRIPS Agreement itself—that courts are not obliged to always apply those two remedies. Both Articles start with the phrase "The judicial authorities shall have the authority to [...]." Judicial authorities shall have the authority, but they are not requested to issue injunctions and account for damages in every case of infringement. Injunctions may not be granted if the ceasing of the infringement would cause an unjustified and disproportionate harm to the public interest or to the legitimate interests of the infringer. This is the consequence of the application of the principle of equity as set by Article 41.1 of the Agreement. The United States Supreme Court affirmed the applicability of the well-established equity principle to patent law in *eBay Inc v. MercExchange* (2006):

> We hold only that the decision whether to grant or deny injunctive relief rests within the equitable discretion of the district courts, and that such discretion must be exercised consistent with traditional principles of equity, in patent disputes no less than in other cases governed by such standards.[234]

Likewise important (even though not binding) is the expression of the rationale of the principle of equity by four of the Supreme Court Justices (Justice Kennedy, with whom Justices Stevens, Souter, and Breyer concurred). The Justices conceded that, although under a rule of equitable discretion, District Courts had previously granted injunctions in patent infringement cases almost automatically. However, they pointed out that the situation had dramatically changed, in view of the rising of the industry of patent "trolls" (a term that the Justices did not use but that fits their description of the facts):

> In cases now arising trial courts should bear in mind that in many instances the nature of the patent being enforced and the economic function of the patent holder present considerations quite unlike earlier cases. An industry has developed in which firms use patents not as a basis for producing and selling goods but, instead, primarily for obtaining licensing fees. [...] For these firms, an injunction, and the potentially serious sanctions arising from its violation, can be employed as a bargaining tool to charge exorbitant fees to companies that seek to buy licenses to practice the patent. [...] When the patented invention is but a small component of the product the companies seek to produce and the threat of an injunction is employed simply for undue leverage in negotiations, legal damages may well be sufficient to compensate for the infringement and an injunction may not serve the public interest. In addition, injunctive relief may have different consequences for the burgeoning number of patents over business methods, which were not of much economic and legal significance in earlier times. The potential vagueness and suspect validity of some of these patents may affect the calculus under the four-factor test. The equitable discretion over injunctions, granted by the Patent Act, is well suited to allow courts to adapt to the rapid technological and legal developments in the patent system.[235]

It is true that Article 41.2 of the TRIPS Agreement determines that procedures "concerning the enforcement of intellectual property rights shall be fair and equitable." Equitable procedures are those that require that the judge treats the various interests at stake in the lawsuit in a balanced manner, namely, those private interests of the

234. In *eBay Inc v. MercExchange* 547 U.S. 388, 393 (2006). The complete opinion can be found at < laws.findlaw.com >.

235. *Ibid.*, at 396-397.

plaintiff and the defendant, as well as the collective interests of society that may be affected by the judgment. Under this principle, the judge may be prevented from issuing an injunction, provisional or definitive, if such an injunction harms the public interest.[236]

However, the refusal to issue an injunction should not be made by the court lightly. As said, systematic refusals of injunctions convert the enforcement of patent rights into pretexts for licensing. But licensing is a by-product of the patentee's core right—the right to say "no." If the patentee is entitled to prohibit third parties from using his/her invention, he should also be entitled to refuse the licensing. The enforcement of rights by NPEs (nonpracticing entities), which are investment funds that acquired patents with the mere intent of enforcing them and extracting royalties from potential infringers, is not a problem as generalized as suggested by the four Justices. The problem of patent trolls is a reality, yes, but mainly, if not only, in the United States, where the exploitation of the patented invention is not an obligation and does not give rise to the grant of compulsory licenses.

As examples of what was said above, two statutes deserve particular attention. One is the patent law of China, which, in its Article 65, provides for a very peculiar—and quite interesting—procedure of enforcement:

> *Article 65.*
>
> *Where a dispute arises as a result of the exploitation of a patent without the authorization of the patentee, that is, the infringement of the patentee's patent right, it shall be resolved through consultation between the parties. Where the parties are unwilling to consult with each other or where the consultation fails, the patentee or any interested party may file a lawsuit in the people's court, or request the departments in charge of patent-related work to deal with the dispute. When the department in charge of patent-related work dealing with the dispute considers that the infringement is established, it may order the infringer to stop the infringing act immediately. If the infringer refuses to accept the order, he may, within 15 days from the date of receipt of the notification of the order, file a lawsuit in the people's court in accordance with the Administrative Procedure Law of the People's Republic of China. If the infringer neither files a lawsuit nor stops the infringing act at the expiration of the period of time, the department in charge of patent-related work may file an application with the people's court for compulsory execution. At the request of the party concerned, the department in charge of patent-related work dealing with the dispute may carry out mediation concerning the amount of compensation for the patent right infringement. If the mediation fails, the parties may file a lawsuit in the people's court in accordance with the Civil Procedure Law of the People's Republic of China.*

The example that comes from China is interesting in the sense that it provides for a differentiated procedure, combining conciliation/mediation with enforcement and, eventually, the mandatory execution of an injunction.

236. *See, e.g.*, *TVA v. Hill*, 437 U.S. 153 (1978). The opinion of the Supreme Court in *eBay Inc.* can be read in exactly the same way.

The other example comes from Oman, with a provision on injunctions that is more than merely procedural. The relevant text is as follows:

Article (66):

. . .

5— *Courts may refuse to grant provisional or definitive injunctions, without prejudice to the payment of damages, when:*

. . .

B— *the injunction causes serious harm to the public interest;*
C— *the patented products or the products manufactured by a patented process are sold by the plaintiff or by a third party with the plaintiff's consent at prices that are deemed excessive taking into account the average purchase power of consumers and the specific nature of the needs the products aim at meeting, and there is no competing product on the market;*
D— *the patent owner has engaged in anti-competitive acts or practices, as determined by the Court or by a competent administrative authority;*
E— *the patent owner is found to have engaged in inequitable conduct during the procurement of the patent letter; . . .*

Of particular importance is the language found in subparagraph B, which reproduces the rationale employed by the United States Supreme Court in the *eBay* opinion. We could say this is the ultimate flexibility that a developing country (and a developed country as well) could introduce in its patent law: the judge, in assessing the weight of the three factors involved in the enforcement of patents—the patentee's private rights, the infringer's private rights, and society's collective rights—may lean toward the latter, albeit not necessarily, and not always.

One final word on remedies is necessary. In general, damages are set by the lawmaker as the result of the losses suffered by the patent holder as a result of the infringement. In addition, as Article 45.2 of the TRIPS Agreement, the patent holder is entitled under the patent laws of a significant number of countries to recover from the infringer the expenses he/she incurred in court (court fees, experts, attorneys).

But assessing damages is not always an easy task—for the simple reason that it is not infrequent that the patent owner has not lost any revenue as a result of the infringement. In this event, punitive damages are in order. However, punitive damages are very frequently set by courts in abstract, i.e., without any specific reference, exactly because of the eventual impossibility to find an exact amount of losses.

For this reason, a few patent laws determine a mechanism of calibration of methods of calculating the compensation to be paid to the patent owner. A relevant example is found in the Industrial Property Act of Brazil. It is Article 210, which provides:

Art. 210. Lost profits [which are the same as the patent owner's damages] *will be determined by the criterion most favorable to the injured party, among the following:*

I— the benefits that the injured party would have received if the violation had not occurred; or
II— the benefits that were received by the perpetrator of the violation; or

III— the compensation that the perpetrator of the violation would have paid to the holder of the violated right for the granting of a license that would have legally allowed him to exploit the property.

This is a very commendable provision, which developing countries (and developed countries as well) should follow.

2.3 Other Matters

The lawmaker of a developing country may have other points for reflection (and legislative action) that make the enforceability of patent rights more adapted to the specific, overall needs of society. We will not discuss those points in detail because the response is generally conditioned by principles and rules that preside over procedural matters, which tend to be very specific to the countries, given that a significant number of them result from court practice and jurisprudence. Those points are as follows:

- Should the law complement the protection of the patentee's legitimate interests with the rules and sanctions that apply in the repression of unfair competition? This question may seem inappropriate, but there are aspects that involve the offense against the interests of the patentee but which do not reach the level of infringement, as is the case, for example, of the use by a third party of some components of a complex invention, but which do not form an entire independent claim, as noted above. Conversely, some aspects of infringement may be more serious than simply using the invention without the patentee's authorization. In this context, it is worth quoting again from the Industrial Property Law of Brazil, which contains this important provision:

  Article 209.

  The injured party is entitled to compensation for losses and damages for losses caused by acts of infringement of industrial property rights and acts of unfair competition not provided for in this Law, which tend to harm the reputation or business of others, to create confusion between commercial, industrial, or service-providing undertakings, or between products and services offered for sale.

- Should the law provide for criminal sanctions in the case of patent infringement? Many laws answer this question affirmatively, but the necessity of those sanctions is not clear. Even though, as explained above, the notion of innocent infringement is not (or should not be) accepted because it contradicts the very essence of the patent system and the principle of publicity that presides over it, the reality is that, particularly in developing countries, infringers are rarely willing or informed infringers—they are what we could identify as *naive infringers*; i.e., third parties who are not aware of the patent system and of the possibility of engaging in searches for patents before adopting certain manufacturing techniques.

- Should the law provide for the payment of punitive (also designated as "exemplary" damages) by infringers? The answer, in general, is provided by the court, not by the lawmaker, but it could be interesting for the latter to take into account the reality of the technology market in a developing country, where *naive infringement* is more common than willing or informed infringement. Punitive damages help make a better assessment of damages when losses are difficult to quantify and have a deterrent or exemplary effect. But the judge should be given the possibility (or the legal duty) of taking the infringer's good faith or naiveté into account and refuse to order the payment of punitive damages. In this case, there would be damages to be compensated, but the unlawful act would not deserve to be chastised with punitive (or exemplary) damages.
- Should the patent law include the so-called *patent linkage* mechanism, in accordance with which while a patent is in force the covered product may not be registered by a third party (a generic manufacturer) with the regulatory authority?

Usually, the patent linkage is provided in the context of pharmaceutical products. In anticipation of the expiry of the patent term, generic manufacturers may engage in experimenting and manufacturing the patent product under the so-called *Bolar exception*. This exception was included in many patent laws around the world after the WTO Dispute Settlement Body decided that the patent law of Canada, which provided for that same exception, was in conformity with Article 30 of the TRIPS Agreement.[237] The question is whether the generic manufacturers may not only submit those data to the regulatory agency but also obtain the marketing approval before the patent expires.

A number of developing countries, persuaded by the United States under free trade agreements (FTAs), have in their laws included a provision that answers negatively to the second leg of that question: while the patent is in force, not only the product may not be commercialized by third parties during the patent term but also the regulatory agency shall not issue the corresponding marketing approval.

237. *See Canada—Patent Protection of Pharmaceutical Products* (WT/DS114/R, of March 17, 2000, para. 7.25), adopted by the Dispute Settlement Body (WT/DS114//Rev. 1, of April 27, 2000). But the Panel added that the products made under the exception could not be warehoused with a view to be sold after the expiry of the patent term. In this regard, section 17 of the Industrial Property Act of Samoa is flawed. The relevant language reads:

> *18. Test batches of patented products—*
> *(1) ... test batches of a patented product may be produced without the consent of the patent owner six (6) months before the expiry of the patent.*
> *(2) Test batches must not be put on the market before the expiry date of the patent.*

These provisions have two problems: first, there is no need for limiting the production of batches made for the purpose of testing to the period of six months before the expiry of the patent; the production of batches may occur at any time during the term of the patent, provided they are exclusively destined to the submission of a request for marketing approval; second, test batches must not be put on the market either before or after the expiry of the patent; once they serve their purpose, they must be destroyed or disposed of in circles outside commercial channels.

This is the case, for example, of the patent law section of the US-Bahrain FTA, which provides:

Article 14.9: Measures related to certain regulated products

. . .

4. *Where a Party permits, as a condition of approving the marketing of a pharmaceutical product, persons, other than the person originally submitting safety or efficacy information, to rely on evidence of safety or efficacy information of a product that was previously approved, such as evidence of prior marketing approval in the Party or in another territory, that Party:*
   (a) *shall implement measures in its marketing approval process to prevent such other persons from marketing a product covered by a patent claiming the product or its approved method of use during the term of that patent, unless by consent or acquiescence of the patent owner; and*
   (b) *shall provide that the patent owner shall be notified of the identity of any such other person who requests marketing approval to enter the market during the term of a patent notified to the approving authority as covering that product.*

The patent linkage mechanism implies that regulatory agencies are under the obligation to request information about the eventual existence of conflicting patent rights before registering or granting marketing approval to certain regulated products. Actually, this is a sort of administrative enforcement of patent rights, not only because it is enforced ex officio by the governmental agencies in question but also because it creates a direct obstacle against the administrative (regulatory) act of registering infringing products, regardless of their being subsequently commercialized or not.

This mechanism has the natural consequence of making it more difficult for generic products (both in the pharmaceutical field and in all other fields that are subject to regulatory monitoring and approval) to enter the market. From the patent holder, the advantage of the linkage is clear: the infringer of his/her patent rights will be held accountable not only for the infringement of the patent rights but also for violation of administrative/health law. The sanctions, therefore, will be more severe. On the generic drug manufacturer side, the linkage has the effect of limiting the effects of the Bolar exception—he/she may obtain the data necessary for having the generic product approved, but cannot get that approval while the patent is in force.

The linkage also makes it impossible for generic drug manufacturers to take calculated risks, that is, to willingly and knowingly engage in unauthorized manufacturing and selling of patented products because, relying on their own interpretation of the patent claims, they believe that there is no patent infringement—either because they believe they have been able to circumvent the claims or because they understand the claims are invalid, hence unenforceable.

An inconvenience of the patent linkage is that it reverses the burden of proof: it is the obligation of the registration applicant to convince the authorities that his/her (generic) product does not infringe any patent rights. Such a measure has the benefit of increasing the protection of the rights of patent owners, but, at the same time, because it discourages the early registration of generic products, it generates an additional barrier against competition with off-patent pharmaceutical products.

Moreover, the linkage requires the establishment of an orange book-like procedure in the countries that have adopted it, with all its complexities and vulnerabilities. And this is perhaps the most serious inconvenience that developing countries may devise in the patent linkage mechanism. After all, accurate information about the existence of valid patents is not available in many WTO Members, where, due to the absence of appropriate structures, patent offices do not keep an efficient record of patents granted.

An extreme, but real, example of the inconveniences that the need for supplying the Ministry of Health with information concerning patents granted comes from a small developing country, which signed an FTA with a large trading partner. Consequently, that country had to adapt its law to the new obligations acquired under the agreement, including the adoption of the patent linkage mechanism. But when the time came for the patent office to provide the required information to the Registration Division of the Ministry of Health, the agency realized they had no records whatsoever of patents granted in the pharmaceutical sector—or in any other sector. The solution was for that country, provisionally, accepting that all patents in force in the large trading partner at that time, and until the expiration of their terms, produced effects against the registration of generic products.

Moreover, the linkage produces effects even when the relevant patents are under administrative or court challenge. So, challenges to the validity of the patent do not necessarily accelerate the market entry of generic products because, given the technical complexity of litigation involving the patent validity, it is not infrequent that a final decision is reached after the expiration of the patent term. The only possible way to overcome this problem is the grant of injunctions by the court with the effect of suspending the challenged patent for the purposes of sanitary registration of generic pharmaceuticals (with all the risks associated to the suspension of patents that in the end may resist the challenge).

However, where a developing country finds it indispensable to introduce patent linkage, and taking into account that the legitimate interests of both patent owners and generic drug manufacturers should be balanced, two solutions should be envisaged:

- first, it should be the burden of the patentee to keep the Ministry of Health informed of the patents granted (and, eventually, cancelled);[238] if the patentee fails to do so timely, the generic company may obtain the regulatory approval

238. This was the solution found by the lawmaker of the Dominican Republic, in transposing to the national legal framework the commitments contained in the free trade agreement with the United States and a number of Central America and Caribbean countries, known as CAFTA-DR. The relevant provision reads:

Article 181.—Information and protection of data for marketing authorization. (*Law no. 20, of 2000, as amended by Law no. 324, of 2006*):

1) *Where a competent national authority requires or permits, as a condition of approving the marketing of a new pharmaceutical or agricultural chemical product, the submission of undisclosed information concerning the safety or efficacy of said product, the competent national authority shall not permit third persons, without the consent of the person that provided the information, to market a product on the basis of: (1) the information, or; (2) the approval granted to the person that submitted the information*

for the product (thus reducing the time necessary for starting the commercialization of that product once the patent expires); and
- second, the fact that marketing approval has been granted by a regulatory agency to a generic product cannot be used as a defense in a lawsuit enforcing patent rights.

This second solution, actually, seems obvious as it stems from general principles of patent law, but it might be nevertheless useful if the lawmaker includes it in the law so as to ease legitimate concerns of research-based pharmaceutical companies that may see in anticipated marketing approvals of generic products a mechanism that facilitates or encourages patent infringement.

The first solution has the great merit of releasing the Ministry of Health from the burden of verifying the accuracy of the information provided by the generic manufacturer when he/she applies for the marketing approval of a similar drug. As noted above, this apparently simple issue may be the cause of serious problems, given that in small countries, with less experience in managing national patent systems, accurate information about patented products is not always available in the patent office.

On a different matter, it is worth noticing that the patent linkage scheme has been established by some WTO Members exclusively in association with the marketing approval of pharmaceutical products. Because the linkage generates more rights to patent owners than those set by Article 28, it constitutes protection more extensive than is required by the Agreement, as mentioned by Article 1.1. It must therefore not contravene the provisions of the Agreement, including those of Article 27.1. In other words, in order to avoid positive discrimination concerning the field of technology, the linkage should be extended to all products whose commercialization depends on the prior approval by government authorities.

As a final note, the concept of patent linkage has a close association with the protection of regulatory data, under Article 39.3 of the TRIPS Agreement, in spite of their being independent. The data concerning a chemical product may be in the public domain—for example, because the inventor has disclosed those data and made them publicly available—and yet a patent may cover the concerned invention. In this case, if the lawmaker accepts the idea of patent linkage, no registration should be possible for a generic product until the expiry of that patent's term in spite of the generic manufacturer's legitimate access to the regulatory data.

Moreover, the protection of regulatory data is usually seen as complementary to the protection that results from a patent. Again, it should be noted that those two legal mechanisms are independent and have a different nature, patent protection being exclusive, whereas regulatory data enjoy protection against unfair practices only. They may exist separately, i.e., not all patentees are entitled to have their data protected, neither all possessors of regulatory data are patent owners. But, undoubtedly, both contribute to securing the rights of inventors of regulated products in avoiding the early

for a period of five years for pharmaceutical products and 10 years for agricultural chemical products from the date of approval in the Dominican Republic.

entry of generic competitors on the market, and they have more efficacy in assisting the inventor to reach that goal if they coexist.

But this should not be a reason for the lawmaker to include provisions dealing with regulatory data in the Patent Act, as, for example, is the case of the statute of Lebanon:

> *Article 47*
>
> . . .
>
> *Secret information that the Authority specifies to be released in order to license use of pharmaceutical preparations and chemical products utilized in agriculture shall not be illegally used for commercial purposes. Such information shall not be released unless the protection and welfare of the public so dictates.*

Regulatory data have a different nature and obey a rationale that is different from patents. Their protection should not be included in a law that primarily deals with the latter but, preferably, should be dealt with along with other acts of unfair competition. Besides the mistake in the conceptual mix-up, the rapprochement of test data and patents in the same patent statute may have the inconvenience of constituting a legislative suggestion that the data give rise to the same exclusionary rights as patents, particularly when the law does not define precisely the scope of the rights that result from the data—and this is exactly the case of Article 42 of the Lebanese law.

CHAPTER 11

Other Issues

The previous chapters have dealt with matters that pertain chiefly to patent law and which, only subsidiarily, may relate to other areas, such as the case of patent linkage, which has a clear association with administrative law.

This last chapter will look at a few issues that, by contrast, have more affinity with other matters of law, and only secondarily—but no less importantly—with patent law.

Let us start with the very scope and functions of the patent office.

1 SHOULD THE COUNTRY HAVE ONE SINGLE OFFICE FOR ALL INTELLECTUAL PROPERTY-RELATED AREAS?

It is common to see both in developed and in developing countries the whole field of intellectual property covered by two agencies of the public administration: the industrial property office, dealing with the registration and the management of industrial property rights; and the copyright office, dealing with the management (and, eventually, the registration in some circumstances) of copyrights and related rights.

This seems to be basically a matter of indifference—unifying the agencies or keeping them separate does not cause significant externalities. However, it should be noted that in some areas of intellectual property, the two agencies may be involved in matters of common interest, such as software, layout-designs, and industrial designs.

It is relevant, therefore, that the lawmaker who opts for keeping two independent agencies establishes a system of regular consultation between them.

It happens, however, that in some countries the lawmaker who opts for the single-agency solution falls into the temptation of giving that agency the authority in matters concerning the enforcement of rights. The issue may be one of finding the appropriate resources: the lawmaker may understand that the judiciary is not properly equipped to settle IP-related disputes, many of which involve extremely complex issues of law and of fact. However, in attributing that task to the IP agency, the lawmaker should not forget that a good deal of litigation involving IP is about invalidation, and here, where the rights depend on registration accorded by the authority, a serious issue of conflicting interests may arise.

In any event, even in those countries where the national IP agency has a mandate to settle disputes involving IP rights, the lawmaker should not forget that the TRIPS Agreement requires, in some instances, that decisions involving the disposition of patent rights be judicially reviewed (Article 31(i) and (j) and Article 32). Part III of the Agreement also provides for the necessity of infringement procedures to be heard by courts, although Article 49 accepts that enforcement be carried out through administrative procedures. Therefore, where the patent office is put in charge of settling disputes, the lawmaker has to identify a higher and independent authority with the mandate of scrutinizing a number of decisions that, under the Agreement, require such review.

2 SHOULD THE PATENT LAW DEAL WITH THE PROFESSION OF PATENT ATTORNEYS?

The patent laws of several countries include provisions on the profession of patent attorneys, defining their qualifications and eligibility for registering as such (usually, through an examination system). Some countries exempt qualified attorneys from that registration, in recognition of their professional status and their entitlement to defend their clients.

Of course, no one can deny the importance of having the profession of patent attorneys regulated, but the patent law does not seem the appropriate place.

3 ON EMPLOYEES' INVENTIONS

The adequate treatment of the relationship between employers and employees is a matter of crucial importance.[239] Two are the reasons that qualify that relationship as such. First, the majority of inventions that are protected by patents around the world are owned by undertakings, not by individual inventors. And second, although the majority of commentators, when they refer to the human rights-related aspect of the patent system, mean the question of prices of patented products, in particular of medicines, and the difficulty of access that the poor have to those products in the absence of governmental help, the real issue concerning human rights is the protection of the employee-inventor in the face of his/her employer.

Indeed, this is an aspect that, as noted above, in the Introduction, is dealt with by Article 27 of the Universal Declaration of Human Rights. It is true that inventions are not explicitly mentioned in that provision, but the reference to scientific production extends to them.

Of course, one can say that the topic of employees' inventions is not specific to developing countries, but the truth is that labor laws are not equally applied in all

239. Henceforth, comments concerning "employers" will cover contractors in general, as well.

countries, with employees' rights receiving less attention and protection from the lawmakers in those very poor countries that struggle to keep their economies afloat. This is a reality, as inconvenient as it may be.

Therefore, although the topic of employees' inventions is left to be regulated by labor laws in a number of countries, the trend in developing countries is to include provisions in their patent laws that seek to set a balance between the rights and obligations of the parties involved. It is indeed commendable that the patent lawmaker pays special attention to this matter. Unsatisfied employees tend to underperform in the exercise of their creativity, and, in the case of those employees who are not hired to invent, they tend to neglect the communication of the inventions made in the course of their professional tasks and with the use of data and resources that belong to the employer.

As far as employees' inventions are concerned, the lawmaker should have two main goals in mind: the various solutions adopted that attribute ownership and remuneration arising from those inventions should not lead to situations of unjust enrichment; and the loyalty by the employee toward the employer should be encouraged, namely by ensuring the early disclosure of inventions, the subsequent support to the employer in his/her efforts to obtain patent protection, and encouraging confidentiality.

Although the solutions found in the patent (and labor) laws concerning the regime of employees' inventions have many variations, it is possible to find some general lines that are common to the generality of those laws. Differences are found in the details, and we will take note of a few of them.

An invention may be made by an employee in three different scenarios.

3.1 Inventions Made by Employees Hired for Inventing

The first scenario is the employee who has been hired to invent. In this case, the existence of a labor contract justifies the transfer of the title to the patent from the inventor to the employer. Thus, the employer is entitled to the patent.

Difficulties may arise in identifying the tasks of the employee as inventing, when the contract does not say it explicitly.

In this regard, there are no predetermined solutions, other than those that we could find in the jurisprudence concerning other disputes in labor courts. Indeed, patent laws or specific regulations on employees' inventions tend to overlook this matter, in spite of its high relevance, given that the allegation by the inventor-employee that he/she has not been hired to invent is frequently raised because, absent such clause, his/her remuneration will be higher.

Anyway, we can suggest here three criteria for ascertaining whether the labor contract which is silent about the specifically inventive nature of the employee's tasks has as its object the obligation to invent. The first criterion is that of the *contractual environment*. According to this criterion, in determining that the employer effectively expects its employees to commit to inventing—that is, to finding new and creative solutions to technical problems in their daily work—is whether the company is regularly engaged in innovating. A regularly innovative company is one that has clear and specific expectations regarding the creative capacity of its employees working in research, development, maintenance, and production. This is measured by the image the company projects of itself: texts on its website and social media, advertising material in the media, promotion of innovation and technical suggestion contests, and internal and external policies to promote and encourage inventive activities. Moreover, many of these companies have internal rules that encourage their employees to submit suggestions for improvements, and they often adopt internal regulations for inventions.

The second criterion is the *causality* or *eventuality* of the invention. The question that must be asked is: is the invention (which the employee claims to have made outside of his/her contractual obligations) an unusual, unexpected event in the sector or department in which the employee is assigned, or, on the contrary, is it just another invention originating in a sector that is a regular, or at least repeated, source of inventions, made by colleagues at the same level and/or performing similar functions? If the first option prevails, then the invention has been made casually or eventually—not systematically, by a person who would be expected to invent.

The third criterion concerns the *autonomy* of the employee in making the invention. Has he/she made the invention on his/her own initiative, without the employer's knowledge and/or encouragement, or has the invention been made in pursuance of specific instructions given by a supervisor, or has the inventor been integrated into a research team with a collective mandate to find an innovative solution for some technical problem? If the second option proves to be true, then we are in the face of what the French doctrine designates as "invention de mission" or "mission invention." But if it is the first option that results from the facts, then the court will tend to find that the invention has not been made in pursuance of the labor contract.

This highlights the importance of taking all three criteria into consideration. The presence of one, or eventually of two, only, may lead to a wrong understanding of the circumstances of the invention.

Under the labor laws of some countries, in addition to the discussion of these criteria, once one or more of them are verified as having occurred, an additional debate emerges: whether initially, the employee had not been hired to invent but, subsequently, his/her tasks have changed.

This is a difficult topic, which in some countries may lead to the nullity of the changes, when they cause harm to the employee (which they cause necessarily if the rights to remuneration for an invention are at stake), but it is specific to labor law, and thus it does not fit in this book.

What is important to retain, in order to find an adequate decision on the attribution of the entitlement to the patent, is that the expectations of the employer at the moment he/she hired the employee are determinative of the real nature of the employees' tasks. That is why those three criteria are helpful, to the extent they help the court determine what the employer's expectations were.

Still concerning the inventions made by employees hired to invent, the lawmaker, following the principle that prohibits unjust enrichment, may order that the employee, in spite of having his/her inventive work paid by his/her regular salary, be paid an extraordinary compensation when the inventions generate unexpectedly high gains for the employer. This element may prove difficult to assess quantitatively, but constitutes a matter of fairness and justice. An example of a statute that contains a provision in this sense is the Patent Act of Ghana, as follows:

> *Section 4—Right to Patent; Naming of Inventor.*
>
> . . .
>
> (5) *Where an invention is made in execution of an employment contract, the right to the patent belongs in the absence of any contractual provisions to the contrary, to the employer.*
>
> (6) *Where the invention has an economic value much greater than the parties could have reasonably foreseen at the time of the conclusion of the contract, the inventor shall be entitled to a special remuneration, which shall be fixed by the court in the absence of an agreement between the parties.*[240]

3.2 Inventions Made by Employees Not Hired for Inventing

It is in regard to inventions made by the employee who was not hired for inventing but who invented in the course of his/her job that patent laws show many variations.

When the employee, for reaching the inventive result, has used data, information, and equipment of the employer, in some countries the employee is entitled to the patent, but the employer is entitled to an exclusive license; in other countries, the patent will belong jointly to the employer and the employee, with the former receiving (and paying for) an exclusive license as regards the half of the patent that belongs to the employee; and, in other countries, the employer is entitled to the patent, and a remuneration has to be paid to the employee in return for the assignment of the right to the patent.

It may happen, however, that the employee who has not been hired to invent made an invention that is not of immediate interest to the employer, in the sense that the invention does not belong to the same technological sector and therefore would have no immediate utility for the employer's operations. In this case, the general solution is to attribute the entitlement to the patent to the employee, but because he/she has used the employer's resources (and, of course, the time or part of the time he/she should be performing the tasks for what he/she had been hired), some laws give the employer the right to express interest in the patent, and even to claim an entitlement—against fair compensation, of course. However, unless the law provides differently, the remuneration to be paid to the employee should correspond to the amount that applies in the case of the assignment of the patent, given that in this case

240. Patent Act, 2003. The patent statute of Ghana is an example of a well-drafted and balanced law, which—with a few improvements—could serve as model for other developing countries with a similar level of development. The high quality of that statute should not come as a surprise. When it was drafted, so as to implement TRIPS obligations, the Director of the Intellectual Property Law Department, in WIPO, in charge of providing legislative assistance, was Dr. James Quashie-Idun, a distinguished jurist national of Ghana, with vast knowledge and understanding of intellectual property. I had the privilege of working under his supervision for a number of years. During that time, I learned from him a good deal of law, prudence, and common sense.

there is no contract covering services that consist of or may lead to inventing. But, in the case the employer has no interest whatsoever, the employee may be sanctioned for wasting the time and the resources that are the employer's property.

3.3 Observations

The lawmaker should be careful not only in regard to apportioning the rights resulting from inventions made by employees in the course of their tasks but also in clarifying the obligations of the employee, which combine that of disclosure—the employee should inform the employer as soon as he/she is certain that an invention has been made—with cooperation with and assistance to the employer in prosecuting the patent application and with confidentiality.

As regards disclosure, the patent law of Mozambique includes a very interesting provision, which reads:

> *Article 46*
>
> *Communication of the invention*
> 1. *The employee shall, as soon as possible, notify the employer in writing, of the invention carried out.*
> 2. *Should the employee fail to comply with the obligations of the above paragraph his rights to the invention shall expire, whether under this Code or those resultant from the contractual provisions relating to the employment relationship.*

This provision seems much better drafted than a corresponding article in the abovementioned Germany's Employee Inventions Act, as follows:

> *Section 5 Duty to Report*
>
> *(1) Any employee making a service invention shall be under a duty to report the invention to his employer immediately in a special notice in text form indicating that said writing constitutes the report of an invention. . . .*

The *don't* in this provision is that with certain frequency the nature of an invention as a *service one*, that is, an invention made by an employee who was hired to invent, is the subject of controversy, namely when the inventive obligations result naturally from the tasks the employee is supposed to perform, but which are not expressly stated in the contract.

It is worth noticing that the topic of employees' inventions has close links with unfair competition and the employee's duty of not engaging in activities that may lead to disclosing confidential information to third parties and/or to exploit those inventions in a way that may be seen as competition with the employer.

For this reason, frequently the provisions that attribute to the employee the entitlement to the patent are meaningless, given that the exploitation of the patented invention or its licensing to third parties—eventually, but not necessarily, competitors of the employer—would entail the communication of information that is confidential and proprietary. Without the employer's express consent to either the use of the invention by the employee or its licensing to a third party, the employee may be subsequently charged of engaging in unfair competition, usually deemed not only a civil but also a criminal offense.

Another matter of relevance is the consideration of who should settle the disputes between employers and employees over inventions made during the course of a contract. The answer, in the absence of an explicit provision, depends on the structure of the national legal and political system. In some countries, specialized labor courts shall take care of the matter. In other countries, civil courts will hear the parties and settle the disputes. Another solution, that has been adopted in a number of countries, is to attribute the matter to arbitration and mediation—which, depending on the quality of the arbitrators, may be the best solution, because usually arbitration does not lead to the same antagonism and bitterness that civil or labor costs do, something that should be avoided at all costs in the context of a relationship between employees and employers.

Another point that is usually covered by patent laws in this context is the determination of a presumption of ownership in the event the employee leaves the job and files a patent application within a predetermined period after the expiry of the contract. The presumption consists of applying to that invention the same regime that applies to employees' inventions because the invention is presumed to have been made before the employee left the job. However, that is a presumption *juris tantum*; i.e., it admits proof to the contrary.

Associated with this same concern of determining the ownership of inventions made in the course of the contract by employees who, after quitting the job, applied for patents is the difficult and sensitive issue of the lawful mobility of employees. In this matter, should the lawmaker include rules dealing with it in the law of patents? The answer is "no," and the reason is that employees' mobility has more to do with trade secrets and unfair competition than with patents.

On a final note, the regime above described concerns not only those employees' inventions that are patented but also those that are kept by the employer as trade secrets. In this regard, the German law on employees' inventions contains another *don't*, when it imposes on the employer the obligation to apply for a patent every time he/she is informed of an invention by an employee. This is how the corresponding provision reads:

> *Section 13 Application for Domestic Industrial Property Protection*
>
> (1) *An employer shall be under a duty—and he shall be solely entitled—to apply for a domestic industrial property right for a service invention reported to him. Where the invention is capable of patent protection, he shall apply for a patent unless, on an evaluation of the industrial applicability of the service invention, protection as a utility model appears more appropriate. The application shall be filed without delay.*

This is a nonsense, to the extent it denies the employer the right to opt for keeping the service invention as a trade secret, with all the attending risks. However, the fact that the employer has decided not to submit the invention to the scrutiny of the patent office should not harm the rights and interests of the employees. But the regime applies to genuine inventions only, provided they reach a minimal lower of inventiveness.

Therefore, those companies that establish internal systems of rewarding suggestions and improvements proposed by employees—which do not reach the inventive level of a patentable invention—are not bound by the regime of employees' inventions. In the case of a dispute between the employer and the author of a suggestion, the court may search inspiration or analogies in the regime that applies to employee's inventions, but that will be an expression of their discretionary authority in the construction of legal loopholes.

3.4 Inventions Made by Civil Servants

The trend in patent statutes is to accord to inventions made by civil servants (researchers in public institutions, academics, etc.) the same treatment, *mutatis mutandis*, that is given to employees' inventions in the private sector.

But three caveats are of great importance and should be addressed by the lawmaker.

First, and following the good example of the US Bayh-Dole Act, of 1980 (which was adopted with a view to dealing with the ownership of inventions made in small businesses, universities and other nonprofit organizations that receive federal funding), the law should allow the entity to acquire ownership in the invention. The lawmaker should also consider the benefits of extending this regime to inventions made within military structures (of course, with special treatment to be dedicated to inventions that affect national security). In addition, the lawmaker might include a suggestion that universities set offices within their organization with the objective (and the expertise) of handling matters relating to patents, in particular their licensing.

Second, inventors located within governmental bodies should be entitled to receive a part of the remuneration gained by the institution. The general practice is to divide the remuneration into three identical parts and attribute one-third to the inventor(s), one-third to the governmental agency or Ministry that has provided the funds (if it is the case), and one-third to the entity (i.e., the university or the research institute). In addition, the law should allow for a flexible approach to this matter, permitting the university to license the exploitation to the inventor, and allowing the latter to open a business, say, a start-up firm, to bring the invention to the market, without the risk of the inventor being later charged of acting in conflict of interest.[241]

241. This useful provision was introduced in Brazil with the enacting of Law No. 10,973, of 2004, which deals with invention and innovation carried out in research institutions, including those associated with public universities. Of particular interest are the provisions that ensure the remuneration of the inventor (from 5% to one-third of the revenue obtained by the institution with the licensing of the invention) and those that permit the inventor to engage in the private exploitation of the invention, for a three-year period (renewable), without the fear of being accused of conflict of interest. This favor is extended to civil servants who are under a regime of exclusive dedication. As a result of this law, patent applications filed by universities and other public institutions started growing, and today a few universities are among the largest applicants of patents in Brazil.

And, third, the public agency that has provided the funds should retain the right to supervise how the rights stemming from publicly funded inventions are to be managed. This idea results from a provision of the Bayh-Dole Act, which reads:

> *§203. March-in rights*
>
> *(a) With respect to any subject invention in which a small business firm or nonprofit organization has acquired title under this chapter, the Federal agency under whose funding agreement the subject invention was made shall have the right, in accordance with such procedures as are provided in regulations promulgated hereunder to require the contractor, an assignee or exclusive licensee of a subject invention to grant a nonexclusive, partially exclusive, or exclusive license in any field of use to a responsible applicant or applicants, upon terms that are reasonable under the circumstances, and if the contractor, assignee, or exclusive licensee refuses such request, to grant such a license itself, if the Federal agency determines that such—. . .*

It should be noted, however, that the supervision power of the agency should be limited to what is really of essential importance. The agency should avoid interfering with the normal management of patent rights, which are of a private nature. Actually, the U.S. Federal Government has never exercised their march-in rights, which have been requested in several cases, including complaints against high prices and medicines and medical devices invented with public funding.

4 SECRET INVENTIONS

The patent laws of a number of developing countries contain references to *secret inventions*, i.e., inventions that are not disclosed to the public. This seems a paradox—a secret patent—given that disclosure and publicity, as already said above, are at the core of the patent system, with two main goals: to ensure the technical teaching of new inventions; and to inform competitors of the acquisition by the inventors of proprietary and exclusive rights in certain inventions. In this last context, a patent is the equivalent of a signboard hanging from a fence on the side of the road, with the saying: "private property; no trespassing."

However, secrecy of patented inventions is necessary when their knowledge presents risks to security, such as those involving the military use of atomic energy or the making of weapons. It is evident that such secrecy may lead to problems of enforceability against infringers because the presumption of knowledge of publicized claims cannot be invoked against them. However, generally, the solution to those cases of infringement is never brought to the light, and they are settled through confidential arbitration. Moreover, when the patent office, in a preliminary assessment (before the publication), understands that an invention may be of interest to national security, and sends it for the analysis of the competent department (usually, the Ministry of Defense), some constraints will apply to the patent, once it is granted, such as limitations to the freedom of licensing and exploiting the invention. Of course, the patentee will be entitled to compensation.

Here are a few examples of patent laws that provide for the secrecy of inventions that involve matters of national secrecy. First, the Patent Act of India, as follows:

157A. Protection of security of India.—Notwithstanding anything contained in this Act, the Central Government shall—

(a) not disclose any information relating to any patentable invention or any application relating to the grant of patent under this Act, which it considers prejudicial to the interest of the security of India;
(b) take any action including the revocation of any patent which it considers necessary in the interest of the security of India by issue of a notification in the Official Gazette to that effect.

Explanation.—For the purposes of this section, the expression "security of India" include any action necessary for the security of India which—

(i) relates to fissionable materials or the materials from which they are derived; or
(ii) relates to the traffic in arms, ammunition and implements of war and to such traffic in other goods and materials as is carried on directly or indirectly for the purpose of supplying a military establishment; or
(iii) is taken in time of war or other emergency in international relations.

In the same token, these are the relevant provisions of the patent statute of Indonesia:

Article 50

(1) If an Invention concerns to the interest of the defense and security of the State, the Minister may decide not to announce the Invention upon consultation with relevant institutions administering government affairs in defense and security of the State.
(2) The Minister notifies the Applicant or his/her Proxy in writing concerning the decision on the Application that is not announced as referred to section (1).
(3) The document of the Application that is not announced consulted with Government institutions as referred to in section (1) is exempted from the provisions as referred to in Article 45 section (1).
(4) The government institutions as referred to in section (1) are required to preserve the confidentiality of the Inventions and Application documents being consulted.

A third example comes from the Patent Act of Israel. The particular care of Israel with matters of national security has led the lawmaker to dedicate it various and extensive provisions, which, for the sake of brevity, will not be quoted in their entirety. The excerpts that follow are aimed at just showing how a lawmaker can deal with this important topic:

Chapter Six: Powers of State

Article One: Powers Required for National Defense

Section 94.

(a) The Minister of Defense may, by order, if he deems it necessary so to do in the interests of National security, including the protection of defense secrets, and after consultation with the Minister of Justice—

(1) order the Registrar to refrain from performing any act which he is required or permitted to do under this Law on a certain application, or to postpone its performance;
(2) prohibit or restrict the publication or release of information concerning a particular application, or in connection with the information in it.
(b) A copy of the order of the Minister of Defense shall be delivered to the applicant.

Section 95.

The Minister of Defense may direct the Registrar to transmit to a person he designated therefore a copy of applications of a certain category, and the Registrar may transmit to the Minister of Defense applications the matter of which appears to him to be relevant to National security or Defense which includes a defense secret, all in order to enable the Minister to weigh whether an order under section 94 should be made in their respect; the Minister of Defense shall decide on every said application not later than four months after it was transmitted, and as long as he has not decided or as long as the said period has not expired, whichever is shorter, the Registrar shall not perform any act in respect of the said applications, except to acknowledge their submission under section 14.

Section 96.

(a) The applicant may contest an order under section 94 before a three member contestations committee appointed by the Minister of Justice, the members of which shall include a judge of the Supreme Court—the chairman of the committee—and a person recommended by the Minister of Defense. . . .

Section 98.

An Israel national, a permanent resident of Israel or any other person who owes allegiance to the State shall not submit any application abroad for a patent for an invention the subject of which is weaponry or ammunition, or which is otherwise of military value, or for an invention with which section 95 deals, and he shall not—directly or indirectly—cause a said application to be submitted, unless one of the following applies:
(1) he received written permission from the Minister of Defense in advance;
(2) he submitted an application in respect of that invention in Israel and within six months after that application was submitted the Minister of Defense did not make an order on it under section 94, or he made such an order, but it is no longer in effect.

Under Article Two of this section, the same provisions above apply to inventions that relate to nuclear energy (sections 99 through 103).

As a final example of how most patent laws deal with the secrecy of inventions that may give rise to national security concerns, the US Patent Act contains two provisions, one dealing with the topic under a general approach, and another dealing with inventions in which the public administration has proprietary interests:

§122. Confidential status of applications; publication of patent applications

. . .

(d) National Security.—No application for patent shall be published under subsection (b)(1) if the publication or disclosure of such invention would be detrimental to the national security. The Director shall establish appropriate procedures

to ensure that such applications are promptly identified and the secrecy of such inventions is maintained in accordance with chapter 17.

. . .

§181. Secrecy of certain inventions and withholding of patent

Whenever publication or disclosure by the publication of an application or by the grant of a patent on an invention in which the Government has a property interest might, in the opinion of the head of the interested Government agency, be detrimental to the national security, the Commissioner of Patents upon being so notified shall order that the invention be kept secret and shall withhold the publication of the application or the grant of a patent therefor under the conditions set forth hereinafter.

These four samples of patent law provisions dealing with inventions that relate to national security permit to identify the two main trends:

- first, patent applications claiming that type of inventions are to be kept secret, this meaning that they will not be published by the patent office; the eventuality of seeking technical subsidies to the examination of those inventions from the specialized industry will be a matter to be dealt with by regulations, but the primary concern is that those inventions shall remain confidential;
- second, the patent applicant shall refrain from applying for patents for those inventions in other countries, except with permission from the competent authority.

A few national lawmakers have added to these provisions language granting the patent applicant the right to be compensated for the restrictions imposed on his commercial exploitation of the invention that result from the duties of secrecy and of not filing abroad. In this regard, the solution found in most laws is that inventions that belong to national security shall be the subject matter of compulsory licenses. This is the case, for example, of the Industrial Property Law of North Macedonia, as follows:

Use of confidential invention

Article 72

(1) The Ministry of Defence shall have the exclusive right to use the confidential invention and have at its availability that invention.
(2) The holder of the right shall be entitled to a one-time compensation for confidential invention which is protected with a patent, regardless if the invention is used for the needs of defence and to what extent.
(3) The amount of the compensation referred to in paragraph (2) of this Article shall be determined amicably by the right holder and the Minister for Defence.
(4) In case agreement is not reached, the holder of the patent right, in accordance with the rules outside the proceedings, may request the court to determine the amount of the compensation.

Anyway, this discussion does not generate controversy. The problem comes when the lawmaker decides to extend secrecy to other inventions on different grounds. An example of this orientation can be found in the patent law of China, as follows:

Article 4. Where an invention-creation for which a patent is applied for relates to national security or other major interests of the State and confidentiality needs to be maintained, the patent application shall be handled in accordance with the relevant prescriptions of the State.

. . .

Article 19. Where any entity or individual intends to file a patent application abroad in a foreign country for any an invention or utility model accomplished in China, it or he shall submit the matter to request the patent administration department under the State Council for confidentiality examination in advance. The procedures and duration etc. of the confidentiality examination shall be carried out in accordance with the regulations of the State Council. . . .

An additional provision in the Chinese patent law, which is not worth being repeated here, imposes sanctions in the case a patent application for an invention originally made in China and that affects national security is filed abroad without permission. Of relevance for this discussion is that Article 4 implies that inventions in other fields not related to national security may also be kept undisclosed.

The same orientation can be found in the Patent Act of Algeria, which reads:

Section 5 Secret Inventions

Article 19. Without prejudice to the material and moral rights of the inventor, inventions of interest to national security and those of particular significance for the public interest may be declared secret. The implementation of the provisions of this article shall be defined by regulation.[242]

Which inventions could be identified as "of particular significance to the public interest"? One may think of inventions of high technical relevance made by a national resident, and that applies to a sector of the economy of particular importance to the country. Let us suppose that a developing country has acquired expertise and international competitiveness in a given technical field, and that a national inventor makes a revolutionary invention, which adds greatly to the success of the national industry. Absent a legal provision dealing with that sort of crucially important inventions, that inventor may hesitate before applying for a patent because of the disclosure that application will necessarily entail. Not only the condition of enabling disclosure would make that inventor vulnerable to intense infringement (which tends to be the fate of the more successful inventions) but also the competitive advantage of that country could be lost—ironically, as a result of the features of the patent system, which is designed to secure the competitive advantages of inventors against their rivals.

It might be understandable that the lawmaker decides to keep that revolutionary invention under secrecy. Significantly, this topic was the subject of discussion in a case that was heard by the English Court of Chancery in 1816 (*In re Lacy's Patent*). At that time, the patent statute that was in force in France, of 1791, allowed for inventors to request that their inventions be kept under secrecy. Having received a patent in England, Mr. Lacy, the British inventor of a process of making French lace by a machine, asked the court for the application of reciprocity. His application for a patent

242. Ordinance n° 03-07 of 19 Joumada El Oula 1424, corresponding to July 19, 2003, concerning patents for invention.

had been rejected because he wanted to keep his invention secret for a period of fifteen months after the grant. Mr. Lacy's argument was that "there was reason to apprehend that if the particular description of the invention should be enrolled within the usual period [six months], copies thereof would be obtained by foreign agents, and transmitted to foreign countries, the inhabitants of which would have the benefit of making use of the invention before his Majesty's subjects could by law make use of the same." Mr. Lacy invoked as a precedent an act that granted another inventor a period of fifteen months after the grant for his submission of the description. The court refused. "His Lordship could not establish a new principle merely to prevent the French from smuggling." The requested extension "was certainly contrary to the general policy of the law, and [his Lordship] could not in justice to the King's subjects affix the great seal to it merely because it was a manufacture which other countries had in common with this."[243]

In conclusion, no lawmaker should see any inconvenience in ordering that inventions concerning national security should be kept secret, provided that the rights and legitimate interests of the inventors are respected. But extending that same treatment to inventions in other fields, as relevant as they may be, should be viewed under the perspective of the fundamental principles and goals of the patent system. The British Court, in 1816, was correct in refusing the temptation of disrupting what is perhaps the most crucial feature of the patent system—to make inventions *patent*, i.e., publicly known—just because disclosure may benefit competitors. After all, that is the essence of the system. And for those inventors who fear competition, they may resort to the indirect protection of trade secrets through the repression of unfair competition. But that should be a matter of a personal decision, with all the risks it entails, not a public policy. If governments started imposing secrecy on relevant inventions, the patent system would be left with the function of securing property rights in inventions of minor value, without interest for competitors, thus losing significance in promoting the transfer and dissemination of technology.

5 ENSURING COMPLIANCE WITH INTERNATIONAL OBLIGATIONS

When discussing the main objectives of developing countries in drafting their patent statutes, it was said that implementing international obligations found in treaties like the Paris Convention and the TRIPS Agreement was one of those. In pursuing such an objective, developing countries are carrying out part of the deal of providing for patent protection in exchange for facilitated market access to the commodities and industrial articles they export to developed countries.

In this token, a number of countries, fearful of the consequences that might result from the inadequate implementation of those international obligations, have included in their laws provisions establishing that, in the case of conflict between national and international law, the latter shall prevail.

243. William Carpmael, Law Reports of Patent Cases, vol. I, at 354, 355, 356 (A. Macintosh, London, 1843).

This is the case of the patent law of Angua and Barbuda, whose section 50 reads:

> *50. Application of treaties*
>
> *The provisions of any international treaty in respect of industrial property to which Antigua and Barbuda is party shall apply to matters dealt with by this Act and, in case of conflict with the provisions of this Act, the provisions of the treaty shall prevail.*

The same solution is found in section 87 of Eswatini's patent law, as follows:

> (10) *In the event of inconsistency between this Act and the provisions of the Treaty or the regulations or administrative instructions made under the Treaty, the Treaty and those regulations and instructions shall prevail.*

Actually, one should always expect to find a number of provisions that are in conflict with both the Paris Convention and the TRIPS Agreement in the patent statutes of developing countries. Two are the reasons that explain this: the first is of a political nature—not always the country's legislative branch is inclined to transforming commitments made by trade negotiators into law; the second is simply the lack of human and financial resources necessary for the preparation of draft laws and regulations that cover a wide range of legal specialities, including, but not limited to, constitutional matters, administration, customs and taxation, technical standards, health and environment, civil and criminal procedures, etc.—not to mention all the numerous branches and subbranches of intellectual property law. So, the matter is seeking the highest level possible of compliance. But, for that matter, developed country Members will never fully implement the TRIPS Agreement either. The number of Panel findings under the WTO Dispute Settlement Mechanism against developed country Members is illustrative of this. Moreover, sometimes, both developing and developed WTO Members show the same implementing flaws, as the cross-complaints of Brazil and the United States involving the local exploitation requirement show.[244]

Therefore, including a provision ensuring the primacy of international law over eventually non-compliant national provisions may operate as an interesting solution. However, according ascendancy to international treaties is useful only when their provisions are sufficiently detailed so as to dispense with their being transposed into national laws. These are the cases—at least to some extent—of the right of priority, in the Paris Convention, and compulsory licenses and enforcement, in the TRIPS Agreement. But that is not helpful when the treaties do not enter into details or when they simply authorize Contracting Parties to opt for some measure among those available.

244. *See supra* note 198 and accompanying text.

Index

A

Abstract inventions, 80
Agenda for Development, 3, 19, 204 (*see also* Development Agenda)
AI (Artificial Intelligence), 27, 38, 39, 65
Albania, 42
Algeria, 120, 237
Amazon.com, 83
Amendments, 127–135
Andean Community of Nations, 82
Andorra, 17
Angola, 17
Antigua and Barbuda, 28, 29, 33, 42, 143, 239
Anti-suit injunctions, 187, 188
APOTEX, 151
Argentina, 19, 29–31
Australia, 17, 18, 38, 63, 86

B

Backlog, 39, 48, 51
Bahamas, 74, 99
Bahrain, 68, 76, 82, 103, 194, 195, 198, 221
Bangui Agreement, 31, 32, 158, 162
Barbados, 120
Barnes and Noble, 83
Belize, 143, 210
Benin, 41
Best mode, 78, 93, 98–100
Bioprospector, 114
Bolar exception, 220, 221
Bolivia, 61
Botswana, 45, 49, 105, 191, 192
Brazil, 16, 17, 19, 20, 47, 50, 51, 62, 70, 72, 81, 86, 98, 101, 102, 130, 143, 144, 158–160, 174, 177, 190, 191, 195, 196, 204, 213, 218, 219, 239
Breeders' exemption, 66–68, 70
Budapest Treaty on the International Recognition of the Deposit of Microorganisms for the Purposes of Patent Procedure, 95
Bulgaria, 71
Burkina Faso, 32
Business methods, 80, 83–85, 216

C

Cambodia, 23, 24
Cameroon, 41
Canada, 151, 153, 155, 192, 199, 200, 220
Cape Verde, 19, 21, 24
CBD *see* Convention on Biological Diversity (CBD)
Central African Republic, 32
Chad, 32
Chemical inventions, 51, 95
Chile, 147, 149
China, 24, 86, 107, 185, 188, 189, 195, 213, 217, 236, 237

Civil servants, 40, 49, 140, 232–233
Colombia, 61, 192
Commercial novelty, 89, 117
Comoros, 32
Competition authority, 145–147, 155, 163, 186, 203–209
Complex products, 7, 173, 186, 187, 189, 212
Compulsory licenses, 145–167
Computer software, 38, 80–82
Congo, 32, 114
Continuation applications, 135
Convention on Biological Diversity (CBD), 106, 109, 110
Cook Islands, 130, 143, 211
Costa Rica, 49, 60, 65, 99, 103, 104, 193
Côte d'Ivoire, 32
COVID, 153, 167
Croatia, 158, 159
Cuba, 14, 15
Czechoslovakia, 71

D

DABUS, 38
Democracy, 48
Development Agenda, 4, 204 (*see also* Agenda for Development)
Differentiation, 23, 24
Disclosure requirement, 92, 94, 95, 97–99, 106, 107, 109–116, 156
Discovery, 34, 70–73, 75, 76, 78, 79
Djibouti, 42
Dominica, 42, 209, 210
Dominican Republic, 70
Double dipping, 169, 170
Draft Treaty Supplementing the Paris Convention as far as Patents are Concerned, 92, 119, 176
Dr. Pallin, 64

E

Ecuador, 61
Egypt, 51
Employees' inventions, 32, 39, 226–233
Enforcement, 11, 12, 15, 45, 48, 86, 96, 129, 149, 157, 185, 187, 188, 203–226, 239
EPC *see* European Patent Convention (EPC)
Equatorial Guinea, 32
Equity, principle of, 216
Ethiopia, 18, 32, 33
European Patent Convention (EPC), 52, 73–75, 77
European Patent Organization (EPO), 52, 78, 100
European Union, 151, 153, 155, 159, 172, 197
Exclusions from patentability, 42, 43, 47, 53, 57, 63, 144
Exhaustion, 168–176
Exploitation requirement, 156–158, 160, 163, 239
Extraterritoriality, 185, 188

F

Farmers' exemption, 66, 67, 70
FDI *see* Foreign direct investment/investors (FDI)
Fernando Henrique Cardoso, 20
Fiji Islands, 131
First sale doctrine, 168
Flexibilities, 4, 11, 22, 117, 206, 215, 218
Foreign direct investment (FDI), 23–25
France, 44, 94, 237
Francis Gurry, 3
FRAND (fair, reasonable, and non-discriminatory), 147, 149, 183, 185, 188
Free Trade Agreement (FTA), 1, 6, 12, 22, 189, 194, 195, 198, 220–222
FTA *see* Free Trade Agreement (FTA)

G

Gabon, 302
GATT 1947, 157, 159, 166, 201

genetic resources (GRs), 1, 68, 105–116
Geneva Treaty on the International Recording of Scientific Discoveries, 71
Germany, 38, 39, 86, 172, 189, 230, 231
Giorgio Agricola, 94
Global chains of value, 169, 186, 189, 204
GRs *see* Genetic resources (GRs)
Grace period, 116–123
Grant-back, 205, 207
GSK, 151
Guatemala, 14, 17, 147, 148
Guinea, 32
Guinea-Bissau, 32
Gulf Cooperation Council (GCC), 12
Guyana, 45, 183, 184, 200, 201, 210, 211

H

Handicrafts, 85–90, 112, 115
Honduras, 83
Human rights, 13–15, 36, 226

I

Iceland, 172
IGC, 144, 124 (*see also* WIPO Intergovernmental Committee on Genetic Resources, Traditional Knowledge and Folklore)
Independence, principle of, 100, 168, 175, 176, 186–188
India, 65, 75, 77, 143, 152, 153, 156–158, 234
Indonesia, 33, 73, 76, 122, 181, 182, 193, 205, 234
Industrial privileges, 94, 116, 156
Industrial Revolution, 85, 94, 156
Inequitable conduct, 101, 141, 218
Information concerning foreign applications, 100–105
Infringement
  cooperative or divided, 210
  direct, 209
  indirect or contributory, 167, 209
  innocent, 192, 210–213, 219
Injunctions, 12, 83, 166, 187, 209, 210, 212, 214–219, 222
Innovation patents, 86, 87
Integrated circuits, 212
Invalidation, 39, 43, 86, 87, 92, 97, 101–105, 109, 116, 129, 130, 135, 139–144, 197, 226
Inventive step, 44, 46, 49, 70, 75, 81, 82, 97, 102, 104, 123–125, 144 (*see also* Non-obviousness)
Israel, 160, 234, 235

J

James Quashie-Idun, 229
Japan, 17, 86, 155
Jeronimo de Ayanz y Beaumont, 92

K

Kenya, 121
Korea, Democratic People's Republic of, 18
Korea, Republic of, 18, 155, 192
Kuwait, 12

L

Lebanon, 47, 210, 224
Licenses of right, 183–184
Liechtenstein, 172
Linkage, patent, 220–223, 225

M

Mail-box, 50
Market segmentation, 151, 170, 207
Maintenance fees, 92, 109, 166, 183
Mali, 32
Mauritania, 41
Microorganisms, 65–71, 95
Morality, 46–48, 52, 59–62, 142
Moral rights, 29–31, 33, 237

Most-favoured-nation (MFN), 22, 114, 172
Mozambique, 42, 122, 230

N

Namibia, 142, 206, 211
National security, 50, 148, 232–238
National treatment, 10, 54, 114, 145, 151, 157, 160, 192, 201
Niger, 41
Nigeria, 174, 175, 179
Non-practicing entities (NPEs), 163, 217
North Macedonia, 31, 37, 50, 236
Non-obviousness, 124, 141 (*see also* Inventive step)
Norway, 172
Novelty, 6, 7, 43, 46, 49, 53, 57, 63, 70, 74, 76, 78, 83, 85, 89, 91, 94, 102, 104, 116–119, 122, 124, 141–144
NPEs *see* Non-practicing entities

O

OAPI, 31, 32, 41, 158
Octavio Paz, 89
Oman, 12, 68, 69, 71, 79, 82, 101–103, 105, 153, 171, 172, 174, 175, 195, 218

P

Panama, 122
Parallel imports, 151, 168, 169, 171–176
PCT (Patent Cooperation Treaty), 2, 16, 54, 57
Person skilled in the art, 93, 95–97, 99, 124
Peru, 61
Pharmaceutical inventions, 6, 20, 54, 80, 196
Philippines, 24, 62, 75, 76, 78, 122, 172
Plant varieties, 19, 65–71, 85, 89, 117
Portugal, 90
PPH (Patent Prosecution Highway), 53, 54, 93, 105, 139
Priority, right of, 5–7, 43, 56, 117, 118, 239
Prior user exception, 176–183
Provisional applications, 56
Punitive damages, 113, 218, 220

Q

Qatar, 12, 162, 179

R

Regulatory data, 223, 224
Retroactive protection, 190–192
Revocation, 44, 116, 142–143, 234
Rwanda, 151
Riyadh Design Law Treaty, 110

S

Samoa, 76, 77, 79, 108, 109
Saudi Arabia, 36, 195
Scientific Revolution, 94
Second uses, 72–79
Secret inventions, 233–238
Senegal, 41
SEP (standard-essential patent), 147, 149, 183–185, 188
Service inventions, 80, 84, 230, 231 (*see also* Abstract inventions)
Shaman, 114, 115
Sierra Leone, 99, 100
South Africa, 38, 82, 132
Soviet Union, 18, 71, 72
Spain, 21, 22
SPLT *see* Substantive Patent Law Treaty (SPLT)
Standard-setting organizations (SSOs), 147, 183, 185
Substantive examination, 38, 42–52, 55, 57, 86, 87, 91, 155, 193, 196
Substantive Patent Law Treaty (SPLT), 3, 120, 133
Supplementary Protection Certificates (SPCs), 197, 198

Swiss claims, 78
Switzerland, 70, 172

T

TCEs (traditional cultural expressions), 110
TK *see* Traditional knowledge (TK)
The Gambia, 46, 201
Therapeutic methods, 63, 64
Tie-in, 206
Togo, 32
Traditional knowledge (TK), 1, 68, 105–116
Transaction costs, 10, 21, 111, 169
Treaty on Intellectual Property in Respect of Integrated Circuits, 212
Trinidad and Tobago, 209
Trolls, 163, 216, 217
Tunisia, 65, 191, 192
Two-step test, 62, 142

U

Ulpianus, 14
Unclean hands doctrine, 146, 148, 167
UNCTAD, 204
Unfair competition, 2, 15, 90, 155, 167, 205, 212, 219, 224, 230, 231, 238
United Arab Emirates, 23, 65
United Kingdom (UK), 185
United States of America (US), 33, 37, 96, 117, 135, 198, 233
Unity of invention, 43, 91–92, 135
Unjust enrichment, 227, 228
Universal Declaration of Human Rights, 13, 226
UPOV, 65–68, 89
Uruguay, 33, 49, 50, 80, 192, 203–206, 212
Uruguay Round, 10, 20, 80
US *see* United States of America
Utility, 85–90
Utility models, 17, 19, 30, 41, 85–90, 117, 159, 162, 164, 174, 212, 231, 237

V

Vanuatu, 42
Vietnam, 107

W

WIPO Intergovernmental Committee on Genetic Resources, Traditional Knowledge and Folklore, 114 (*see also* IGC)
WIPO Model Law for Developing Countries for Inventions, 34, 101
WIPO Treaty on Intellectual Property, Genetic Resources, and Associated Traditional Knowledge, 109–111, 115, 116

www.ingramcontent.com/pod-product-compliance
Lightning Source LLC
LaVergne TN
LVHW020000031026
849161LV00021B/773